1001

Things Everyone Should

Know About

Women's History

1001

Things Everyone Should Know About

Women's History

CONSTANCE JONES

MAIN STREET BOOKS

DOUBLEDAY
New York London Toronto Sydney Auckland

A Main Street Book
PUBLISHED BY DOUBLEDAY
a division of Random House, Inc.
1540 Broadway, New York, New York 10036

MAIN STREET BOOKS, DOUBLEDAY, and the portrayal of a building with a tree
are trademarks of Doubleday, a division of Random House, Inc.

1001 Things Everyone Should Know About Women's History was published
in hardcover by Doubleday in 1998. The Main Street Books Edition is published
by arrangement with Doubleday.

Book design by Bonni Leon-Berman

The Library of Congress Cataloging-in-Publication Data

Jones, Constance.
1001 things everyone should know about women's history /
Constance Jones.—1st
Main Street Books ed.
p.   cm.
Originally published: New York : Doubleday, 1998.
Includes bibliographical references and index.
1. Women—History—Miscellanea.   2. Women—Biography—Miscellanea.
I. Title: One thousand one things everyone should know about women's
history.   II. Title: One thousand and one things everyone should know about
women's history.   III. Title.
HQ1121 .J634   2000
305.4´09—dc21   99-056835

ISBN 0-385-48387-2
Copyright © 1998 by Constance Jones

For my nieces,

Alyssa and Diana

Acknowledgments

I'D LIKE TO THANK a number of people for making this book a reality: editor Rob Robertson for the original idea; my agent, Gordon Kato, for bringing the project to my attention and taking care of the details; Carleen Brice for her work on the Economics, Work and Business section; Deidre Elliott for her contributions to the Science, Medicine and Technology and Daily Life sections; Heather Lewis for her help with the Arts and Entertainment, Sports and Adventure and Wild Women sections; Athena Angelos for her tireless and professional picture research; editors Frances Jones and Denell Downum for seeing the book through to completion; and my partner, Jackie Kohler, for her incredible faith in me during a time of transition.

Contents

Introduction 1

Introduction

FEW PEOPLE TODAY WOULD debate that women around the world have achieved great accomplishments and done amazing things since the dawn of human history, and few would deny that this fact has too often been neglected by historians. While the history of women has not been forgotten, most laypeople would agree that even those historians who specialize in the subject have unfortunately tended to turn it into a dull and tedious affair. Tantalized by random facts picked up along the way, many people rightly suspect that there is a lot more to women's history than suffrage and discrimination. Indeed, women have played a significant and varied role in history, and have experienced fascinating successes and failures in every field—we just haven't heard enough about them.

1001 Things Everyone Should Know About Women's History represents one attempt to help turn the tables. By no means comprehensive, it gives but a glimpse of the achievements of women, both celebrated and unknown, who have pursued their passions in all arenas of human endeavor. In presenting a wide variety of facts, the book hints at the complexity and excitement of women's history, serving as a different kind of introduction to the topic. From its pages there emerges a fascinating story: the story of people from all walks of life, all eras of history and all corners of the earth who are linked by nothing more—and nothing less—than the common fact of their sex.

Here is a look at both the essential and the esoteric people, places, issues and events of women's history. The fundamentals are amply covered alongside a healthy smattering of amusing, startling and scandalous tidbits—the stuff that can make history so entertaining. You will meet politicians, artists, parents, athletes, physicians, laborers, teachers, soldiers, criminals, spiritual leaders, citizens, entertainers, poets, scientists, philanthropists, homemakers, diplomats, musicians, inventors, lovers, entrepreneurs, journalists, farmers, activists, civil servants and thrill-seekers of every stripe. In the process you may learn more than you expected to, without realizing it.

Broken down into broad areas of interest, this book illuminates the lives, words, works and legacies of women in ten categories: Government, Law and Politics; Religion and Humanitarianism; Education and Academia; Science, Medicine and Technology; Economics, Work and Business; Daily Life; Literature and Journalism;

Arts and Entertainment; Sports and Adventure; and Wild Women. You can read the book straight through or use the category divisions to locate the topic you seek quickly and easily. Or you can flip randomly to any page of the book and find a surprising fact. Scores of rare and familiar illustrations will pique your curiosity and bring the text to life wherever you pause.

1001 Things Everyone Should Know About Women's History includes mini-biographies, capsulized anecdotes, short-and-sweet analyses and a generous dose of salient quotations and excerpts from historical sources. In this survey of all historical periods, the emphasis naturally falls more heavily on the nineteenth and twentieth centuries, when women have been most active in public life. Likewise, information on women from all parts of the world is weighted in favor of Europe and the United States, where women have had the advantage of greater opportunities.

Built on a foundation of careful research, the material presented in these pages often takes an unconventional spin meant to provide a fresh, contemporary perspective. The inclusion or exclusion of specific topics or personalities is firmly situated in the context of existing scholarship but guided by a spirit of vitality and candor—the notion that history is *fun*. The book provides the kind of straightforward, lively and sometimes humorous treatment rarely found in academic writing, an approach that complements the selection of subject matter. Those familiar with women's history will no doubt find something new in these pages, while newcomers to the field will find a trove of fascinating details. So turn the page and enjoy!

Part

ONE

Government, Law and Politics

FOUR ANCIENT QUEENS

1. The Queen of Sheba

Reigning in the tenth century B.C.E., Balkis was the celebrated queen who met with King Solomon of Israel. According to the Bible, which refers to her only as the Queen of Sheba, she traveled to Jerusalem to learn what she could of Solomon's legendary wisdom. She arrived "with a very great retinue, with camels bearing spices,

The Queen of Sheba.

and very much gold, and precious stones," evidence of the wealth of her people. Balkis was one of the earliest rulers of Sheba, located in southwestern Arabia where the Republic of Yemen now lies. It was one of the region's more powerful states until the second century B.C.E. and profited greatly from trade routes to Palestine.

2. Semiramis (d. 807 B.C.E.)

After the death of her husband, King Shamshi-Adad V, the Assyrian queen known as Semiramis ruled as regent for her son from 811 to 807 B.C.E. Semiramis defeated the Medes and Chaldeans in war and imported some elements of Babylonian religion. Legend erroneously attributes the building of Babylon to her; it also holds that she ordered the execution of lovers who failed to please her.

3. Salome Alexandra (d. 67 B.C.E.)

Married to two successive kings of Judea, Salome Alexandra became king herself in 76 B.C.E. following the death of her second husband. She carried on the rule of the Maccabees, or Hasmoneans, a family of leaders instrumental in winning freedom for the Jews. During her reign she played a pivotal role in a battle between two Jewish sects, supporting the Pharisees in their bitter dispute with the Sadducees. Her intervention helped the Pharisees, originally known as the Hasidim, oust their rivals from positions of religious and political influence. Credited as the originators of rabbinic Judaism, the Pharisees believed every aspect of life should be governed according to divine law.

4. *Cleopatra* (69–30 B.C.E.)

Ascending the Egyptian throne as co-ruler with her brother Ptolemy XIII in 51 B.C.E., Cleopatra struggled with him for two years before he usurped her power. Another two years elapsed before Julius Caesar came to her aid and vanquished Ptolemy. Leaving the government in the hands of her younger brother—now her husband as well—Cleopatra moved to Rome as Caesar's mistress. Caesar was soon assassinated, however, and she returned to Egypt and murdered her brother to make her son, Cesarion, her co-ruler. In 42 B.C.E., she started her famed love affair with Marc Antony. After a few years in Egypt, he returned to Rome and married the sister of Octavian, the future emperor. Cleopatra reunited with him in 36 B.C.E. while he led a military campaign against the Parthians; he divorced his wife and they married. They lived together in Egypt until Octavian declared a war of vengeance. Joining Antony in battle, Cleopatra stood by him until the naval engagement at Actium in 31 B.C.E. Convinced they could not win, they fled to Alexandria. There, a rumor of Cleopatra's death induced Antony to kill himself; Cleopatra soon did the same by allowing an asp to bite her. Octavian then executed Cesarion and made Egypt a province of the Roman Empire.

WARRIOR QUEENS

5. *Empress Jingo* (c. 169–269)

The military ambitions of Empress Jingo had a profound influence on the early cultural development of Japan. She became regent of Japan for her son Ojin when her husband, Emperor Chuai, died. According to tradition, she sent a large army to invade Korea, which she conquered by 203. She ruled Japan for sixty-nine years, fending off a number of challenges to her authority. Her conquest of Korea opened several centuries of cultural exchange between the two countries that brought not only Korean but Chinese elements into Japanese civilization. Empress Jingo lives on in Japanese tradition as a great ruler and goddess.

6. *Zenobia* (d. after 274)

One of history's great warrior queens, Zenobia ruled her domain with an eye toward enlarging it as much as possible. She reigned over Palmyra, a city on the northern edge of the Syrian Desert, with her husband, Odenathus,

Zenobia.

during the third century. When the king was assassinated in 267—possibly with the collusion of his queen—Zenobia gained control of the prospering city-state, reigning as regent for her young son. Feigning loyalty to Rome, she went out to conquer nearby peoples. Military campaigns expanded her dominion to Syria, Egypt and Asia Minor, and she announced her independence from Rome. In 272, Emperor Lucius Domitius Aurelian invaded her realm and captured its outlying areas, then laid siege to Palmyra itself. When the city fell, Aurelian captured Zenobia and left Palmyra in ruins. He put Zenobia on display in Rome before sending her to live on an estate at nearby Tibur.

7. *The Kahina*

In the eighth century, a Berber leader known as the kahina (meaning "prophetess" or "sorceress") repelled invading Arabs to maintain the independence of the region occupied by modern Tunisia. She achieved this by uniting the Berber and Byzantine armies and led an independent state for several years until she died in battle.

8. *Aethelflaed* (d. 918)

Queen of the Anglo-Saxon state of Mercia, in what is now central England, Aethelflaed fought alongside her husband and brother to defend her people against Welsh and Viking (Danish) invaders. After her husband's death in 911, she ruled alone but lost none of the bravery that made her such an effective warrior. She was also noted for the imposing fortifications she built to protect Mercia.

9. *Tamara* (c. 1160–1212)

Queen of the Asian empire of Georgia, Tamara guided her land to the height of its power. She rode into battle with her army, earning the sobriquet "King Tamara," and was famed for her brilliant statesmanship and military strategy. Her conquest of neighboring Russians, Turks, Persians and Armenians marked the peak of Georgia's prosperity and vitality. Reputedly insatiable in matters carnal, she was nonetheless canonized by the Georgian church.

Two Virgin Queens

10. *Queen Elizabeth I* (1533–1603)

The daughter of Henry VIII and Anne Boleyn ushered England into the Renaissance and transformed it into one of history's greatest world powers. She had to fight for the throne because Henry beheaded her mother to marry Jane Seymour, who bore his only legitimate son, Edward VI. Imprisoned for asserting her birthright, she finally took the crown in 1558, after the death of Edward and the reign of her half-sister Mary Tudor. As queen, she made Protestantism the official religion of England and ushered in an era of peace, prosperity and exceptional cultural advancement. She successfully quelled plots and intrigue in her court—notably the tumult over Mary Stuart, Queen of Scots—and contained disputes with Spain, routing the formidable Spanish Armada in 1588. Establishing England's dominance as a naval power, she secured extensive claims in the New

World, thereby inaugurating more than four centuries of staggering growth for the British Empire.

11. Queen Christina (1626–1689)

Inheriting the throne of Sweden at the age of six, this only child received a boy's upbringing while several regents managed her kingdom. She was crowned in 1644 and started a reign fraught with war, economic crisis, dissension and revolt. Expanding the power of the crown, she forced Swedish witch-hunters to end their abuses; she also restricted the use of the death penalty to certain murderers. She was a renowned patron of the humanities and embraced the work of French philosopher René Descartes. In 1654, she selected a successor and abdicated, leading to speculation that she preferred not to fulfill her royal obligation to marry and bear children. She subsequently converted to Roman Catholicism and moved to Italy, where she tried to take the throne of Naples and then Poland. A patron of Bernini, Corelli and Scarlatti, she died in genteel poverty.

African Queens

12. The Queens of Meroë

The civilization of Meroë in the ancient African empire of Nubia reached its apex under the rule of a long line of queens. Bartare, who ruled from 284 to 277 B.C.E. was the first. Others of note included Shanakdakhete (r. 177–155 B.C.E.), Amanerinas (r. 99–84 B.C.E.), Amanishakete (41–12 B.C.E.), Amanitere (12 B.C.E.–12 C.E.) and Amanikhatashan (62–94 C.E.). Promoting commerce, ironworking and other valuable pursuits, they also commissioned Meroë's most ambitious public building programs and restored its great urban temples.

13. The Start of Something Big

The Hausa, one of Africa's great civilizations during the fifteenth to eighteenth centuries, built their vibrant walled city-states on foundations laid by women. A dynasty of Habe queens ruled the lower Niger River region in the tenth and eleventh centuries, until the last of them married the king of Baghdad, initiating a line of Habe kings.

14. Kasa

From 1341 to 1360, the famed west African kingdom of Mali was ruled by a monarch known simply as Kasa, the Mandinke word for "queen."

15. Awura Pokou

Queen of the Baule of western Africa from approximately 1735 to 1750, Awura Pokou led her people to independence in a new home. As the Asante Confederacy sought to exert greater control over the tribes in its dominion, the Baule queen rebelled and took her people farther west, to the area now occupied by the Ivory Coast.

TWELVE AMBITIOUS QUEENS

16. *Dynasty Builder*

Empress Wu Zitian, or Wu Chao, started her career as a concubine in the seventh century, then married up to become empress. Upon the emperor's death she took over, won the war with Korea, and went on to rule for fifty years. Although pitiless toward anyone who stood in her way, she was a skillful administrator who improved conditions for women and ushered in the "golden age" of the T'ang dynasty.

17. *Empress Irene* (752–803)

Coming to power at the death of her husband, Emperor Leo IV, Irene ruled the eastern Roman Empire as regent for her son. As empress, she reestablished the traditional divinity of Christian icons, slowing a movement away from the worship of images. The decree that accomplished this launched a period of great creativity in Byzantine art. Constantine VI, her son, assumed the throne in 790 and banished her, then accepted her return as co-ruler. Irene then arrested him, had him blinded and threw him into prison, reclaiming sole power over the empire. Eventually, the aristocracy dethroned her and banished her to the Aegean island of Lesbos.

18. *Zoë and Theodora*

Together and separately, these sisters ruled the eastern Roman Empire from 1028 to 1056, curbing corruption in the Church and the government. Although Theodora was older, Zoë became empress first, in 1028. Theodora plotted to overthrow her sister, but instead became co-empress with Zoë and her husband, Constantine IX, in 1042. When Zoë died in 1050 and Constantine in 1055, Theodora became the empire's sole ruler.

19. *Islamic Influences*

During the thirteenth century, at least two women managed to overcome Muslim tradition to become leaders of their people. Raziy'yat-uddin succeeded her father as ruler of the Delhi slave dynasty in India, while Shahar al-Dur pre-

Theodora.

vailed over her rival son to claim the throne of Egypt.

20. *Isabella of Castille* (1451–1504)

Best known as the patron of Columbus's voyages to North America, Isabella had an enormous impact on the history of Spain and the history of the world. She married Ferdinand of Aragón in 1469, before succeeding to the throne of Castile and León. Her authority expanded in 1479, when Ferdinand gained the throne of Aragón. Uniting the kingdoms and strengthening the monarchy, she harbored far greater ambitions than her husband. She earned her reputation as the "crusading warrior queen" by mounting battles against the Islamic Moors, the last of whom

Isabella of Castille.

she expelled from the Iberian Peninsula in 1492. In addition to her successful strategizing, her endurance in battle and her skilled horsemanship were instrumental in securing Spain. Fanatically devoted to the Roman Catholic Church, she not only rid her domain of Muslims but also expelled the Jews and instituted the Inquisition to exterminate Christian heretics. She saw Christopher Columbus's proposal of exploration as a possible means to augment both Spanish and Catholic power and funded the ocean voyage that was to change the world. When Columbus returned, word of his luck rapidly spread throughout Europe but Isabella maintained Spain's edge in the New World by immediately sending him back. Not long after her death, Spain controlled the entire Caribbean region, as well as large tracts of North and Central America.

21. *Catherine de Médicis* (1519–1589)

The queen of France and mother of three French kings, Catherine was born in Florence, Italy, into the fantastically wealthy and powerful Medici family. She married a French duke who became King Henry II in 1547, and spent several relatively quiet years as a wife and mother. However, after her husband and her first son, King Francis II, died, she took control of France as regent for her second son, King Charles IX. Even after he came of age, she kept a tight grip on the reins of power. In order to protect the power of the crown, she intervened in the conflict brewing between Roman Catholics and Protestant Huguenots. Civil war broke out in

1562, and again in 1567, but in both cases Catherine used political machinations and royal edicts to end the fighting and preserve her power. Still fearful of the Huguenots, though, she plotted to kill their leader. In 1572 her plot unfolded in the Saint Bartholomew's Day Massacre, which left fifty thousand Huguenots dead. Two years later her third son, Henry III, became king and her power waned. By then, however, she had managed to marry one daughter to King Philip II of Spain and another to the next king of France. She also encouraged the advancement of French learning, art and architecture, adding a wing to the Louvre, building the Tuileries gardens and the château of Monceau, and assembling a celebrated library of rare manuscripts.

22. *Maria Theresa* (1717–1780)

The archduchess of Austria and queen of Hungary and Bohemia, Maria Theresa was the daughter, wife and mother to several successive emperors of the Holy Roman Empire (and bore a total of sixteen children, including Marie Antoinette). Her 1740 succession to her father's throne set off the War of the Austrian Succession, in which the rulers of Bavaria, Poland, Saxony, Prussia and Spain challenged her claim to the hereditary dominions of her family, the Habsburgs.

Presuming a woman would not stand up to them, her male opponents found themselves fighting an eight-year war that all but the king of Prussia lost. Maria Theresa then supervised a twelve-year period of vigorous economic development in Austria. An alliance she made with France shattered the peace in 1756, igniting the

Seven Years' War. Austria lost that war, but Maria Theresa continued to consolidate her family's power in the region, acquiring part of Poland in a deal with Russia and Prussia.

23. *Catherine the Great* (1729–1796)

A German woman presided over one of the most fascinating periods of Russian history. In her teens, Sophie Friederike Auguste von Anhalt-Zerbst moved to Russia, adopted the name Yekaterina Alekseyevna and married the man who became Czar Peter III. From then on, she considered herself a Russian. Her passion for Russia, as well as her passion for power, prompted her to overthrow her witless husband almost as soon as he ascended the throne in 1762. Proclaiming herself Empress Catherine II, she set about expanding Russian territory. Her conquests of Poland and Turkey gained the em-

Catherine the Great.

pire territory in Crimea and the Ukraine, boosting the population under her control from 20 million to 36 million. She secularized the vast lands held by the Russian church, pushed for legal reform and promoted intellectual and cultural life, at least until the French Revolution. Thereafter, she tightened her grip on the Russian people. Under her reign, millions of free peasants were reduced to serfdom.

24. *Queen Victoria* (1819–1901)

Ascending the throne at the age of eighteen, Victoria at first seemed to accept the English monarch's customarily advisory role. However, with the encouragement of her husband, Prince Albert, she started to assert her authority, demanding that Parliament follow her orders. From 1850 on, she had a direct hand in England's political affairs, shaping the country's foreign and domestic policy in such areas as the reorganization of colonial authority in India. She abandoned many of her ceremonial functions after the 1861 death of Prince Albert, but continued to exert great influence on the nation's prime ministers. Among them, she was an ally of the conservative Disraeli but she objected to the liberal philosophy of Gladstone. In 1876, she assumed the title of empress of India; she also forcefully protected Britain's interests in South Africa during the Boer War. Over the course of her sixty-three-year reign—the longest in England's history—Victoria enjoyed enormous popularity among her subjects. She remade the role and image of the English monarchy and came to represent the strength of Britain at the height of its colonial power. At the same time, a large, prosperous middle class emerged and embraced the conservative morality now associated with the Victorian age.

25. *Tz'u Hsi* (1835–1908)

Entering the court of Emperor I-chu as a concubine, Tz'u Hsi became de facto ruler of China within six years, as regent for her son, Emperor Tsai-ch'un. When he died in 1873, she continued her rule as regent for her nephew, Tsai't'ien. She ruled until 1889 as China's absolute monarch, exerting an iron will and a conservative philosophy. After a brief period of retirement, she resumed control in 1898 in order to curtail her nephew's attempts at liberalizing China's foreign policy. She backed the Boxer Rebellion of 1900, in which nationalists protested growing foreign influence. When the rebellion failed she fled the court, but then reversed her politics and supported wide-ranging reforms. Renowned for her violent temper and her taste for opium, she was known to some as "Old Buddha" and to others as "the Dowager Empress."

WOMEN OF INFLUENCE

26. *Livia* (56–29 C.E.)

The third wife of the first emperor of Rome, Livia had great political influence during an important era of Roman history. Her second husband, Augustus, was the adopted heir of Julius Caesar and was instrumental in bringing order to Rome after Caesar's assassination. Through the years of political and military machinations,

Livia had Augustus's ear. She also had his only child, a daughter named Julia, who became notorious for her dissolute ways. But in recognition of her political support, Augustus granted Livia the honorary title Julia Augusta. Augustus also adopted Tiberius, a son from her first marriage, and named him his successor as emperor. When Augustus died and Tiberius became emperor, Livia grew even more powerful in public affairs. In the provinces, Livia was considered divine even during her lifetime, and at least one temple was built in honor of her and Tiberius. In 42 C.E. her grandson Claudius officially deified her.

27. Galla Placidia (c. 390–450)

Born ten years after Christianity became the official religion of Rome, the daughter of Theodosius the Great became ruler of the western Roman Empire. Her father died when she was five, leaving the throne to her eleven-year-old brother, Flavius Honorius, whose guardians took actual control. The empire slowly disintegrated under constant attack by Alaric, the Visigoth king, especially after he sacked Rome in 410 and kidnapped Placidia. She married first Alaric's successor and then Constantius, a Roman general, but rumors surrounded her rather too close relationship with Honorius. In 421, Honorius proclaimed Placidia and her husband Augusta and Augustus when he made Augustus his co-ruler. Placidia's son inherited the crown in 425, initiating Placidia's fifteen-year rule of the western empire on his behalf. After he took over as Emperor Valentian III, she turned her attention to her rebellious daughter, Honoria. She refused to allow Honoria to marry

Attila the Hun, who had been threatening the empire for some time. But when Placidia died, Attila tried to claim Roman territory in Honoria's name; Rome refused to recognize the claim, and Attila invaded Gaul.

28. Eleanor of Aquitaine (c. 1122–1204)

Heir to Aquitaine, a region representing about a third of modern France, Eleanor had her hand in many of the major political events of her time. At fifteen she married France's King Louis VII, whom she joined in fighting the Crusades. After fifteen years she divorced him to marry Henry II of England. France rejected the claim of the new English queen to Aquitaine, launching a French-English conflict that lasted four centuries. The mother of Richard the Lion-Hearted and John Lackland—both future kings of England—she backed their 1173 efforts to overthrow her unfaithful husband. Henry II placed her in confinement until 1189, but she thwarted his attempt to divorce her and lay claim to Aquitaine. When Richard became king and left for the Crusades, Eleanor managed England's affairs until his return, at one point preventing John from usurping the throne. She subsequently reconciled her sons and, after John succeeded Richard as king, quelled a rebellion by her grandson Arthur.

29. Queen Mother

In memory of his mother, Queen Nandi (1760–1827), the Zulu leader Shaka ordered the ritual execution of hundreds in 1827. She had advised him as he built the Zulu empire in southeastern Africa; soon after she died, he went insane and was killed by his brothers.

30. Anna Ella Carroll (1815–1893)

This Maryland-born American political writer put her pen to use for the Union during the Civil War. In 1861 she published *War Powers of the General Government,* a defense of President Lincoln's decision to use military power against the South; a year later she published *Relation of the National Government to the Revolted Citizens Defined,* which described Lincoln's views on the constitutional issues raised by secession. Her ideas on military strategy became part of General Grant's Tennessee River plan, which ultimately precipitated Sherman's famous march.

31. Wartime Propagandists

Instrumental to the Japanese effort in World War II, Tokyo Rose broadcast propaganda to American troops stationed in the South Pacific. Her real name was Iva Ikuko Toguri D'Aquino, and she was a California-born Japanese-American. In the European theater, Tokyo Rose had a counterpart in Axis Sally, an American named Mildred Gillars who broadcast Nazi propaganda to U.S. forces. The Allies eventually captured and imprisoned her.

32. Eva Perón (1919–1952)

The second wife of Argentine leader Juan Perón took an active role in politics, working unofficially to improve conditions for women and the working classes. Her commitment to social causes arose in part from her humble background, and she won the heart of Argentina's proletariat, who nicknamed her Evita. She met Perón while working as a popular radio soap opera actress and married him in 1945, the year before he became president. Although never appointed to government office, she served as her husband's link to labor. She organized working women, successfully pressed for women's suffrage and championed accessible health care. Ardently supported by the *descamisados* ("shirtless ones"), she infuriated many powerful politicians; the military prevented her from running for vice president in 1951.

33. Jiang Quing (1914–1991)

Third wife of Chinese leader Mao Zedong, Jiang Quing played an important part in the Communist revolution but ended her life in disgrace. Working as an actress in the 1930s, she joined the Communist Party, where she met and married Mao in 1937. When, under Mao's leadership, the Communists took over the Chinese government in 1949, Jiang became an important figure in the arts. She promoted the rejection of traditional forms and themes in favor of work centered around Mao's creed, and was a moving force behind the harsh Cultural Revolution of 1966 to 1969. Her influence with her husband made her one of China's most powerful figures until his death in 1976. As power shifted, she was arrested with three others and charged with treason and other crimes against the people. The so-called Gang of Four were tried and convicted in 1980, with Jiang's death sentence reduced to life imprisonment a few years later. Chinese authorities termed her 1991 death a suicide.

34. Center of Controversy

On October 6, 1991, a University of Oklahoma law professor named Anita Hill set off a political and social firestorm when she publicly accused Supreme Court nominee Clarence Thomas of sexual harassment. While she had been working for Thomas at the Department of Education in 1981, she charged, he had pressured her for dates and described his sexual proclivities to her. The harassment continued after Hill and Thomas transferred to the Equal Employment Opportunity Commission, which Hill quit in 1983. Hill's revelations forced the Senate Judiciary Committee to convene hearings that were broadcast live across the U.S. The hearings sparked heated public debate over sexual harassment and, by extension, women's position in society. The Senate's confirmation of Thomas angered many women, inciting severe political backlash against many politicians in the 1992 elections. A turning point in American politics, the episode revived concern for women's rights and reshaped the public's attitude toward government.

Two Truly Noble Queens

35. *Jadwiga* (c. 1373–1401)

This Polish queen lived only twenty-eight years, but hers is considered one of Poland's most distinguished reigns. Married to Wladyslaw II in 1386, she excelled at international relations, both diplomatic and military. She also promoted Christianity and founded the University of Cracow.

36. *Queen Margaret* (1353–1412)

Daughter of King Valdemar IV of Denmark and wife of King Haakon VI of Norway, Margaret ruled both countries as regent for her son from 1376 until he died in 1387. The people of Norway and Denmark immediately elected her joint sovereign, and in 1389 the people of Sweden offered her the throne in exchange for expelling their inept king. Taking the king prisoner, she pursued her conquest of Sweden to victory in 1397. She then joined Sweden, Norway and Denmark into the Union of Kalmar, crowning her nephew Eric of Pomerania king. Lasting until 1523, the union represented the largest monarchy in Europe at that time.

Royal Pains in the Ass

37. *Roman Suds*

Intrepid and loyal, Agrippina I (c. 14 B.C.E.–33 C.E.) assisted her husband, Germanicus Caesar, in his military campaigns on behalf of Rome. She also gave birth to the infamous Caligula and to a daughter, Agrippina II (c. 15–59 C.E.), who shared her daring but perhaps not her decency. Married three times, Agrippina the Younger was the mother of the nefarious Nero. After persuading her third husband and uncle, Emperor Claudius, to name Nero his successor, she is thought to have poisoned him. One of Claudius's previous wives, the notoriously dissipated Valeria Messalina, had tried to depose him, but succeeded instead in getting herself executed. More effective in her plotting against Claudius,

Agrippina II finally met her match in Nero, who had her assassinated, perhaps at the behest of his wife, Poppaea Sabina (d. 69 C.E.). Nero, of course, went on to a colorful career as one of Rome's most profligate and heartless rulers.

38. Mary, Queen of Scots
(1542–1587)

Ruler of Scotland from the time she was six days old, Mary Stuart caused uproars in Scotland and England because of her fervent adherence to Roman Catholicism. She was raised in France and in 1558 married the French king, Henry II, acquiring the refinements of French culture in addition to its religion. When her husband died, she returned to Scotland and pronounced herself absolute monarch in 1561. She married her cousin Henry Stewart and named him king, then decreed Roman Catholicism the religion of the land. Angered by her actions, her nobles plotted several insurrections, finally forcing her out of her own court with her infant son. By then, Henry had died and she eloped with the Earl of Bothwell. Her marriage outraged her nobles and prompted her supporters to abandon her, leaving her no option but to abdicate in favor of her son, who became James VI of Scotland. She was thrown into prison but managed to escape and raise an army of six thousand, but the Scots overpowered her and she fled to England in 1568. There, Elizabeth I had her imprisoned. Mary's supporters made several unsuccessful attempts to oust Elizabeth and install the Catholic queen, bringing her under suspicion. In 1586, she was convicted of conspiracy against Elizabeth, who had her beheaded.

SOLDIERS

39. Chinese Amazon

According to Chinese legend, Hua Mu-Lan became a soldier in the fifth century after winning a sword fight with her father. Posing as a man, she fought valiantly for twelve years, inspiring her commander to offer her his daughter's hand.

40. Daring Duo

In the seventh century, two Arabian women helped start the expansion of the Arab empire across the Middle East and into Europe and Africa. An army commander named Khaula allied with a chief named Waferia to crush the Greek army.

41. Japanese Warrior

In thirteenth-century Japan, a female samurai named Tomoe was ranked among the finest fighters in Japanese history. Records of the time describe her as "a match for a thousand warriors and fit to meet either God or the devil."

42. Deborah Sampson (1760–1827)

This free African-American from Plymouth, Massachusetts, was inspired by intense patriotism to serve in the Continental Army during the American Revolution. In 1782, she secretly sewed a man's suit and adopted the alias Robert Shurtleff, then enlisted in a town where no one knew her. Sampson's unusual height and stamina allowed her to conceal her gender while serving in the Fourth Regiment, even af-

Deborah Sampson delivering a letter to
George Washington.

44. Woman of Valor

For her work as a Union Army nurse and surgeon during the Civil War, Dr. Mary Edwards became in 1865 the first woman to receive the United States Medal of Honor. The army rescinded the medal in 1917, claiming her "gallantry" had not been proven; two years later she died. In 1977 the army finally reinstated the honor.

45. The Other Allies

American women served in vital support roles in the military during World War II. They came to be identified by a jumble of acronyms: Army WACs and WAACs, Navy WAVES and Coast Guard SPARS filled noncombat posts in order to free their male colleagues for combat duty.

46. Etched in Stone

Of more than 58,000 names inscribed on the Vietnam Veterans Memorial in Washington, D.C., eight belong to women. Nearby stands a separate monument to the American women who served in Vietnam. It was dedicated on Veterans Day, 1994, a dozen years after the original memorial.

47. Modern Warriors

ter she was wounded at the Battle of Tarrytown. She extracted musket balls from her own leg and returned to duty, then was shot in the shoulder at the Battle of Yorktown. When she came down with brain fever, a doctor discovered her sex. He kept her secret but she was soon discharged for health reasons. After the war, her adventures came to light and she went on the lecture circuit. With the help of Paul Revere, she secured a soldier's pension from the State of Massachusetts and from the federal government.

Thirty thousand American women served in combat support roles during the Persian Gulf War of 1991. Although banned from combat, they were instrumental to the effort as communications, technical and medical personnel.

43. Cossack Cross-Dresser

Abandoning her husband and posing as a man, Nadezhada Durova (1783–1866) served eight years in one of Russia's Cossack regiments and rose to the rank of cavalry officer.

48.

"I volunteered to go to the Gulf. I was attached to the 24th Infantry Division, the unit that spearheaded the end-ground attack. Our support outfit was in just as much danger as the combat element. The Iraqi weapons had just as much capability of hitting us as the men in front. The difference was that we didn't have the capability to defend ourselves like the combat troops. . . . No normal person wants to go into combat. Soldiers are the last people who want to. But we've volunteered. We understand our commitment. Everybody raises a hand, male and female, and swears to support and defend the same Constitution. Women are competent, capable and committed. We are an integral part of the best-trained military force in the world. The services should have the flexibility to assign the best-qualified person to the job, regardless of gender. That's the bottom line." —Captain Carol Barkalow, August 5, 1991

LAWS AND LAWYERS

49. The Code of Hammurabi

The world's first recorded legal code, framed by the ruler of the Babylonian empire in the late eighteenth century B.C.E. formalized the far-ranging rights of the realm's women. Women shared equal authority with men over their children, they could will their property to whomever they pleased, and upon marriage they—not their husbands—received a dowry.

50. Early Equality

Archaeologists studying ruins of Mycenae—a culture that thrived in Bronze Age Greece—have discovered writing tablets that suggest men and women shared equal legal status in one of Europe's first states.

51. Legal History I

The first female lawyer known to history practiced in Babylonia 550 years before the Christian era.

52.

"The husband and the wife are one person in law; that is, the very being or legal existence of the woman is suspended during her marriage, or at least, is consolidated into that of her husband." —Sir William Blackstone, *Commentaries on the Laws of England,* 1765

53. Sub-Citizens

In ancient Athens, even women of the citizen class were legally subordinated to men. Their fathers, brothers, husbands or sons controlled their wealth and their children, and the laws that protected them did so only insofar as that protection benefited their male guardians. Forbidden from taking any form of legal action, they were also formally excluded from government, politics and warfare.

54. Law of the Twelve Tables

Written from 451 to 450 B.C.E., the Twelve Tables represented ancient Rome's first legal code. Many of the laws defined women's place in society: under male authority. Detailed directives established who controlled a woman's destiny at each stage of her life—which man or boy determined whether she was to live free or to be enslaved and, indeed, whether she lived at all. Other rules covered the inheritance of property by women and the freedom from male authority enjoyed by vestal virgins.

55. Legal History II

At the University of Bologna, a woman named Bettisia Gozzadini held the judicial chair for ten years, between 1239 and 1249.

56. Margaret Brent
(c. 1600–1671)

Long before the first American woman was admitted to the bar, Margaret Brent practiced law in the British colonies. Born in England, she never married but crossed the Atlantic at age thirty-eight and was the first woman to receive a land grant in the colony of Maryland. She became one of the colony's largest landowners and became involved with local politics. In 1644 she assembled a militia for the colony's defense, and in 1647 she served as executor of the estate of Leonard Calvert, Maryland's governor. Denied the right to vote in the colonial assembly, she nevertheless played a central role in local development, bringing her legal acumen to bear in more lawsuits than any other American from 1642 to 1650.

57.

"Women developed law and its application to life in the germs of family rule and tribal custom quite as much as did men; but when statutes took the place of tradition, and courts superseded personal judgeship, and when a special class of lawyers was needed to define and administer laws, which grew more difficult to understand with growing complexity of social relationship, men alone entered that profes-

sion." —Anna Garlin Spencer, *Woman's Share in Social Culture,* 1912

58. Chattel and Their Chattel

In the nineteenth century, American women of all classes and races were accorded the same legal status as children and slaves. Any income they made and any inheritances they received belonged to their husbands. Their children were considered the sole property of their husbands as well. Without the permission of their husbands or closest male relatives, they could not make investments, sign contracts, make wills or bring lawsuits. Except under severely restricted circumstances, they could not divorce their husbands. Under pressure from women's rights activists, states gradually began to grant property rights to women in the 1860s.

59. The Combination Law

In 1851, Germany's Combination Law outlawed women's participation in political associations or meetings. The law was reversed in 1884, but women's legal rights remained tenuous well into the twentieth century.

60. Women at the Bar

In 1869, Arabella Mansfield of Iowa became the first American woman admitted to the bar. By 1890 many law schools admitted women and nearly two hundred women practiced law in the United States, although many were excluded from the courtroom.

61. Belva Lockwood (1830–1917)

One of the first American women admitted to the bar, Belva Lockwood started practicing law

Belva Lockwood.

crimination. She then lobbied Congress for three years, finally winning passage of a law she drafted permitting women to practice before the Supreme Court. Lockwood was the first woman lawyer to take advantage of the law and argue a case before the highest court in the land. Her 1879 appearance there forced every lower federal court to accept women lawyers as well. She continued to press for women's rights: She forced the federal government to pay women the same wages as men; she ran for president in 1884 and 1888 as the Equal Rights Party candidate; she wrote legislation that extended suffrage to women in Oklahoma, Arizona and New Mexico; and she won damages of $5 million from the U.S. for displaced Cherokees.

62. Equal Rights Amendment

In 1972 Congress passed the Equal Rights Amendment (ERA), guaranteeing that "equality of rights under the law shall not be denied or abridged by the United States or by any State on account of sex." The amendment went to the states for ratification, backed by activists prepared for a long, hard fight. But the required number of states failed to ratify the ERA within the ten-year deadline, spelling the end of the amendment for the time being.

63. Supreme Justice

Sandra Day O'Connor (1930–), the first woman to serve on the U.S. Supreme Court, was nominated by President Ronald Reagan in 1981. Historically conservative, O'Connor nonetheless worried pro-life activists because of her unclear stance on abortion. The Senate approved her 99–0; since then she has become the Court's

in Washington, D.C., in 1873. An exponent of women's rights, she was particularly concerned with winning equity for women in the legal profession. She had to struggle to gain admission to law school, to receive a diploma when she finished and to gain access to courts in order to argue cases. In 1876, when a federal judge refused to hear her in court, Lockwood turned to the Supreme Court, which rejected her claim of dis-

moderate conservative, siding with liberal members on some issues, such as sexual harassment, and with its conservative members on others. In 1992 she gained a female colleague in Ruth Bader Ginsburg (1933–), nominated by President Bill Clinton. Ginsburg brought a clearly liberal sensibility to the bench, but she has also proved a moderate jurist.

On Women's Rights

64.

"In the new code of laws which I suppose it will be necessary for you to make, I desire you would remember the ladies and be more generous and favorable to them than your ancestors. Do not put such unlimited power in the hands of the husbands. Remember, all men would be tyrants if they could. If particular care and attention is not paid to the ladies, we are determined to foment a rebellion, and will not hold ourselves bound by any laws in which we have no voice or representation." —Abigail Adams, in a letter to John Adams, 1776

65.

"Consider, I address you as a legislator, whether, when men contend for their freedom, and to be allowed to judge for themselves respecting their own happiness, it be not inconsistent and unjust to subjugate women, even though you firmly believe that you are acting in the manner best calculated to promote their happiness? Who made man the exclusive judge, if women partake with

him the gift of reason?" —Mary Wollstonecraft, in a letter to Talleyrand, 1791

66.

"Even admitting that Eve was the greater sinner, it seems to me man might be satisfied with the dominion he has claimed and exercised for nearly six thousand years, and that more true nobility would be manifested by endeavoring to raise the fallen and invigorate the weak, than by keeping woman in subjection. But I ask no favors for my sex. I surrender not our claim to equality. All I ask of our brethren is, that they will take their feet from off our necks and permit us to stand upright on that ground which God designed us to occupy." —Sarah Moore Grimké, in a letter to Angelina Grimké, 1837

67.

"When not one man, in the million, shall I say? no, not in the hundred million, can rise above the belief that Woman was made *for Man*,— when such traits as these are daily forced upon the attention, can we feel that Man will always do justice to the interests of Woman? Can we think that he takes a sufficiently discerning and religious view of her office and destiny *ever* to do her justice, except when prompted by sentiment—accidentally or transiently . . . ?" —Margaret Fuller, *Woman in the Nineteenth Century,* 1845

68.

"A discussion of the rights of animals would be regarded with far more complacency by many of what are called the *wise* and the *good* of our land, than would a discussion of the rights of women. It is, in their estimation, to be guilty of evil thoughts, to think that woman is entitled to equal rights with man. Many who have at last made the discovery that the negroes have some rights as well as other members of the human family, have yet to be convinced that women are entitled to any." —Frederick Douglass, 1848

69.

"That man over there says that women need to be helped into carriages, and lifted over ditches, and to have the best place everywhere. Nobody ever helps me into carriages, or over mud-puddles, or gives me any best place! And ain't I a woman? Look at me! Look at my arm! I have ploughed and planted, and gathered into barns, and no man could head me! And ain't I a woman? I could work as much and eat as much as a man—when I could get it—and bear the lash as well! And ain't I a woman? I have borne thirteen children, and seen them most all sold off to slavery, and when I cried out with my mother's grief, none but Jesus heard me! And ain't I a woman?" —Sojourner Truth, 1851

70.

"How has this Women's Rights movement been treated in this country, on the right hand and the left? This nation ridicules and derides this movement, and spits upon it, as fit only to be cast out and trampled underfoot. This is not ignorance. They know all about the truth. It is the natural outbreak of tyranny. It is because the tyrants and usurpers are alarmed. They have been and are called to judgement, and they dread the examination and exposure of

their position and character." —William Lloyd Garrison, 1853

71.

"The prejudice against color, of which we hear so much, is no stronger than that against sex. It is produced by the same cause, and manifested very much in the same way. The negro's skin and the woman's sex are both *prima facie* evidence that they were intended to be in subjection to the white Saxon man." —Elizabeth Cady Stanton, 1860

72.

"Men their rights and nothing more; women their rights and nothing less." —Susan B. Anthony and Elizabeth Cady Stanton in *The Revolution,* 1868

73.

"Men do not want solely the obedience of women, they want their sentiments. All men, except the most brutish, desire to have, in the woman most nearly connected with them, not a forced slave but a willing one, not a slave merely, but a favourite." —John Stuart Mill, *The Subjection of Women,* 1869

74.

"Of my two 'handicaps,' being female put many more obstacles in my path than being black." —Shirley Chisolm, *Unbought and Unbossed,* 1970

75.

"The Equal Rights Amendment is about a socialist, anti-family political movement that encourages women to leave their husbands, kill their children, practice witchcraft, destroy capitalism and become lesbians." —Pat Robertson, 1994

The Fight for Suffrage

76. National Society for Women's Suffrage

In 1867, a group of British suffragists that included Dame Millicent Garrett Fawcett and Lydia Becker founded England's first national suffrage organization. John Stuart Mill supported the group, under whose auspices Becker became the first woman to lecture publicly on the issue.

77. Minor v. Happersett

In St. Louis, Virginia L. Minor tried to vote in November 1872 and was denied the privilege by Reese Happersett, the registrar of voters. Refusing to accept the status quo, Minor sued Happersett for $10,000, claiming he violated her constitutional rights on the grounds she was a woman. She lost in the circuit court of St. Louis County and before the Missouri Supreme Court, so she took her case to Washington. In their arguments before the Supreme Court, her attorneys stated that "There can be no division of citizenship, either of its rights or its duties. There can be no half-way citizenship. Woman, as a citizen of the United States, is entitled to all the benefits of that position, and liable to all its obligations, or to none." The Supreme Court disagreed in 1875, deciding unanimously that the U.S. Constitution did not require the State of

Women vote in Wyoming, 1869.

Missouri to allow Minor to vote. "When the Constitution of the United States was adopted," the justices wrote in their decision, "... in no State were all citizens permitted to vote. Each State determined for itself who should have that power." The Supreme Court's decision in *Minor* v. *Happersett* made it easier for states to prohibit women from voting, a practice that would continue for many years.

78. Another Double Standard

After the Civil War, the U.S. Congress enacted the Fourteenth and Fifteenth Amendments to the Constitution, granting suffrage to African-American men. Nevertheless, a woman suffrage amendment to the Constitution was defeated in 1897.

79. *The Wild West*

The booming Western states led the way in American woman suffrage, granting women the vote before the more staid Eastern states did. In 1890 Wyoming was admitted to the Union as the first state that allowed women to vote. Colorado (1893), Utah and Idaho (both 1896) attained the same status within the decade, and Western women began to demonstrate their importance as voters on the state level. These four suffrage states stood alone for several years, until lobbying and demonstrations by the National American Woman Suffrage Association began to yield results. Washington State permitted women to vote in 1910, California in 1911 and Arizona, Kansas and Oregon in 1912. Montana and Nevada voted for suffrage in 1914, followed by New York in 1917 and Michigan, Oklahoma and South Dakota in 1918. Fourteen other states enacted limited suffrage in presidential primaries before the passage of the Nineteenth Amendment.

80. *World Citizens*

It took a century for nations with democratically elected governments to adopt universal woman suffrage. The very first country to allow all women to vote at the national level was New Zealand, which did so in 1893. Other nations slowly followed suit, and by the 1980s all but a few Muslim countries embraced woman suffrage.

1906 Finland
1908 Australia
1913 Norway
1916 Denmark, Iceland
1917 Soviet Union, the Netherlands
1918 Canada, Luxembourg
1919 Austria, Czechoslovakia, Germany, Italy, Poland, Sweden
1920 United States
1923 The Philippines
1928 Great Britain, Puerto Rico
1929 Ecuador
1930 South Africa
1931 Spain
1932 Brazil, Uruguay
1934 Turkey, Cuba
1941 Panama
1944 France
1945 Guatemala, Japan
1946 Italy, Mexico, Argentina
1947 Bolivia, China
1948 Belgium, South Korea, Israel
1949 Chile, India, Indonesia, Syria
1950 El Salvador
1954 Belize, Honduras
1956 Egypt, Greece, Nicaragua, Peru
1957 Tunisia
1958 Algeria, Mauritius
1961 The Bahamas, Cameroon
1962 Monaco
1963 Iran
1964 Libya, San Marino
1965 Afghanistan
1966 Barbados, Botswana
1968 Ireland
1970 Andorra
1971 Switzerland
1974 China
1977 Liechtenstein
1980 Cape Verde
1985 Bangladesh

81. Battle on the Home Front

World War I broke down the last barriers to woman suffrage in the U.S. While the nation's men shipped out to fight in Europe, women on the home front flooded into factories to manufacture armaments and equipment and volunteered their free time to raise funds and assemble care packages. Some even went overseas to drive ambulances or to serve as nurses. At war's end, only a few elected officials dared speak out against giving the vote to women.

82. The Nineteenth Amendment

On January 10, 1918, the U.S. House of Representatives passed the woman suffrage amendment, known as the Anthony Amendment in honor of Susan B. Anthony. The Senate approved the amendment on June 4, 1919, and fourteen months later Tennessee became the thirty-sixth state to ratify it. On August 26, 1920, the Nineteenth Amendment was officially added to the Constitution of the United States. It reads: "The right of citizens of the United States to vote shall not be denied or abridged by the United States or any State on account of sex." American women finally gained one of the most basic rights of citizens in a democracy.

SUFFRAGISTS AND THEIR SENTIMENTS

83. Elizabeth Cady Stanton
(1815–1902)

Intellectually gifted as a child, women's rights leader Elizabeth Cady Stanton first learned the realities of sexism from her father, a stern judge who once remarked to her, "Oh, my daughter, would that you were a boy!" An avid student, she excelled in Greek and read law informally at her father's office before marrying. At her wedding, the young feminist refused to use the word "obey" in her vows; she also insisted on keeping her family name, using it for the rest of her life in conjunction with her husband's name. Her honeymoon at the 1840 World Anti-Slavery Convention in London proved a turning point in her life, for there she met Lucretia Mott, an older feminist who became her mentor. In 1848 the two women called the first Women's Rights Convention, held in Stanton's hometown of Seneca Falls, New York. Stanton drafted the convention's "Declaration of Sentiments and Resolutions," establishing herself as a leader of the women's rights movement. In 1851 she met Susan B. Anthony and the two women launched a fruitful, lifelong partnership. They published the women's rights newspaper *The Revolution,* agitated for women's property rights and in the 1880s co-authored the first three volumes of the massive, six-volume *History of Woman Suffrage.* After the Civil War, as the focus of the women's movement shifted increasingly toward suffrage,

Cady Stanton tried to keep other, equally important issues on the agenda. She critiqued the sexism of organized Christianity in *The Woman's Bible* (1895), toured the lecture circuit and spoke out for women's education. Toward the end of her life, Stanton viewed the next generation of feminists with satisfaction: "Of one thing men may be assured," she wrote, "and that is, that the next generation will not argue the question of women's rights with the infinite patience we have displayed during half a century."

84. Emmeline Pankhurst
(1858–1928)

The single most powerful force within the British woman suffrage movement, Emmeline Pankhurst helped found the National Society for Women's Suffrage in 1867 and wrote England's first woman suffrage bill in the late 1860s. In the 1870s she authored and pressed for passage of the Married Women's Property Act, which passed in 1882. Founding the Women's Franchise League in 1889, she was instrumental in passage of an 1894 bill permitting married women to vote in local elections. She became increasingly frustrated with Parliament's refusal to grant universal woman suffrage and with the conservatism of existing suffrage groups, so in 1903 she founded the Women's Social and Political Union (WSPU) to agitate for the cause. The group adopted militant tactics that drew wide public attention to the woman suffrage issue, holding large demonstrations and marches as well as boycotts and pickets. Some members harassed anti-suffrage politicians, broke windows and even set off bombs to get their message across. When WSPU members—including Pankhurst and her two daughters, Christabel and Estelle—were thrown into prison, they conducted hunger strikes to continue their protest. Pankhurst and her supporters suspended their protests during World War I and garnered growing public support through their contributions to the war effort. Protesting resumed after the war, and Pankhurst lived just long enough to see British women win universal suffrage in 1928.

85.

"It always seems to me when the anti-suffrage members of the Government criticize militancy in women that it is very like beasts of prey reproaching gentler animals who turn in desperate resistance when at the point of death."
—Emmeline Pankhurst, 1912

86.

"If it turned out that Britain could only be governed by riot and violence I am game for that sort of thing. But I mean to have a try at the other thing first—when the vote is won! . . . When we have done that, then we will help the men to solve the problems of the twentieth century. Plainly they can't settle them without us."
—Christabel Pankhurst, in a letter to Henry Harben, 1913

87. Alice Paul (1885–1977)

This Quaker social worker radicalized the woman suffrage movement early in the twentieth century, infusing it with a burst of energy essential to its imminent success. A 1905 graduate of Swarthmore College with master's and doctorate degrees from the University of Pennsylvania, Paul learned activism at the feet of England's militant suffragists. In 1912 she returned to the U.S. and joined the National American Woman Suffrage Association, then left to establish a more aggressive organization. That group, the Congressional Union for Woman Suffrage (which in 1917 became the National Woman's Party), set up picket lines and conducted dramatic demonstrations in Washington, D.C. On March 3, 1913, Woodrow Wilson's inauguration day, Paul led eight thousand protestors, twenty-six floats, ten bands and six chariots in a protest march past half a million spectators. It took five of the U.S. Army's cavalry units to subdue the violence that broke out and left more than two hundred people injured. The publicity boosted donations and helped the suffragists gather close to half a million signatures on a petition demanding passage of a constitutional amendment. Paul continued to picket the Capitol and the White House and landed in jail with many of her colleagues, where they conducted hunger strikes and other actions. In 1917, during Wilson's second inauguration, Paul led a daring march around the White House, helping to ensure that the next inaugural would seat the first president elected, in part, by women's votes.

88. Sole Survivor

Only one of the participants in the 1848 Women's Rights Convention, Charlotte Woodward, lived to vote after passage of the Nineteenth Amendment. She was nineteen years old at Seneca Falls, and ninety-one when she voted in 1920.

89. Martyr for Votes

Far more militant than the American suffrage movement, the drive for women's votes in England spawned riots, acts of terrorism and other radical incidents. In the name of woman suffrage, one activist threw herself onto the racetrack at Epsom Downs and was trampled to death by horses.

REBELS AND RADICALS

90. In Quest of Independence

The people of ancient Vietnam spent centuries fighting off Chinese invaders and deposing Chinese conquerors. Among the most famous resisters of Chinese rule are several women, two of whom led the first major uprising. In the year 39, sisters Trung Trac and Trung Nhi, both widows of aristocrats killed by the Chinese, led a revolt and installed Trung Trac, the elder, as the head of an independent state. Within four years the Chinese reconquered the area, but Vietnamese resistance continued for the next thousand years. Women took the initiative in many of the uprisings: Phung Thi Chinh fought while pregnant, pausing to give birth and strap her baby onto her back before resuming the battle. In 240, Trien Au assembled an army and battled for six months before meeting defeat. Known as "the Vietnamese Joan of Arc," the virgin warrior killed herself rather than surrender to the Chinese.

A few years later, thousands followed a twenty-three-year-old peasant named Trieu Thi Tinh in an unsuccessful revolt; she, too, committed suicide in the face of Chinese capture. The tradition of women warriors survives in the twentieth century: The Anti-Colonialist Women's

Association, formed in 1930, pressed for the independence and reunification of Vietnam, and during the Vietnam War, American soldiers reported that women fighting for North Vietnam were even tougher than their male comrades.

91. *Olympe de Gouges* (d. 1793)

A supporter of the French Revolution, this political writer nonetheless voiced criticism of some of its leaders and philosophies. Author of various tracts on education and women's rights, she gained wide notoriety in 1791, when she published a fearless response to the revolution's *Declaration of the Rights of Man and of the Citizen.* That document, which championed the virtues of equality and individual freedom, conspicuously neglected to mention women's rights. Gouges composed a *Declaration of the Rights of Women and of Citizenesses* (1791) to make the point that the revolution should support legal, economic and social equality for women. The male leadership of the insurrection scoffed at her proposals and would happily have ignored her if she hadn't spoken up on behalf of the deposed King Louis XVI, whom she thought should not be executed. Her final offense was to criticize the violent techniques of Robespierre, who had initiated the Reign of Terror against anyone perceived as an enemy of the revolution. Gouges immediately fell into that category and was executed in 1793.

92. *Some Revolution*

The French Revolution, founded on the humanist ideals of the Enlightenment, emphatically denied women equal rights with men. Although women were vital to the revolution's success, staging massive demonstrations, circulating petitions and pamphlets and even fighting, they soon understood the limits of the rallying cry *"Liberté, Égalité, Fraternité."* In 1793 the French Revolutionary Convention voted to ban women's political clubs, prohibit women from taking part in any political activity and exclude women from citizenship. Théroigne de Méricourt, who dared to organize women fighters and to demand equal rights for women, was beaten by a mob and locked up in an insane asylum until her death.

93. *Louise Michel* (1830–1905)

One of France's leading anarchists started her political career as a feminist, founding in 1866 a women's rights organization dedicated to the prevention of prostitution and the improvement of women's wages and education. In 1871 she joined the revolutionary Paris Commune, but her increasingly radical politics got her exiled in 1873. She returned to France when general amnesty was declared in 1880 and immediately resumed her anarchist agitating. Sentenced to six years' imprisonment in 1883, she refused a pardon and agreed to move to London upon her release. When she came home to Paris in 1896, however, she resumed lecturing and anarchist agitating. She also published several books over the course of her career.

94. *Victoria Woodhull* (1838–1927)

In 1872 the Equal Rights Party nominated Victoria Woodhull its candidate for president of the United States. An outspoken and controversial figure, she was the daughter of a medicine-show proprietor and an afficionado of the supernatural. With her sister Tennessee Claflin, she worked as a psychic, as a Wall Street stockbroker and as publisher of *Woodhull and Claflin's Weekly,* a feminist paper in which she discussed prostitution, abortion and other topics considered shocking in Victorian America. Woodhull was the first in America to publish Karl Marx's *Communist Manifesto,* but most shocking of all was her enthusiastic endorsement of "free love." In a special issue of her paper, she printed an exposé of an adulterous affair between noted clergyman Henry Ward Beecher and a parishioner; she was arrested for publishing obscene material and her presidential campaign came to an end.

95. *Rosa Luxemburg*
(1870–1919)

Born in Poland, Luxemburg had to leave her homeland at the age of eighteen because of her affiliations with the radical underground. She studied at the University of Zürich, where she adopted Marxism and got involved in the socialist movement. After helping to found the Polish Communist Party, she moved to Berlin in 1898 and joined the German Social Democratic Party (SPD). The Russian Revolution of 1905 took her to Warsaw and landed her in prison; when she was released in 1907 she returned to Berlin to teach at the SPD school. Fervently opposed to Germany's endeavors in World War I, she established the Spartacists, a revolutionary branch of the SPD, with Karl Liebknecht. She went to jail for her antiwar activities and after her release continued her radical activities. During the vio-

lent 1919 Spartacist uprising, she was arrested and killed by German troops.

96. *Red Emma*

Emma Goldman (1869–1940) immigrated from Russia to the U.S. in 1885 and became one of the most famous radicals of her time. An anarchist who also involved herself in socialist causes, she was jailed several times for spreading her antigovernment message. She founded and edited an anarchist periodical, *Mother Earth,* and traveled extensively to speak out on feminism, pacifism and socialism. Deported to the Soviet Union in 1919, she was soon disheartened by that country's failure to fulfill socialist ideals. She moved to London and later contributed her energies to the Spanish Civil War.

Rosa Luxemburg.

97.

"There is no such thing as a good government."
—Emma Goldman

98. Hannah Szenes
(1921–1944)

A poet before the outbreak of World War II, this Hungarian Jew was a fierce Nazi resister. Her Zionist convictions prompted her to emigrate to Palestine, where she joined the Palestine underground army. Backed by that group, she parachuted into Nazi-held Yugoslavia to organize Jewish resistance there. But before she could start her mission she was captured by the Nazis, who brutally tortured her to extract resistance secrets. Szenes, however, would not talk and was executed by a firing squad.

99. Pivotal Protestor

The Stonewall Riot, which launched the gay rights movement, started when a woman resisted arrest. Late on Friday night, June 27, 1969, New York City police raided the Stonewall Inn, a gay bar in Greenwich Village. They began ejecting the patrons from the bar one at a time, detaining some and letting others go. Those released by the police gathered across the street to watch. When a woman being ejected from the bar put up a struggle, the police turned rough and a riot ensued. Bottles and rocks flew as the crowd on the street grew larger. A fire started in the bar and the police turned a firehose on the crowd. By the time more police arrived and cleared the scene, close to two thousand angry people had gathered in front of the Stonewall Inn. Tensions remained high and scattered disturbances broke out in the days that followed. Lesbians and gay men formed the Gay Liberation Front (GLF) to agitate for their civil rights. Word of events in New York spread across the country, prompting gays in other cities to join the movement that summer. Gay rights organizations multiplied rapidly and began pressing for recognition and respect.

CIVIL RIGHTS MOVEMENT

100. The Back of the Bus

On December 1, 1955, Rosa Parks (1913–   ) propelled the civil rights movement into a new stage of activism when she refused to give up her seat and move to the back of a Montgomery, Alabama, bus so a white rider could sit down. It wasn't the first time she'd done so, but it was the first time a bus driver had her arrested for it. Parks had served as secretary of the NAACP's local chapter for twelve years, and had been kicked off Montgomery buses more than once for refusing to follow the rules of segregation. Her arrest set off the yearlong boycott in which hundreds of African-Americans walked or carpooled to work rather than ride the buses. Pressure on local authorities to change their policies spawned a lawsuit that ultimately made its way to the U.S. Supreme Court. In November 1956, the court ruled in *Browder* v. *Gayle* that Alabama's bus segregation laws were unconstitutional. The boycott, and the legal victory, provided new momentum to the growing civil rights movement.

101. Fannie Lou Hamer (1918–1977)

A sharecropper's daughter advanced the rights of African-American voters by making an unauthorized appearance at the 1964 Democratic National Convention. Leading members of the Mississippi Freedom Democratic Party into the Atlantic City convention hall, she charged that Mississippi's all-white delegation should not be seated because it was the product of presidential primaries that had illegally excluded black voters. She failed to unseat the delegation, but her testimony was broadcast live on national television and drew attention to discrimination against African-American voters in the South. In addition, the Democratic Party voted not to seat future delegations selected illegally; the subsequent revision of the party's rules forced Southern Democrats to allow at least some minority voters into the polls. Hamer, who endured beatings, eviction, job loss and other harassment because of her voter activism both before and after the convention, later lost a race for state senate. She uttered her most famous phrase in a hearing before a congressional committee: "I am sick and tired of being sick and tired."

102. Discrimination in the Movement

Although countless African-American women worked on behalf of the civil rights movement, it was led by men on the local, state and national levels. Some of these leaders felt attention to women's concerns would divert the movement from its primary goals; others believed women were not capable of leadership. Nevertheless, women learned about activism within the movement and eventually put their skills to work in the women's movement.

103.

"On the road to equality there is no better place for blacks to detour around American values than in forgoing its example in the treatment of its women and the organization of its family life." —Rep. Eleanor Holmes Norton, 1970

THREE FIRST STEPS OF SECOND-WAVE FEMINISM

104. The Feminine Mystique

Frustrated by the limitations of her life, a suburban American homemaker in 1963 published an indictment of women's restriction to passive, domestic roles. Within a year, readers bought 3 million copies of Betty Friedan's book, which showed countless American women they were not alone in their unhappiness. As women spoke with each other, wrote to Friedan and read whatever they could find on the topic, they began to understand the depth of their oppression. Friedan later wrote: "I and every other woman I knew had been living a lie, and all the doctors who treated us and the experts who studied us were perpetuating that lie, and our homes and schools and churches and politics and professions were built around that lie. If women were really *people*—no more, no less— then all the things that kept them from being full people in our society would have to be changed. And women, once they broke through the feminine mystique and took themselves seriously as people, would see their place on a false pedestal, even their glorification as sexual objects, for the putdown it was." Unflinching in its portrayal of women's second-class status, *The Feminine Mystique* triggered the women's movement of the late twentieth century, making it one of the most important books of its time.

105. *National Organization for Women*

Although the U.S. government banned sex discrimination in employment early in the 1960s, federal officials made little effort to enforce the legislation. The budding women's movement made this failing the target of its first organized action on the national level. In 1965 a group of women went to Washington, D.C., to pressure the government to enforce its own laws, but they made no headway with the male officials they met. Angered, Betty Friedan and a circle of women lawyers, union leaders and government workers decided to form a national organization to agitate for women's rights. The National Organization for Women (NOW) formed in 1966 as a forum for feminist ideas and a force to lobby government, industry, universities and other institutions to end sexist practices. According to its statement of purpose, NOW vowed to "take *action* to bring women into full participation in the mainstream of American society now, exercising all the privileges and responsibilities thereof, in truly equal partnership with men."

106. *Women's Strike for Equality*

In the 1960s the growing American feminist movement spawned scores of activist groups dedicated to various aspects of women's fight for equal rights. Many of these feminists joined forces to hold the National Women's Strike for Equality on August 26, 1970, the fiftieth anniversary of the passage of the Nineteenth Amendment. In New York City, fifty thousand women linked arms and marched down Fifth Avenue to demand equal rights in employment, education, politics and other spheres. The strike, a peaceful event involving not only activists but homemakers, secretaries, teachers and women from all walks of life, brought feminism into the mainstream and awakened even more women and men to the realities of sexism. It helped mobilize grassroots activism around the nation, inspiring demonstrations, boycotts, lectures, petitions, articles and lobbying on behalf of women's rights.

POLITICIANS

107. *Governing the Nile*

From the establishment of Egypt's first dynasty around 3200 B.C.E., aristocratic Egyptian women enjoyed considerable political power. Pharaohs inherited the throne from their mother's side of the family; their queens occasionally ruled on their behalf during periods of illness. Queen Aahhotep I, for instance, ruled around 1570 to 1546 B.C.E. and played a vital role in reuniting the kingdom after a period of civil strife. Endowed with the same legal rights as their male counterparts, lesser royal women trained for government service and participated in foreign as well as domestic affairs.

108. The Fu

As early as 1700 B.C.E., aristocratic Chinese women known as *fu* participated in Chinese politics. Rising simultaneously with the Shang, or Yin, dynasty—China's first—they commanded armies and held various civil offices, overseeing agriculture, religion and tax collection. The *fu* remained active for many centuries.

109. Unsung Diplomat

One of her people's delegates at peace talks with the British, Asante Princess Akyaawa Yikwan brought the negotiations to a successful conclusion. In 1831 the two nations signed a peace treaty that improved conditions for the Asante, at least for the time being.

110. Mary E. Lease (1853–1933)

When agrarian revolt swept through the American Midwest in the 1880s, this Kansas attorney rose to prominence as a Populist activist and political candidate with a talent for spellbinding oratory. On one especially memorable occasion, she told her audience, "What you farmers need to do is to raise less corn and more *hell!* Wall Street owns the country. It is no longer a government of the people, by the people and for the people, but a government of Wall Street, by Wall Street and for Wall Street. The great common people of this country are slaves, and monopoly is the master."

111. Two Firsts

British labor leader Margaret G. Bondfield became the country's first woman cabinet member in 1929, a year after women gained the vote. Fifty years later, Parliament elected Margaret Thatcher the first woman prime minister of Great Britain; she held the office for eleven years, until 1990.

112. Margaret Chase Smith
(1897–1995)

As a congresswoman for Maine, Smith served in the U.S. House of Representatives from 1940 to 1948, and in the Senate from 1948 to 1972. She was the first woman elected to both houses of Congress, and the first to win a Senate seat without serving previously by appointment. An independent, she took a moderate stance on most issues and criticized all forms of extremism, notably Senator Joseph McCarthy's Communist witch-hunt. In 1950, in the midst of that frenzy, she delivered an eloquent speech denouncing McCarthy's tactics. The speech, which became known as "A Declaration of Conscience," appealed to the Senate to protect the free-speech and free-association rights upon which McCarthy was trampling.

113. Geraldine Ferraro (1935–   )

In 1984 Geraldine Ferraro became the first woman to run as the vice-presidential candidate for a major American political party. She started her career as an attorney in private practice, then became an assistant district attorney in Queens, New York. After serving from 1974 to 1978, she was elected to the U.S. House of Representatives. Queens voters reelected her in 1980 and 1982, and her popularity grew. So did her power within the Democratic Party, which appointed her head of its platform committee in 1984. Soon Walter F. Mondale chose her as his running mate in his campaign for the party's presidential nomination. Mondale and Ferraro won the nomination, but in November 1984 they lost the national election. Ferraro retired from politics until 1992, when she campaigned to become one of New York's U.S. senators. She lost that election but remained an influential figure in national and feminist politics, and in early 1998 announced her intention to again seek a U.S. Senate seat from New York.

114. Taking Power

Between 1963, when the American women's movement took off, and the elections of 1988, women tripled their presence in elected office on the local, state and national levels. Their numbers skyrocketed in 1992, "The Year of the Woman," when the number of women in the U.S. Senate doubled from three to six, the number in the House of Representatives rose to forty-seven from twenty-eight and women came to hold 20 percent of statewide executive and legislative offices.

115. EMILY's List

Founded to help pro-choice, Democratic women win election to Congress, this fund-raising organization takes its name from the acronym for "Early Money Is Like Yeast." The group and its individual members specialize in making contributions to campaigns at the crucial, early stages—a total of $8.2 million during the 1994 elections alone.

116. Carol Mosely Braun
(1947–)

In 1992, an African-American woman won a seat in the U.S. Senate for the first time. Carol Mosely Braun, a civil servant from Chicago, defeated incumbent Senator Alan J. Dixon in the Democratic primaries and then beat her Republican opponent by a wide margin to represent Illinois in national office. Her rapid ascent from obscurity came in the wake of the Anita Hill–Clarence Thomas fiasco on Capitol Hill, in which Dixon supported Thomas. The Cook County recorder of deeds since 1989, Braun had previously served ten years as a representative to the Illinois state senate and had worked as an assistant U.S. attorney. As for many other women campaigning for office in 1992, anger over the Hill-Thomas hearings prompted her to run. Her victory in a state known for racial tension demonstrated the fervor of the electorate's hope that women could put an end to politics as usual.

ACTIVISTS AND ACTIVISM

117. Protestor's Paradox

Women who fought for the abolition of slavery in the U.S. did so in the face of a basic contradiction: Some of the most important figures in the movement were women, yet they worked to secure for African-Americans rights they themselves did not enjoy. The humiliation of abolitionist women intensified in the summer of 1840. At the World Anti-Slavery Convention, held in London and attended by the leading abolitionists of the day, women were refused seats on the convention floor and were denied the right to participate in discussions or vote on the issues before the assembly. The affront enraged many women attendees, inspiring them to launch a movement for women's rights.

118. Seneca Falls

In 1848 Lucretia Mott and Elizabeth Cady Stanton organized the first Women's Rights Convention in Seneca Falls, New York. The delegates discussed the problems facing women and adopted a "Declaration of Sentiments and Resolutions," modeled after the Declaration of Independence. Signed by one hundred of the three hundred convention attendees, the declaration asserted that "all men and women are created equal" and outlined "a history of repeated injuries and usurpations on the part of man toward women" by presenting a list of grievances. Among those were the disfranchisement of women, the denial of women's property rights, lack of access to decent education and employment, the existence of a double standard of morality for men and women and the psychological tyranny of men over women. In the declaration, the delegates demanded "immediate admission to all the rights and privileges which belong to [women] as citizens of the United States."

119. The Underground Railroad

From the 1780s until Emancipation, thousands of escaped American slaves made their way to the Northern states and Canada via the Underground Railroad. The most famous conductor on the Railroad was Harriet Tubman, an escaped slave who returned to the South nineteen times to guide a total of three hundred slaves to freedom. Another conductor, fugitive slave Ann Wood, led a group of boys and girls to the North, losing two of her charges in a gunfight with slave catchers.

120. Sarah Winnemucca
(c. 1844–1891)

This daughter of Paiute Chief Winnemucca worked to secure decent treatment for her people from the whites who forced them off their Nevada land. Born Thocmetony, she kept house in her early teens for a white businessman who gave her the name Sarah. There she learned English and Spanish in addition to the three Indian languages she already knew. As tensions intensified between Paiutes and white settlers, Winnemucca lost most of her family in the fighting and moved to an Oregon reservation with her people. She interceded with the U.S. authorities for food, blankets and housing, which were promised but not delivered. Emerging as a national figure, she gave lectures on the mistreatment of Native Americans, traveled to Washington, D.C., to negotiate with the president and the interior secretary, wrote *Life Among the Piutes* (sic) and started an Indian school.

121. Maude de Victor (1937–)

In the years following the Vietnam War, one Veterans Administration employee became convinced that the mysterious ailments reported by many American veterans had a single cause. Maude de Victor, an African-American veterans benefits counselor in the Chicago office of the VA, blamed their health problems on Agent Orange, a chemical defoliant used by the U.S. military to destroy enemy crops and cover. The military, including the VA, denied Agent Orange was harmful. De Victor first heard complaints about Agent Orange in 1977, but when she submitted claims on behalf of veterans and their widows, the VA refused to pay their benefits. Tracking down military officials, chemical manufacturers and scientists, De Victor learned that the government had known of Agent Orange's dangers. Mapping the use of the chemical in Vietnam, she compiled more than fifty case histories that showed a link between Agent Orange and a host of medical problems. The VA dismissed her findings and ordered her to stop investigating. Instead, she turned to the press. A CBS affiliate in Chicago aired an exposé on March 23, 1978, setting off a torrent of publicity. Agent Orange–related claims began to pour into the VA, which still refused to act. Frustrated, De Victor quit the VA in 1981, but by then her work had inspired veterans to form organizations and file class-action suits. In 1985, the Vietnam veterans injured by Agent Orange were finally awarded millions of dollars in compensation.

122. *Irish Peacemakers*

In 1976 Mairead Corrigan (1944–   ) and Betty Williams (1943–   ), two Roman Catholic women from Northern Ireland, won the Nobel Peace Prize for their efforts to bring peace to their feuding homeland. Since 1968, Roman Catholics have agitated to end the discrimination they experience in a predominantly Protestant country. When Britain tried to take control of Northern Ireland's government, the violence escalated. In 1976 Mairead Corrigan and Betty Williams founded the Peace People in a courageous attempt to unite Catholics and Protestants. The Nobel Committee recognized the importance of their pacifist efforts even though the fighting has continued.

123. *Yelena Bonner* (1924–   )

Best known as the wife of Soviet physicist and dissident Andrei Sakharov, Yelena Bonner has had a long career as an activist in her own right. Working alongside her husband to protest human rights abuses in the Soviet Union, she dedicated herself to political reform. In 1975, when the Soviet government refused Sakharov the right to travel, Bonner went to Oslo to accept his Nobel Peace Prize and deliver his speech. The following year she founded a dissident group to advance civil liberties. She led the group's efforts until 1984, when she was sentenced to internal exile with her husband. Sakharov died in 1989, shortly after the fall of the Soviet Union, but Bonner continued to agitate for human rights in the new Russian republic. In 1990 she opposed the award of the Nobel Peace Prize to former Soviet premier Mikhail Gorbachev, and in 1995 she resigned from Boris Yeltsin's human rights commission to protest the Russian president's war against Chechnya. She currently heads the Sakharov Foundation, a human rights think tank.

124. *Phyllis Schlafly* (1924–   )

This conservative lawyer is president of the Eagle Forum, which she founded in 1972, and editor of *The Phyllis Schlafly Report* and *The Eagle Forum Newsletter*. She rose to national prominence in the 1970s as the driving force behind STOP-ERA, an organization dedicated to preventing ratification of the Equal Rights Amendment. Wielding scare tactics about single-sex public toilets, the drafting of women into the armed services and the threat to traditional family structure and women's roles, Schlafly was instrumental in the amendment's failure. Part of that campaign was the 1977 "pro-life, pro-family" convention she organized in Houston as a challenge to the International Women's Year meeting that drew twenty thousand women to the city. Hundreds of conservative women rallied around her to protest not only the ERA but abortion rights, gay rights and other liberal concepts. Schlafly has since carried on her work with the Eagle Forum, attacking issues such as sex education and federal funding of the arts, day care and family leave. In 1990 she founded the Republican National Coalition for Life, which helped draft the uncompromising anti-choice plank in the party's 1992 platform. Her politics have allied her with the Christian right and groups such as Concerned Women for America, led by Beverly LaHaye.

125. *Winnie Mandela* (1934–)

After her husband, Nelson Mandela, was jailed in 1964, Winnie Mandela carried on his work with the anti-apartheid African National Congress (ANC). Her political activities put her in jail from 1969 to 1970, then prompted the South African government to declare her a banned person in 1976. Despite orders to the contrary, she continued her struggle against apartheid, sometimes alienating her husband's supporters with her aggressive tactics. When Nelson Mandela was freed in 1990, she was defending herself against accusations that she ordered the 1988 beating of four young black men, one of whom died. She appealed her conviction on kidnapping charges and went to work in the ANC's social welfare department, but new evidence in the case forced her to resign her various ANC appointments in 1992. She separated

from her husband and lost her final appeal, avoiding a prison term by paying fines. Regaining her presidency of the ANC Women's League, she also won an appointment in the new government formed by Nelson Mandela. In 1994 she became South Africa's deputy minister of arts, culture, science and technology. Mandela's image, however, remained sullied. In 1997 she defended herself before South Africa's Truth and Reconciliation Commission, denying charges that she ordered torture and murders in Soweto in the late 1980s. Her integrity in question, Mandela declined the Women's League nomination as a candidate for deputy president of the ANC, most likely ending her political career.

126. *Daw Aung San Suu Kyi* (1945–)

The leader of Burma's human rights and democracy movement received the Nobel Peace Prize in 1991, while under house arrest by the Burmese military. Her commitment to the Burmese people is no accident, as she was born to politically active parents: Her mother was a noted diplomat and her father, assassinated in 1947, was the founder of democratic Burma. Educated in India and England, where she graduated from Oxford University, Daw Aung San Suu Kyi studied Gandhi's philosophy of nonviolence. She took these principles with her when she returned to Burma in 1988. There, she spoke out against the repression imposed by Burma's military dictatorship and helped found the National League for Democracy. Through nonviolence, she foiled government efforts to block free elections in which her party won 80 percent of the seats in parliament. The military refused to yield to the democratically elected government, in 1989 placing Daw Aung San Suu Kyi under house arrest. She turned down several opportunities to go into exile, choosing instead to remain in her homeland. While confined to her home, she published *Freedom from Fear and Other Writings* (1991). Released in August 1995, she resumed her life of political activism.

127. *Wilma Mankiller* (1945–)

In 1985, the members of the Cherokee Nation elected Wilma Mankiller their chief, making her the first woman to lead a major Native American tribe. An Indian-rights activist and worker since the late 1960s, she focused her attention as chief on education, health care and community development, as well as promoting Cherokee business ventures. During her tenure as chief, tribal membership rose from 55,000 to 156,000, and Mankiller was selected to head the Inter-Tribal Council of Oklahoma. She resigned as Cherokee chief in 1994 to continue her work in other capacities.

128. *Rigoberta Menchú* (1959–)

In 1992 the Nobel Committee awarded the Nobel Peace Prize to Rigoberta Menchú, a Guatemalan who has spent most of her life fighting for social justice in her homeland and for respect for indigenous peoples throughout the Americas. A Quiché Indian who grew up in poverty, she joined various political groups involved in the ongoing war between the Guatemalan military and rebel guerrillas. In the

1970s that war claimed the lives of her father, her sixteen-year-old brother and her mother. Menchú fled to Mexico in 1981, where she gradually gained international attention as a vigorous advocate of human, and particularly Indian, rights. She spoke out in favor of rebellion against Guatemala's military government and led the Committee of Peasant Unity, which her father had once headed. In 1983 she published a book, *I Rigoberta Menchú,* describing her life as an example of the oppression suffered by her people. In 1986 her homeland returned to civilian rule, but human rights abuses and guerrilla fighting continued. The government still accused Menchú of supporting violent guerrilla

Wilma Mankiller.

groups, but her Nobel Peace Prize drew the world's attention to official abuses in Guatemala.

ABORTION RIGHTS

129. A Little History

In ancient times, abortion was a common and uncontroversial form of birth control. Only with the spread of the world's major religions—notably Islam and Christianity—did the practice come to be viewed as problematic. These reservations did not take legal form until the nineteenth century, when England's Parliament outlawed abortion. Other nations, including the U.S., subsequently passed a variety of laws limiting abortion. The pendulum began to swing back in 1920, when the Soviet Union legalized abortion on demand. After World War II, Japan and a number of Eastern European nations did so as well. Today, about one fifth of the world's population live in countries that permit abortion only to save a woman's life, 40 percent in countries that allow it under a broader array of circumstances, and 40 percent in countries where women can freely choose abortion before a designated point in the pregnancy.

130. Early U.S. Legislation

Before the 1820s, abortion was legal and unrestricted throughout the U.S. Connecticut was the first state to impose any restrictions on the practice, enacting in 1821 a law that prohibited abortion after "quickening"—the first dis-

cernible movement of the fetus. By 1860 laws in twenty states limited abortion, and in the next twenty years more than twenty states and territories followed suit.

131. Doctors' Opinion

The American Medical Association formally denounced abortion in 1859. As its statements on the issue clearly indicated, the rationale behind its position had nothing to do with science but rather with morality and with a desire to control women. According to an 1871 report by the organization's Committee on Criminal Abortion, the women who aborts "becomes unmindful of the course marked out for her by Providence . . . [and] . . . overlooks the duties imposed on her by the marriage contract."

132. Roe v. Wade

By 1965, abortion—except under the most dire circumstances—was a crime in every state of the U.S. Women seeking to terminate a pregnancy had to do so furtively, often turning to "back alley" abortionists without medical credentials. That all changed in 1973, when the U.S. Supreme Court issued its ruling in *Roe* v. *Wade,* a case that had originated in Texas. There, Norma McCorvey adopted a pseudonym, Jane Roe, to sue the Dallas County district attorney, Henry Wade, for the right to have an abortion. When she won, Wade took the case to the Supreme Court, which also ruled in McCorvey's favor. Abortion, the Court ruled, is protected by constitutional guarantees of the right to privacy, except when the fetus develops to the point where it can survive outside the womb. The Court defined that point as the beginning of the third trimester of pregnancy. During the third trimester, states can regulate abortion except when the mother's life is at risk. States cannot regulate abortion during the first trimester, or during the second trimester if the procedure would endanger a woman's health. Since 1973, the Court's decision in *Roe* v. *Wade* has been challenged several times; the Court has, for the most part, stood by its original ruling but has allowed states to impose some additional restrictions on abortion.

133. *Operation Rescue*

Founded by Randall Terry, a charismatic high school dropout, Operation Rescue dominated the headlines of the abortion rights debate during the late 1980s and early 1990s. The group specialized in weeklong "rescues" across the U.S., staging pickets, demonstrations and blockades that prevented women from entering abortion clinics. Its approximately forty thousand members professed a far-right brand of fundamentalist Christianity and referred to abortion as murder. Although they claimed to practice nonviolent civil disobedience, their tactics included verbal and sometimes physical harassment of women who showed up for appointments at blockaded clinics. Waving photographs of aborted fetuses, singing hymns and shouting "Don't kill your baby!" to clinic clients, members of Operation Rescue made their group an enduring symbol of the radical pro-life movement.

MODERN HEADS OF STATE

134. *Golda Meir* (1898–1978)

Born in Russia and raised in the U.S., Golda Meir embraced Zionism as a teenager and went on to help found Israel. She moved to Palestine with her husband in 1921 and immediately started working with various social and political groups. Head of the Jewish Agency from 1946 to 1948, she signed the Israeli declaration of independence and won election to the first Knesset, or parliament. She served as minister to Moscow, minister of labor, and foreign minister during the 1950s and 1960s and became prime minister in 1969, at the age of seventy-one. In 1974 she retired from politics, but she remained active as a lecturer until her death.

135. *Indira Gandhi* (1917–1984)

The only child of Jawaharlal Nehru, the first prime minister of India, became prime minister herself and had a controversial career that ended in assassination. She graduated from Oxford University and participated in India's rebellion against British colonialism. The 1947 success of that movement placed her father in power, making her an influential insider. A leader of the Congress Party, she became minister of information and broadcasting after her father's death in 1964. She liberalized Indian broadcasting before becoming prime minister in 1966. Five years later her party won the elections by a landslide, but opponents later charged her with violating election laws. Convicted in 1975, she claimed to be the victim of political plotting and refused to resign. She declared a national state of emergency, restricting civil rights and arresting dissenters even after the Supreme Court reversed her conviction. Under attack from various quarters, she called a general election in 1977 and lost. Undaunted, she engineered her party's comeback in 1980 and once again assumed leadership of India. But on October 31, 1984, Sikhs in her security detachment assassinated her. She was succeeded by her son Rajiv, who died in a bombing in 1991.

136. Violeta Barrios de Chamorro
(1929–)

Elected president of Nicaragua in 1990, Chamorro is respected by some of the world's human rights leaders but doubted by others. She entered politics in 1978 when her husband, a newspaper publisher at odds with dictator Anastasio Somoza, was killed. The following year Somoza fled the country in the midst of virtual civil war, and a military Sandinista junta took power. Chamorro supported first the leftist Sandinistas and then the opposing contra guerrillas. The National Opposition Union, a U.S.-backed anti-Sandinista coalition of fourteen political parties, gained power in 1990 and tapped her for the presidency. She implemented a variety of economic, military and political reforms meant to stabilize the country, but conditions remained volatile. Her appointment of former Sandinistas to important posts provoked the contras and fighting broke out again. Chamorro managed to secure foreign aid from several nations, but she has been criticized for filling government posts with relatives.

137. Corazon Aquino
(1933–)

In 1986 the Philippines gained its first woman president. The widow of Liberal Party leader Benigno Aquino, she rose to power in the tumult that ended in the fall of Ferdinand Marcos. Aquino entered the political arena in 1972, when Marcos imposed martial law and jailed her husband. Corazon moved with Benigno to the U.S. upon his release and exile in 1980. Three years later he was killed upon his return to the Philippines, but she ran for the presidency against Marcos in 1986. Fraud and violence cost her the election, but when Marcos declared himself the winner, the army revolted and the people staged huge demonstrations. In the chaos, Marcos fled to the U.S. and Aquino took office, setting up a provisional government. Although she repaired the constitution and oversaw free elections, ongoing economic problems and political unrest convinced her not to run for a second exhausting term in 1992.

138. Benazir Bhutto
(1953–)

The daughter of a Pakistani prime minister, Bhutto was the first woman prime minister of a Muslim country. When General Muhammad Zia deposed her father in 1977 and executed him in 1979, she was put under house arrest as the head of the opposition Pakistan People's Party. Exiled in 1984, she returned in 1986 when political parties once again became legal. She resumed her leadership of the PPP and in 1988 was elected prime minister when Zia died in a mysterious plane crash. In 1990 President

Ghulam Ishaq Khan charged her with corruption and dismissed her, and the PPP lost the elections that followed. Now an opposition leader, she was suspected of plotting against the ruling party and was exiled from the capital city in 1992. But she won the elections of 1993 and became prime minister once again.

Part

TWO

Religion and Humanitarianism

GODDESSES, SPIRITS AND DEMONS

139. Venus Figurines

Across Europe, from France to Russia to Turkey, archaeologists have unearthed scores of prehistoric stone, ivory and clay figurines representing the female form. They date from the Paleolithic and Neolithic eras, spanning the time frame from about 25000 B.C.E. to 2000 B.C.E. The earlier Paleolithic examples feature large breasts, buttocks and thighs, while the later Neolithic ones show less pronounced sexual characteristics. Despite the differences, the discovery of these female figurines (far fewer male figurines have been found) has prompted speculation about prehistoric religion. The notion that prehistoric Europeans may have worshiped female deities—hence the term "Venus" or "Goddess" figurines—has sparked debate. Some feminists have asserted the primacy of goddess worship and speculated that male deities arose much later as men established dominance over women. Judging from the sexual features of the figurines, such goddess worship would seem to have centered around fertility. Others voice doubts about the existence of a unified religion and the significance of the figurines' gender. Perhaps the figurines were actually amulets used in women's coming-of-age rituals or to enhance fertility, or they represented mythological entities or priestesses. Still another theory suggests they were simply children's toys. Whichever explanation is correct, however, the prehistoric tendency to craft representations of the female rather than of the male indicates that women of the time enjoyed elevated spiritual and/or social importance.

140. Isis

The ancient Egyptian goddess of fertility and motherhood was believed to have a taste for carnal pleasure and to wield great supernatural powers. Daughter of the earth god and the sky goddess, she was both sister and wife to the god Osiris, who presided over the dead, as well as the mother of the god Horus, whose domain was the day. A cult formed around Isis, reaching its Egyptian peak during the Thirtieth Dynasty (fourth century B.C.E.). But the goddess's influence reached far beyond the borders of Egypt. She gained followers throughout ancient Greece and became identified with Demeter, the Greek goddess of fertility and the earth. In ancient Rome, Isis became immensely popular and her worship extravagant to the point of debauchery. Not until Christianity appeared in the first century did her fortunes wane. Egyptians continued to worship Isis into the sixth century.

141. Kali

The Hindu goddess of time (her name is the Sanskrit word for time), Kali is omnipotent, with absolute power over all earthly things. She is also the mistress of the god Shiva, whose destructiveness she rivals if not outstrips. Black, grimacing, her teeth dripping with blood, Kali boasts four arms. Each arm has symbolic meaning: One holds a sword and one a human head, while another obliterates fear and the fourth confers happiness. Her followers seek these last two benefits through animal sacrifice. Tradition holds that devotees of Kali used to engage in human sacrifice; the Thugs, a clandestine Indian group of murderers, appealed to her for assistance.

Deir, a Hindu idol.

142. Rashkas

In female form, these Hindu evil spirits seduce mortals with their exquisite beauty. Habitués of graveyards, they feed on human flesh.

143. Aphrodite

Also known as Venus, the goddess of love and beauty was said to have been born from the sea. Her presence brings light, laughter, pleasure and joy; her absence results in misery and ugliness. Aphrodite was also the mother of Eros, aka Cupid, the god of love, who could bring both ecstasy and pain to mortals. Ancient myth indi-

rectly attributes to her the start of the Trojan War, for she caused Paris, the Trojan prince, to kidnap Helen, the wife of King Menelaus of Greece. Asked by Zeus to decide which goddess was more beautiful—Aphrodite or Hera or Athena—Paris chose Aphrodite, who bribed him by promising him the world's most beautiful woman, Helen. Aphrodite probably came to classical mythology by way of religions from the East and still endures in Christianity. One of her priestesses, a sacred prostitute, became Saint Margaret of Antioch, and Aphrodite shared many traits with early notions of the Virgin Mary. Today, love potions are known as aphrodisiacs.

144. Artemis

Twin sister of Apollo, daughter of Zeus and Leto, Artemis is also called Diana and Cynthia in classical mythology. She was the gods' chief hunter and the goddess of the hunt, of childbirth, of nature and of the harvest. She hunted with bow

The goddess Diana, or Artemis.

and arrows, just as her brother did, sometimes turning her weapons upon offensive mortals. The patron of youth—especially young women—and of wild animals—especially the deer and the bear—she was pure of heart and fair of figure. Artemis was associated with the moon, but she had a dark side as well in the form of Hecate, goddess of the underworld and of evil. Joining life and death, she could bless the dying with a quick and painless passing; she was said to be especially merciful to women who died in childbirth.

145. Sul or Sulis

This Celtic goddess, worshiped for centuries before the rise of Christianity, has been identified with Athena/Minerva, the chief goddess of ancient Greece and Rome. In the fourth century B.C.E. she became the patron of the city of Bath (then called Aquae Sulis), whose healing springs were used until the fourth century.

146. Eastre

Long before the crucifixion of Christ, the Saxons worshiped a pantheon that included Eastre, the goddess of spring. Each year they held a spring-time celebration in her honor, even after the Romans invaded their territory. In 325, Emperor Constantine took steps to further the growth of Christianity by declaring that the Saxon festival would become a celebration of Christ's resurrection. Ever since then, the Christian calendar has included Easter.

147. Coatlicue

Each morning, according to Aztec belief, the earth goddess Coatlicue gave birth to her son Huitzilopochtli, the god of war and of the sun.

Each evening he died and became a hummingbird, as the Aztecs believed of warriors who fell in battle. Coatlicue then gathered the hummingbird feathers that fell from the night sky, taking them into her bosom to conceive Huitzilopochtli once more. Coatlicue was also the mother of Coyolxauhqui, the moon goddess, who was murdered by Huitzilopochtli.

148. Pelé and Hi'iaka

The Hawaiians honored Pelé, goddess of the volcanoes, by making leis of lehua flowers and throwing them into the sacred crater of Kilauea. Pelé's younger sister, Hi'iaka-i-ka-poli-o-Pelé, watched over the lehua groves, which Pelé had given to her as a gift. According to legend, Pelé once destroyed the holy groves in a fit of jealousy, suspecting her sister of seducing Pelé's dream lover, Lohi'au. Uncowed, Hi'iaka draped two lehua leis around Lohi'au's neck and one around her own, and before Pelé's eyes she sang him a love song. Today, tradition holds that worshipers on their way to Kilauea should not pick lehua before they arrive, for if they do it will rain. But they may pick the flowers on their way home as souvenirs of their pilgrimage.

MYTHICAL FIGURES

149. Lilith

According to a Hebrew legend, God created Adam's first wife, Lilith, at the same time he created Adam, placing them in Eden together. But they quarreled when Lilith refused to fulfill her womanly destiny of obedience, and she was cast out of Eden. She became a demon who lived in the air and, according to Arabic legend, married the devil and gave birth to various evil spirits. Lilith, the "night hag," was regarded as a menace to pregnant women and newborn children, not only in Jewish and Arabic folklore but in Babylonian mythology as well.

150. Eve

According to the Bible, God created the first woman as a companion and helpmeet for Adam, the lonely citizen of Eden. Where God made Adam in his own image, he made Eve from one of Adam's ribs, defining her as ancillary and inferior from the start. She further proved her lesser nature by succumbing to the serpent's wiles and eating the fruit of the tree of knowledge of good and evil; even worse, she induced Adam to eat it as well. This original sin awakened their sexuality and doomed the offspring of Eve, "the mother of all living," to be born in sin and to live in sorrow. As punishment, God cast Adam and Eve out of paradise and ordained that women would bow to the will of men. In the three thousand-odd years since this story was first written down, it has served as justification for women's oppression under Judeo-Christian tradition. Tertullian, an early Christian scholar in second- and third-century Rome, summed up the moral of the story in an essay entitled "The

The Creation of Woman by Michelangelo.

Grooming of Women." He wrote, "And do you not know that you are Eve? She still lives in this world, as God's judgement on your sex. Live then, for you must, as an accused. The devil is in you. You broke the seal of the Tree. You were the first to abandon God's law. You were the one who deceived man, whom the devil knew not how to vanquish. It was you who so easily overcame him who was made in the image of God. For your wages you have death, which brought death even to the Son of God."

151. Judith

The biblical book of Judith tells of a (probably fictional) pious and plucky widow who delivered the Jews from a siege laid by the Assyrians. Demoralized by the siege, the Israelites began to doubt their God. Judith became impatient with their weakness and took it upon herself to assassinate the Assyrian king, Holofernes. Disguised as an informer, she entered the enemy's camp and secured an invitation to dinner in Holofernes's tent. When the king got drunk and passed out, Judith chopped his head off with a sword and carried it off in a sack. Her trophy emboldened the Israelites, who attacked the Assyrians. Their leader dead, the unnerved Assyrians retreated. Afterward, Judith led the celebration.

152. Pandora

Roman mythology includes the tale of Pandora, the first woman, who was created by Zeus from earth and water. An act of revenge against Prometheus, who had angered Zeus, women were invented as a curse upon men, an irresistible and disastrous temptation to evil.

Pandora was blamed for all the misfortune suffered by humankind, which resulted from her typically female nosiness. The gods gave her a box, forbidding her ever to open it, but Pandora could not resist. When she lifted the lid, she released all the evils the gods had placed inside—plague, misfortune, heartache. But the box also contained one good—hope—that has since sustained mortals through their endless trials.

153. Sibyls

In Greek and Roman mythology, mortals often turned to certain wise women for help and guidance through life's tribulations. Living in remote locations, sometimes in caves, these sybils were endowed with prophetic powers and delivered their messages in Greek hexameters. The earliest mention of a sibyl states that she foretold the Trojan War. Eventually, classical mythology included ten sibyls, identified by where they lived. Prophesies that supposedly came from these women were preserved in the Sibylline Books, which resided in the temple of Jupiter at Rome. These volumes were ordered burned in 405 by an increasingly Christianized government.

154. Present at the Creation

In the creation myth of the Norse people, three female Norns guarded the holy well that watered Yggdrasil, the ash tree that held the universe together. These three—Urda representing the past, Verdandi representing the present, and Skuld representing the future—watched over the sacred white water while the gods gathered there daily to judge mortals.

155. Valkyries

Odin, ruler of the Norse gods who inhabited Asgard, was attended by the Valkyries, maidens who also waited on the gods at mealtime. Their chief duty, however, was to decide who would live and who would die in battle. At Odin's request, led by the Valkyrie Brunhild, they made their choice and rode through the air to carry the heroic dead to Odin at Valhalla. According to *Elder Edda,* the book of Norse mythology, brave warriors about to die had visions of "Maidens excellent in beauty, / Riding their steeds in shining armor, / Solemn and deep in thought, / With their white hands beckoning."

156. Pope Joan

The legend of Pope Joan arose in the thirteenth century. According to the tale, Joan disguised herself as a man to study philosophy, then became a monk. Rising to the rank of cardinal under Pope Leo IV, she was elected pope in 855. She was unmasked three years later when she went into labor during a procession to Rome's Lateran Basilica; an angry mob stoned her to death. The story was so compelling that it went down as fact in official Church history. Pope Clement VII removed "Pope John VIII" from the record in 1601, but the legend lived on. Historians later discovered the roots of the fable in the life of Marozia, who controlled the papacy for many years by having her son (Sergius), her grandson and her great-grandson elected to the post.

ROLE MODELS (OR NOT)

157. Sarah

Sometime between 2000 and 1500 B.C.E., the first wife of Abraham bore him a son, Isaac, from whom the Jewish nation descended. Sarah married her half-brother in the city of Ur, where they were called Sarai and Abram. God directed them to leave the city, so they lived a nomadic life, waiting for God to grant them the promised male heir and to make of Abram "a great nation." When God reaffirmed these promises by a covenant, the couple's names were changed to Sarah and Abraham. But no son arrived, and Sarah passed her childbearing years. She sent her Egyptian handmaid, Hagar, to Abraham to bear a son, and Ishmael was born when Abraham was eighty-six. The Muslims consider Ishmael the progenitor of the Arab people. Finally, Sarah gave birth to Isaac, when Abraham was one hundred and she was a bit younger. As the woman through whom God fulfilled the first part of his covenant with Abraham and as the mother of the Jews, Sarah has been revered in Judaism throughout history.

158. Delilah

A classic biblical bad girl, Delilah brought her lover to ruin. She was the mistress of Samson, an Israelite judge, who as a Nazarite consecrated to God had lived his entire life without a single haircut. Endowed as a result with supernatural strength, he used it against the pagan Philistines, killing many of them. But when he took a lover, the Philistines bribed her to find out the source of his strength so he could be overcome. Delilah wheedled and cajoled Samson, finally using her feminine wiles to persuade him to reveal his secret. She then called the Philistines to cut off his hair while he slept, for which she received 1,100 pieces of silver from each of the Philistine leaders. They blinded, enslaved and put Samson on display, but his hair grew back and he pulled a building down on himself and three thousand Philistines. Delilah's fate is unclear.

159. *Beruriah*

Although traditional Jewish teaching prohibits women from studying or teaching the Torah, this second-century woman was reputedly "capable of reading three hundred traditions of three hundred masters in a winter's night." Daughter of the martyred Rabbi Hanania ben Teradyon and wife of Rabbi Meir, Beruriah defied the famed assertion of Rabbi Eliazar that "to teach Torah to one's daughter is to teach her obscenities." (Ironically, Rabbi Eliazar's wife, Ima Shalom, numbered among the more learned Jews of the first century.) Even today, scholars of the Torah hold Beruriah's work in high regard.

160. *Fatimah* (600–632)

The daughter of Muhammad by his influential and pious first wife ranks among the four perfect women venerated in Islam. "The Shining One" traveled with her father on his famous journey from Mecca to Medina, and was said to be a virgin when she bore three sons. She married Ali, a cousin of Muhammad and the fourth Muslim caliph, supporting him in his rivalry against Abu Bakr, the first caliph. Her husband, sons and grandsons became the twelve holy ones associated with the hours of the day. Their descendants are said to be the founders of the Fatimid dynasty of northern Africa.

161. *Saint Dympna*

This seventh-century Irish princess was killed while attempting to escape the clutches of her pagan father, who had incestuous designs on her. Martyred in the name of chastity and Christian virtue, she has since become the patron saint of those suffering from nervous and mental diseases.

Saint Dympna.

162. Saint Christina the Astonishing
(1150–1224)

This young woman was sainted after supposedly rising from the dead at her funeral. Laid in an open coffin after suffering an apparently fatal seizure, Christina revived in the midst of the requiem mass. She thereafter dressed in rags and roamed the wilds to escape the smell of human sin, begging for food and perching on trees, rocks and fences to pray. Rumored to be immune to fire, cold and injury, she terrified all who saw her and escaped all attempts to confine her. Butler's *Lives of the Saints* notes that "there is little in the recorded history of Christina of Brusthem to make us think she was other than a pathological case."

163. Patron Saints

Among the many Roman Catholic saints associated with specific aspects of daily life are the following women:

Agatha—nurses
Agnes—girls
Anne—women in labor
Apollonia—dentists
Barbara—architects
Brigid—scholars
Catherine of Alexandria—philosophers, preachers, students
Catherine of Bologna—art
Catherine of Siena—fire prevention
Cecilia—musicians
Clare of Assisi—television
Elizabeth of Hungary—bakers
Lidwina—skaters
Martha—cooks, servants
Monica—married women, mothers
Paula—widows

164. A Living Buddha

Born in 1941, the Tibetan girl Doujebamo was designated a living Buddha (enlightened one) at the age of four. Fourteen years later she escaped Tibet with the Dalai Lama when the Chinese invaded. She soon returned to the people who revered her, renouncing her title to serve in the National People's Congress.

LEADERS, PREACHERS AND VISIONARIES

165. Nefertiti

Immortalized in a famous bust that is one of the finest examples of ancient Egyptian art, this fourteenth-century B.C.E. Egyptian queen shaped Egyptian religion with her husband, the pharaoh Akhenaten. She encouraged him to proclaim Aten, the sun god, Egypt's sole deity, making him the first pharaoh to establish monotheism. According to cuneiform inscriptions, Nefertiti may also have served as a priest, a post traditionally filled by male pharaohs.

166. Deborah

One of the seven Israelite prophetesses of old, Deborah lived in the twelfth century B.C.E. Her leadership was instrumental in the defeat of the Canaanites, one of the tribes that oppressed Israel. She celebrated the triumph in The Song of Deborah, which is recorded in the biblical book of Judges. The song is considered one of the oldest works of Hebrew literature.

167. *Aisha bint Abi-Bakr* (614–678)

Muhammad had nine wives, the third of whom—his favorite—lives on in Islam as the "Mother of Believers" and the "Prophetess." Aisha bint Abi-Bakr was the daughter of the first Muslim caliph, Abu Bakr. She was instrumental in the downfall of the caliph Uthman and backed her father during his struggle for power against Ali, the husband of Fatimah. Fighting Ali, she was captured at the Battle of the Camel and executed.

168. *Paranazin*

Montezuma, ruler of the Aztec empire before the arrival of the Spanish conquistadors, had a prophetess for a sister. Records indicate she spent much of her time in a cataleptic trance, remaining motionless in one position for as long as the trance lasted. When she emerged from a trance she uttered prophesies. Shortly before the European invaders arrived, she forecast their approach and warned that Montezuma's empire would soon topple.

169. *Joan of Arc* (1412–1431)

The patron saint of France, called Jeanne d'Arc in her native tongue, followed heavenly voices to win a decisive battle of the Hundred Years' War against England. Saint Joan first heard the voices when she was twelve years old and became convinced she had a divine mission to help the Dauphin, the future King Charles VII. In 1429 she took her message to the Dauphin, who gave her a military command. She donned

Joan of Arc.

armor and led French troops against the English siege of Orléans. When the English retreated Joan escorted Charles to his coronation; she continued to fight the war—without the king's approval—until the Burgundians captured her and sold her to the English in 1430. The English delivered Joan to a French ecclesiastical court at Rouen, where she was charged with witchcraft. The clerics objected to her masculine clothing and her belief that she was accountable to God rather than to the Roman Catholic Church. When sentenced to death, Joan repented and her life was spared, but she resumed wearing men's clothing in prison and was condemned by a government court. She burned at the stake on May 30, 1431, but in 1456 the Church pronounced her innocent. Joan of Arc became a French national hero and a symbol of courage and fidelity. She was beatified in 1909 and canonized in 1920.

170. Mother Shipton

Born about 1488, this English woman claimed to be a prophet and as a result she was accused of witchcraft. She was acquitted, however, and gained followers both before and after her death at seventy-three. Her prophesies were first published in a 1641 pamphlet that endeavored to establish their correspondence to recent events; a similar tract appeared in 1677. In 1862 another publication related her predictions to the technological developments of the Industrial Revolution and included her prediction that the world would end in 1881.

171. Anne Hutchinson
(1591–1643)

This free-thinking woman was persecuted for her religious views by the very people who moved to the wilds of North America in search of religious freedom. Hutchinson immigrated from England to the Massachusetts Bay Colony in 1634 and settled in Boston. She was admired for her piety and intelligence, and soon started a series of meetings at which women—and, later, men—gathered to hear her thoughts. Her central teaching was the doctrine of antinomianism, which holds that faith in salvation through Christ frees the Christian from Old Testament law. Puritan leaders saw Hutchinson as a threat to their strict legal and moral order, but she had many supporters as well. The political fallout of the controversy found her in court

in 1637 defending herself against charges of "traducing the ministers" of the Puritan faith. Summarily found guilty, Hutchinson was excommunicated from the church and banished from the colony. Hutchinson moved first to Rhode Island and then to New York, where she was killed by Indians in August 1643.

172. Jeanne Marie Bouvier de la Motte Guyon (1648–1717)

Known as Madame Guyon, this wealthy French widow gained notoriety as a mystic. One of the ideas she promoted was quietism, the pursuit of spiritual growth through meditation. In 1688 the archbishop of Paris jailed her for her heretical writings, but the wife of King Louis XIV secured her release the following year. Guyon resumed her work and was imprisoned again from 1695 to 1703. The terms of her release required her to leave Paris, so she moved to the countryside and turned to charitable work. At her death she declared her complete accord with Roman Catholic teachings.

173. Vita Kimba

When Europeans arrived in Africa, one of their stated goals in conquering the continent was to bring Christianity to its inhabitants. Protestant and Catholic missionaries found a problematic audience among the practitioners of traditional African religions, who tended to blend elements of old and new beliefs into an amalgam that bore little resemblance to European faiths. Among the African leaders who accepted some but not all of the missionaries' message was Vita Kimba, a priestess and prophetess in the seventeenth- and eighteenth-century Congo.

Declaring that she had been Saint Anthony in a former life, she promoted her own version of Catholicism, which included a healthy dose of the African religion she had long practiced. In 1706, when a Catholic priest caught wind of her activities, Vita Kimba was burned at the stake as a heretic.

174. Ann Lee (1736–1784)

This uneducated, working-class woman from Manchester, England, brought the Shaker society, a radical offshoot of the Religious Society of Friends (popularly known as Quakers), to America. She joined the group in 1758 and became its leader in 1770. Known as Mother Ann, she had visions and claimed that she represented the second coming of Christ. Leaving England with eight believers in 1774, she founded a Shaker outpost in Watervliet, New York, in 1776. There, she and her followers lived a life of celibacy, simplicity and communal ownership of property. The American movement burgeoned, spawning eighteen more communities and attracting six thousand adherents within fifty years. The Shakers became renowned for the characteristic style of their handcrafted furniture and household implements before the movement began to fade after the mid-nineteenth century.

175. Mary Baker Eddy (1821–1910)

Physically frail, emotionally fragile and beset with family difficulties, this New Hampshire native seems an unlikely founder of a major world religion, but Mary Baker Eddy remains the only woman to have done so. For the first forty-five years of her life, she struggled through various illnesses, battled depression and morphine addiction and suffered several nervous breakdowns. Meanwhile, her first marriage left her a widow with one son, whom she was incapable of raising; her second ended in divorce. Eddy finally found some relief in the teachings of Phineas Quimby, a hypnotist who preached the power of mind over matter. After healing herself of injuries sustained in a serious fall, she elaborated on Quimby's ideas to create a philosophy of her own. She outlined her beliefs in *Science and Health with Key to the Scriptures* (1875) and soon gained a loyal following in the Boston area. Her third husband, Asa Eddy, encouraged her to found a church, which she did in 1879. The First Church of Christ, Scientist, soon included the Metaphysical College and published the *Christian Science Journal* (later the *Christian Science Monitor*). Known mostly for the belief that all disease can be cured through prayer, Eddy and her church encountered criticism and fought lawsuits even as the ranks of Christian Scientists continued to grow. By 1887, Eddy reacquired her morphine habit; she lived in seclusion until her death.

176. Antoinette Louisa Brown Blackwell (1825–1921)

Sister-in-law to Elizabeth Blackwell, the first American woman to earn a medical degree, Antoinette Louisa Brown Blackwell was the first woman minister of a church in the United States. Her preaching career began early, when as a nine-year-old she delivered sermons at her hometown Congregational church. She went on to graduate from Oberlin College and Oberlin

Theological Seminary, numbering among the first American women to do so. Engaged by the Unitarian Church, she was known as a vivacious speaker. Blackwell was also a reformer, campaigning for women's rights, abolition and temperance. She made her last appearance at the pulpit when she was ninety.

177. Helena Petrovna Blavatsky
(1831–1891)

A founder and the most important leader of the Theosophical Society, Helena Blavatsky promulgated the occult philosophy known as theosophy. She left her native Russia at sixteen and traveled widely, supposedly studying with Hindu mahatmas for seven years. A close brush with death attracted her to spiritualism—communication with the dead—and convinced her she had psychic abilities. Arriving in New York City in 1873, Blavatsky soon became a leading theosophist, teaching that spirit becomes matter and matter becomes spirit in a cycle of purification. The human spirit, she asserted, is gradually perfected through repeated reincarnation, eventually leaving the impure physical world altogether to achieve a divine state. Blavatsky became an American citizen but moved to India in 1878. Her claims of her own advanced spiritual development earned her many detractors, who called her a charlatan and accused her of plagiarism, but she remained unshaken to her death.

178. Anna Howard Shaw
(1847–1919)

This English-born suffragist and physician came to the United States as a child and became a Methodist minister at the age of twenty-four. Her application for official ordination was denied in 1878 and she was stripped of her license to preach. But she served as a preacher until the mid-1880s, when she earned her medical degree. She then started lecturing on the suffrage circuit and became a major figure in the fight for women's right to vote.

179. Nehanda of Zimbabwe
(c. 1863–1898)

This priestess and prophetess of her people's traditional religion led the Shona in an 1898 revolt against white attempts to dominate them. The colonial ambitions of Cecil Rhodes in southern Africa lent Nehanda's hereditary position even greater importance, as she was responsible for preserving Shona culture. Whites captured her and tried to force her to convert to Christianity, knowing that if she did her people's resistance would crumble. Nehanda refused and was executed.

180. Aimee Semple McPherson
(1890–1944)

A prototypical evangelist, Aimee Semple McPherson gained widespread fame for her colorful preaching style and faith-healing flair. Born in Ontario, Canada, she served as a Pentecostal missionary to China from 1908 to 1909. She then traveled across the United States, delivering her fire-and-brimstone message via radio and in person. Based at her huge Angelus Temple in Los Angeles, opened in 1923, she preached for twenty years, and in 1927 founded the Pentecostal International Church of the Foursquare Gospel. McPherson had thou-

Aimee Semple McPherson.

but works of nonfiction, such as *For the New Intellectual* (1961) and *The Virtue of Selfishness* (1965).

182. Mother Teresa of Calcutta

(1910–1997)

This 1979 winner of the Nobel Peace Prize has been hailed for her selfless devotion to helping the sickest and poorest members of society. She was born in Albania and took her vows as a Roman Catholic nun in 1937, serving as principal of a Calcutta high school until 1948. That year, she obtained special permission to leave teaching to work among the city's sick and dying. She founded the Missionaries of Charity and opened the Nirmal Hriday ("Pure Heart") Home for Dying Destitutes in Calcutta. As her ministry grew, she established missions throughout the world that continue to carry on her work.

sands of followers, but she aroused controversy as well. After her May 1926 disappearance while swimming in the Pacific Ocean, she reappeared five weeks later and claimed to have been kidnapped. She was tried and acquitted of perjury in the case. She died at the age of fifty-four.

183. Reactionary Reformer

In the 1970s, Christian fundamentalist entertainer Anita Bryant launched a campaign against homosexuality in her home state of Florida. Bryant believed that what she called a "sick segment of society" represented a threat to the morals of American youth. "Homosexuals do not suffer discrimination when they keep their perversions in the privacy of their own homes," she declared. "Homosexuals cannot reproduce—so they must recruit. And to freshen their ranks, they must recruit the youth of America."

181. Ayn Rand (1905–1982)

The author of such novels as *The Fountainhead* (1943) and *Atlas Shrugged* (1957), Ayn Rand attracted a cult of followers who embraced her philosophies of objectivism and rational selfishness. Her works promoted the idea that pursuing one's own best interests represents the highest human good. She not only wrote novels

(right) Anita Bryant.

184. A Mind-Body Connection

The 1980s saw the full flowering of the New Age movement in modern society, which encompassed spiritual beliefs and practices from channeling to crystal healing. One of the major figures of the New Age is Louise Hay, most famous for her book *You Can Heal Your Life* (1984). Hay's basic philosophy is that one's thoughts have a profound impact on the circumstances of one's life, particularly with regard to physical health. She attributes detailed symbolism to each part of the body and links specific illnesses and symptoms to specific emotional characteristics. To cure disease, one must let go of negative patterns of thinking and feeling through the recitation of positive affirmations. She claims to have used these techniques to cure herself of cancer.

PRINCIPLES, BELIEFS AND STRICTURES

185. Yin and Yang

Chinese philosophy contains the concept of yin and yang, the essential female (yin) and male (yang) properties of nature. Originated about 2800 B.C.E. by Emperor Fu Hsi, the construct predicates health and harmony on the perfect balance of yin and yang. In that perfect balance, however, the female is held to be subordinate to the male.

186. Nidda

This Talmudic text outlines Jewish law concerning women's "impurity," considered to be contagious. It bars menstruating women from the temple and requires their seclusion for several days after their period. It also excludes them from society for forty days after giving birth to a boy and for eighty days after giving birth to a girl.

187. Mahayana Buddhism

This branch of Buddhism holds that the differences between men and women are insignificant, and that women are essential spiritual guides and comrades for men. Abundant in female symbolism, this tantric tradition is historically associated with Tibet. Tibetan nuns were famous for their spiritual accomplishments.

188. Talk About Enlightenment . . .

Originator of one of the world's great religions, the Buddha recognized the spiritual potential of women. In 550 B.C.E., when his aunt Mahaprajapati asked him for permission to found an order of nuns, he granted her request, opening the door to spiritual opportunity for devout women.

189. The Ramayana

Illustrating the principles of Hinduism, this epic Sanskrit poem idealizes women's ability to endure great suffering. In the story, Sita goes into exile with her husband, Prince Rama, when his right to the throne is challenged. Kidnapped by the demon king Ravana, Sita is rescued by Rama but suspected (by others) of infidelity with her captor. Rama takes the throne but Sita remains in exile, where she bears his sons and lives for many years before reuniting with her husband.

190. The Mahabharata

This epic Sanskrit poem defines total wifely submission as a Hindu woman's highest duty. Quite a bit longer than the *Ramayana,* the *Mahabharata* contains the famous *Bhagavad-Gita,* a dialogue on the meaning of life. The work centers on the story of two related royal families, who compete to control the same kingdom. Throughout, the female characters who represent virtue are those who fulfill their dharma by standing by their husbands until death.

191. Virginity

Many religions hold virginity to be an essential component of female virtue, Christianity being but one obvious example. Early in the Christian era, Mary, the mother of God's son, was established as the female ideal. Many Christians came to believe that Mary was not only a virgin at Jesus' conception and birth but that she remained a virgin throughout her life, epitomizing virtue and purity. Others considered her completely untainted by sin, even the original sin into which the Bible holds that all people are born. Virginity could be so highly prized that public opinion of a woman's moral fiber seemed to hinge almost entirely upon it.

192. The Cult of the Virgin

No female figure—actual or allegorical—looms larger in Christianity than Mary, the mother of Jesus. She appears in the Gospels only peripherally, but by the second century she was revered as the Mother of God, as the Virgin Mary and as the Holy or Blessed Virgin. Veneration of Mary intensified between the fourth and seventh centuries, when the Church added several feast days in her honor to the calendar. Among some Christians, Mary inspired a cultish following in the thirteenth to fifteenth centuries. She took on godlike qualities as the intercessor between sinners and a severe God, the one to whom supplicants turned for mercy. During this time Roman Catholics adopted the rosary, a form of prayer in which they recite ten Hail Marys for every one Our Father; they also originated various litanies and benedictions that address Mary as the Refuge of Sinners, the Mystical Rose and other symbolic titles. The Roman Catholic Church developed the doctrine of the Immaculate Conception (Mary was conceived without original sin) and the Assumption (upon her death Mary ascended bodily to heaven). In this context, believers saw Mary not only as good but as perfect, and women especially were urged, and attempted, to emulate her.

193. *The Woman's Bible*

Late in the nineteenth century, feminist Elizabeth Cady Stanton wrote *The Woman's Bible* to offer a vision of Christianity free of sexism. "The Bible teaches that woman brought sin and death into the world, that she precipitated the fall of the race . . ." reads the introduction. "Marriage for her was to be a condition of bondage, maternity a period of suffering and anguish, and in silence and subjection, she was to play the role of a dependent. . . ." Stanton was vilified for her religious views, but the publication of *The Woman's Bible* marked a milestone on the long road toward women's equality. The Victorian ideal of womanhood was dead.

194.

"[The] primordial event is the murder/dismemberment of the Goddess—that is, the Self-affirming be-ing of women. It might seem confusing that in patriarchy 'the true sin is forgetting' this deed, since its ideologies deny that there ever was, is, or can be female divinity, whose existence would be a prerequisite for her murder. However, since the fathers' ritual is the realm of reversals, such confusion should be expected. The purpose of such contrived confusion is to prevent us from committing the 'true sin' against patriarchal rule/ritual, that is, remembering that as long as we are alive the Goddess still lives. The radical 'sin' is re-membering the Goddess in the full sense, that is, recognizing that the attempt to murder her—mythically and existentially—is radically wrong, and demonstrating through our own be-ing that this deed is not final/irrevocable. The deed can be revoked by re-invoking the Goddess within, which involves 'forgetting' to kill female divinity, that is, our Selves." —Mary Day, *Gyn/Ecology: The Metaethics of Radical Feminism* (1978)

195. *Contemporary Christian Fundamentalism, Part I*

"It is wrong for any girl to wear a garment that arouses in any man desires that cannot be righteously fulfilled outside of marriage. The Bible also warns us not to be so masculine that we threaten men. If your talk is spiritual, but your look is cold, hard, carnal and calculating, the outside is what's believed." —Diane Hay, instructor at Bob Jones University, Greenville, South Carolina.

196. *Contemporary Christian Fundamentalism, Part II*

"Yes, religion and politics do mix. America is a nation based on biblical principles. Christian values dominate our government. The test of those values is the Bible. Politicians who do not use the Bible to guide their public and private lives do not belong in office." —Beverly LaHaye, President of Concerned Women for America

LAY PRACTICES

197. The Veil

Although he promoted female equality in many matters, Muhammad, the founder of Islam, stood firm on marital subservience and female modesty. He introduced the veil to Arab society, veiling his own wives to protect them from the roving eyes of his followers. The practice spread and became even stricter in some regions, where women were required to cover themselves head to toe outside the home.

Veiled Muslim women, mid-twentieth century.

198. Mormon Women

Founded early in the nineteenth century in New York State, Mormonism identifies itself as the only true form of Christianity. Historical and recent accounts indicate that women's position in this socially conservative sect has been one of subservience. Not only are women banned from the church hierarchy, they are expected to accept male dominion in family matters. Mormons privately took up polygamy, in which men extend their marital authority over several wives, while still under the leadership of Joseph Smith, founder of the church. "Gentile" antipathy for the custom contributed to Smith's murder in 1844, but by 1852 up to one fifth of Mormons openly practiced and preached it. In 1876, Ann Eliza Webb Young attacked polygamy in her exposé, *Wife No. 19, or The Story of a Life in Bondage.* The U.S. government applied legal and even military pressure to the Mormons until 1890, when the church officially disavowed polygamy. But small numbers of believers continued to take multiple wives in spite of the threat of religious and legal sanction. In 1979, Sonia Johnson was excommunicated for her advocacy of the Equal Rights Amendment; in 1981 she published *From Housewife to Heretic.*

199. Modern Islamic Fundamentalism

Today, women in some Islamic nations face harsh punishments if they violate religious strictures on their behavior. In 1975, the Iranian Revolutionary Council passed a law requiring all women to wear the chador (garb that hides all but the eyes) in public; that law was repealed in 1979 after women protested. Nevertheless, religious enforcers may still apprehend women who dress or behave immodestly in the streets. In Saudi Arabia, women are prohibited from driving automobiles because some interpretations of Islamic law assert that driving dishonors them. In 1990, when Saudi women protested the ban, the government only strengthened the law.

200. The Goddess Revival

The modern women's movement has brought attention not only to women's economic and social lives but to their spiritual lives as well. The confidence of feminist awareness and New Age thinking has led to a revival of interest in goddess worship. Many women have sought spiritual identity in various goddess-based belief systems. These typically encompass a respect for the natural environment and a humility regarding humankind's place in the cosmos. Most often, the modern goddess cults reject the major institutionalized religions, but much to the dismay of the Roman Catholic Church, some women have sought to incorporate the goddess into that belief system.

DANGEROUS WOMEN

201. True Confessions

Doing daily battle with all manner of tribulations and temptations, women have traditionally found one of their greatest comforts in religion. Seeking solace from monks and priests, Roman Catholic women of the Middle Ages frequently shared more than their thoughts. Clerics easily won the trust of their female parishioners, and religious fervor easily crossed the line to physical intimacy. Literature of the time describes many monks and priests who threw themselves into their work body and soul.

202. Malleus Maleficarum

From the eleventh through the seventeenth centuries, but especially after the Reformation, Christian Europe was obsessed with witchcraft. The Church led the assault, applying the term witch to miscellaneous accused heretics who did not fit into various other categories, such as Jews. Reflecting the Church's belief in woman's inherent evilness, three quarters of those so prosecuted were women. They were charged with harming their communities by means of black magic and with engaging in a variety of sexual excesses and perversions. In 1486, two German monks wrote *Malleus Maleficarum* ("The Hammer of Witches"), used thereafter as the definitive guide to witch-hunting. The text described the proper procedures for identifying, trying and burning witches at the stake, recommending torture as an investigative tool. Equipped with this handbook, officials prosecuted about 100,000 women for witchcraft by the end of the seventeenth century, executing perhaps sixty thousand.

203. The Marks of a Witch

When confronted with a witchcraft suspect, officials followed an intricate set of guidelines for determining the accused's guilt or innocence. Many of these reflected the profoundly misogynistic nature of the witch-hunts. Witches were thought to bear various physical marks, so suspects were stripped and examined intimately at trial. Professional examiners sought a "devil's mark" left somewhere on the body when Satan seduced the supposed witch. As this mark was supposed to be insensible to pain, examination consisted of "pricking" the suspect all over her body with special sharp instruments resembling daggers. Another aspect of the examination involved searching for "witches' teats," used to suckle imps and familiars. Any blemish resembling an extra nipple was damning. Other signs of a woman's guilt included her inability to weep and her failure to sink when thrown into water.

204. New England Witch Trials

Beginning in the 1640s and raging throughout colonial New England for the rest of the seventeenth century, the mania for witch-hunting cul-

minated in the 1692 to 1693 witch trials in Salem, Massachusetts. In a climate of social and economic upheaval, communities focused their anxieties on scapegoats whom they called witches. These individuals were accused of causing just about every kind of misfortune that could befall a colonial town, from arguments and illness to arson and adultery. Of the nearly 250 people formally tried as witches (115 in Salem alone), an overwhelming number—80 percent—were women. The typical "witch" was between forty and sixty years old, although women as young as twenty-five faced trial. She generally came from the lower class, had few or no children and had previously been accused of other crimes. More significantly, most women accused of witchcraft did not conform to expectations of what a lady should be—they were

A witch trial in seventeenth-century Salem, Massachusetts.

spirited, independent and stubborn. A significant proportion also practiced as midwives or healers. In all, about thirty women were executed during the panic, compared with four or five men, mostly husbands of supposed witches.

The Holy Life

205. Taoism

Women who practice Taoism have three possible roles. Lay believers strive to live by Taoist principles of piety, altruism and family harmony. Nuns and church officials conduct religious rituals, study and teach the faith. Saints and goddesses provide guidance and help to mortals and serve as role models.

206. Vestal Virgins

From ancient times in many cultures, the sexual purity of women was directly associated with the well-being of entire societies: If its women were wanton, a nation would fall. Official virgins thus served the purpose of preserving society. So it was in Rome, where an order of six virgins kept a symbolic flame burning in the temple of Vesta, the goddess of the hearth. Drawn from upper-class families, vestal virgins assumed their duties at the

age of ten and served for thirty years, during which time they could be buried alive for violating their oath of chastity. They enjoyed many social privileges in return for their service to the state, and they were freed from many of the legal and economic strictures borne by Roman women. The cult of Vesta endured for nearly a thousand years, finally dissolving in 394.

207. The Early Church

New Testament and other contemporary accounts indicate that women played an essential role in the establishment of Christianity. During Jesus' lifetime, women accepted his teachings in greater numbers than men, and some of his most loyal and influential followers were women, such as Mary Magdalene. Jesus had no qualms about dealing with women directly, and his preaching made little distinction between the roles and rewards of devout men and women. Women figure prominently in many important episodes recounted in the Gospels. After Jesus' death, women served the Church on

The goddess Vesta.

roughly equal footing with men, preaching and organizing. It was not until the Church began to assume a more formal, institutionalized structure that women were relegated to the shadows.

208. Desert Mothers

Among the first in the long and colorful line of ascetic Christian hermits were the desert mothers, who spent years at a time in the parched wilderness of the Mediterranean region. In the fourth century, an abbess named Sara lived in the desert for forty years, while in the fifth century the historian Palladius estimated that three thousand women hermits were scattered throughout the desert of Egypt. They included a reformed prostitute named Mary the Egyptian, who retreated to the desert after her conversion to do penance.

209. Siddah

From its inception, female practitioners known as *siddah* were renowned for their accomplishments in tantric Buddhism, which focuses on meditation and other rituals. In the late eighth century, the *siddah* Yeshay Tsongyal, known as the Great Bliss Queen, was held to epitomize tantric wisdom.

210. Broken Vows

In the early Middle Ages, the number of cloistered nuns in Europe expanded rapidly as patrician parents disposed of their "excess" daughters at Roman Catholic convents. Most families could not afford to assemble large enough dowries to attract well-born husbands for more than two or three daughters. Any additional daughters were sent to the convents as child oblates, there to live out their lives. Because such nuns came to convents with an emolument, a generous donation required to support them throughout their life, the popularity of oblation made some convents extremely wealthy. When the number of cloistered nuns started to drop in the thirteenth century, overflowing convent coffers afforded the remaining nuns a lavish lifestyle. Many dropped all but the vaguest religious pretenses; nuns who had been pledged unwillingly ventured freely outside the convent walls and invited lay visitors—including men—inside for all manner of entertainment. Appalled members of the community denounced the convents as bordellos and, indeed, numerous cases of fornication with nuns and illegitimate births were recorded and prosecuted in the courts. The most notorious institution was the Benedictine convent of Sant' Angelo di Contorta in Venice, which was so flagrantly debauched that the pope shut it down in 1474.

211. The End of the Beguines

Many devout Christian women of the early Renaissance found traditional ecclesiastical institutions, such as convents, incompatible with their religious impulses. For those who wished to dedicate their lives to God, an alternate retreat from the world was called for. Without guidance from the Church, and largely without the involvement of men, communities of celibate women called the Beguines began to form in thirteenth-century Germany. The Beguines adopted chastity and poverty as the means whereby to emulate Christ. They wore plain clothing and lived communally, supporting themselves by the work of their own hands. From about 1280 to 1320, the Beguine movement mushroomed, even though the mainstream Roman Catholic Church found it somewhat heretical. In and around the city of Cologne, for instance, 169 Beguine communities sheltered perhaps 1,500 women of the city's total population of twenty thousand. The number of Beguines plummeted after 1318, when the Church formally declared it spurious. Nonetheless, many so-called holy women individually continued similar practices even after the Beguines became extinct.

212. *Eastern Orthodox Paradox*

Led by the patriarch of Constantinople, the Eastern Orthodox or Greek Orthodox Church is divided into a number of geographical patriarchates. The canon of this patriarchal church is at least as conservative as Roman Catholic teaching when it comes to the role of women, with a remarkable exception. Well before the rise of the modern women's movement, the patriarch of Moscow and All Russia, head of the Russian Orthodox Church, permitted women to serve as priestesses.

STEPS FORWARD

213. *Reform in the Nineteenth Century*

In the nineteenth century, American women set massive efforts in motion on behalf of the less fortunate, working to eradicate slavery, to broaden access to public education and to relieve the plight of the urban poor. Temperance, prison reform and better care for the mentally ill attracted their attention as well. Many middle-class women got involved in the anti-slavery movement and other reform efforts. In most

Russian priestesses
in the early twentieth century.

cases, they formed women's groups based in their churches and operated in concert with separate men's organizations, usually in an auxiliary capacity. But when women attempted to join male-dominated groups or to exert an influence that went beyond support, they were often reminded of their "proper sphere" and dismissed.

214. Temperance

Alcohol's place in American life has deep roots leading back to ancient times. From colonial days, ale and rum were part of the daily diet of American adults and children alike, but in the early years of the nineteenth century, drunkenness became alarmingly widespread. Men did most of the drinking, but women felt its impact in domestic abuse, strained family finances and, in some cases, outright destitution. The temperance movement was, from its start, an overwhelmingly female phenomenon, as women fought to save their families and society through a ban on alcohol. In 1826 women were instrumental in founding the American Society for the Promotion of Temperance, and in 1833 they attended America's first national temperance convention in large numbers.

215. Discriminating Abolitionists

Women were not allowed to participate in the 1840 World's Anti-Slavery Convention in London. Women delegates were allowed to attend, but they were forced to listen from behind a curtain in the balcony.

216. Pacifism

In the early twentieth century, women social reformers turned their attentions to pacifism.

Anti-war activists believed that peace was an essential component of social advancement. To promote world peace, they founded organizations such as the Women's Peace Party, the Women's International League for Peace and Freedom, and the Women's Peace Society. In addition to ending war, these groups dedicated themselves to improving women's economic, social and political lot.

IN LEAGUE

217. An Abolition First

In 1832, African-American women in Salem, Massachusetts, formed the first female antislavery society.

218. The WCTU

In the 1870s the temperance movement gained strength from a religious revival that swept the country. The Women's Christian Temperance Union formed in 1873, excluding men from its membership and working to improve women's lives in various ways. The organization took its campaign international, battling alcohol in Australia, Japan, Britain and elsewhere. It persevered until the passage of the Eighteenth Amendment to the U.S. Constitution in 1919, which launched the era of Prohibition.

219. The YWCA

Founded in Great Britain in 1877, the Young Women's Christian Association had as its original goal the salvation of young women's souls. It soon blossomed into much more, however, introducing programs meant to help women in more concrete ways. Women could find inexpensive rooms and meals at YWCAs around the world, join YWCA industrial clubs at factories, stores and mills, take classes in topics ranging from literacy to child care or improve their physical fitness at YWCA athletic facilities. The YWCA remains a vital organization today.

220. Hadassah

Hadassah, the Women's Zionist Organization of America, was founded in 1912 by Baltimore-born Henrietta Szold. Under Szold's leadership the group sought to educate American Jews and to build schools, hospitals and other humanitarian facilities for Jews in Palestine. Szold moved to Palestine in 1920 to oversee Hadassah's efforts there, while 1,500 chapters opened across the United States. In Israel, Hadassah operates the Hadassah Medical Organization, the Hadassah College of Technology and the Hadassah Career Counseling Institute. Its activities in the U.S. focus on women's health care, education and the Zionist youth movement.

221. Senior Women

Women activists and reformers have been particularly prominent in the senior citizens' rights movement, which is not surprising in light of women's longer average lifespan and the harsh economic realities faced by so many widows. In 1971, Maggie Kuhn founded the Gray Panthers to advocate on behalf of senior citizens; a number of American women's organizations work closely with the American Association of Retired People (AARP) to gain better long-term health care benefits for ailing seniors.

222. MADD

Founded in 1980 by Candy Lightner, Mothers Against Drunk Driving has helped reduce the rate of alcohol-related automobile accidents. A leader in alcohol education in the schools, the group was instrumental in popularizing such safety practices as the designated driver.

223. Peaceful Protests

In 1981 women opposed to nuclear weapons set up camp at Greenham Common Airbase in England. The peaceful encampment attracted women protestors from around the world, who pitched tents and maintained a remarkable presence at the site. Across the Atlantic, the Women's Peace Encampment formed in Seneca Falls, New York, in 1983. In the town where the first women's rights convention was held (in 1848), women of many nationalities gathered to protest nuclear proliferation. Both camps sustained their protests for several years.

WOMEN WHO CARED

224. Dorothea Dix (1802–1887)

Originally a teacher, opening and operating a girls' school in Boston, Dix left behind her career of fifteen years in 1841, when she started visiting almshouses and prisons. Appalled at the conditions she found, she spent two years touring Massachusetts institutions. The report she submitted to the state legislature resulted in substantial reforms in Massachusetts; she then went on to similar success in twenty states and Canada and had a strong influence on several

European countries. At her urging, governments established institutions for the impoverished and mentally ill, no longer treating them like criminals.

225. Abolitionist Leaders

Some of America's greatest abolitionists were women. Among those leading the fight against slavery were Angelina and Sarah Grimké, Sojourner Truth, Lucretia Mott, Lydia Maria Child, Harriet Tubman and Frances Wright. Such women founded influential anti-slavery societies and published some of the movement's most compelling books and articles.

226. Civil Rights Pioneers

In an age when women were almost completely prohibited from public speaking, Maria W. Miller Stewart (1803–1879) delivered a series of four daring speeches in Boston. Addresses such as "Religion and the Pure Principles of Morality, the Sure Foundation on Which We Must Build" urged her fellow African-Americans to educate and improve themselves in order to end slavery, secure their rights and better their lives. Another African-American woman, Sarah Parker Remond (1826–c. 1887), toured the British Isles delivering anti-slavery lectures.

Julia Ward Howe.

women's rights movement, helping to found the National Woman Suffrage Association and other organizations. As a peace activist she led the United States wing of the Woman's International Peace Association. She also became the first woman to be elected to the American Academy of Arts and Letters.

227. Julia Ward Howe (1819–1910)

Known to many as the author of "The Battle Hymn of the Republic," which she wrote after visiting a Union Army camp during the Civil War, Julia Ward Howe was a reformer as well as an author. Before the war she was active in the anti-slavery movement and published articles on the topic. She later got involved in the

228. Clara Barton (1821–1912)

The founder of the Red Cross found her calling during the Civil War, when she worked with wounded soldiers as a volunteer. She organized a search for missing soldiers after the war, then turned her attention to Europe from 1869 to 1873, opening hospitals during the Franco-Prussian War. When the American Red Cross Society formed in 1881, she was elected its president, filling that post until 1904. As a delegate to the 1884 International Peace Convention in Geneva, she secured worldwide recognition of the Red Cross as a neutral provider of wartime and peacetime disaster relief. Among the Red Cross relief efforts she supervised were those during the Spanish-American War, after the 1889 Johnstown, Pennsylvania, flood and during the Boer War in South Africa.

229. Susette La Flesche Tibbles

Native-American activist Susette La Flesche Tibbles (her Indian name was Inshta Theumba, or "Bright Eyes") worked on behalf of her people in the late nineteenth century, when the United States government was completing its expulsion of Native Americans from lands desired by white settlers. She succeeded in persuading officials to enact reforms that granted land allotments and citizenship rights to individual Indians.

230. Bertha von Suttner

Winner of the 1905 Nobel Peace Prize, Austrian novelist and activist Bertha von Suttner was a leading figure in the global peace movement of her time. In 1891 she founded the Austrian Society of Friends for Peace, for which she edited the pacifist journal *Die Waffen nieder!* She is reported to have persuaded Bernard Nobel to establish the Nobel prizes.

231. Jane Addams (1860–1935)

This social worker spearheaded the settlement house phenomenon in the United States and won the 1931 Nobel Peace Prize. Born and educated in Illinois, she opened Chicago's Hull House in 1889 with Ellen Gates Starr. At Hull House, the residents of Chicago's poor neighborhoods found assistance in many forms, from education to health care. Addams lived and worked there for the rest of her life, but her activities reached the entire world. She helped found the National Progressive Party in 1912, the Woman's Peace Party in 1915 and the American Civil Liberties Union (ACLU) in 1920. As president of the Women's International League for Peace and Freedom, she participated in women's conferences in Europe and the United States. Addams also wrote several highly regarded books, including *Democracy and Social Ethics* (1902), *Newer Ideals of Peace* (1907), *Twenty Years at Hull House* (1910) and *Peace and Bread in Time of War* (1922).

232. Christian Soldier

Evangeline Cory Booth (1865–1950), daughter of Salvation Army founder William Booth, led the charitable organization during one of its most active periods. Born in London, she worked with the Salvation Army in England and Canada before moving to the United States to serve there. As commander from 1904 to 1934, she oversaw the delivery of spiritual and material assistance to Allied soldiers during World War I. For her efforts, the U.S. government awarded her the Distinguished Service Medal. Booth served as International General of the World Wide Salvation Army from 1934 until she retired in 1939.

233. Emily Greene Balch (1867–1961)

Inspired by the plight of the poor to study economics, Balch worked for world peace while teaching at Wellesley College. During World War I, she attended an international women's conference at The Hague, then traveled Europe with some of her fellow delegates, attempting to persuade national leaders to put an end to the war. When the United States entered the war, Balch's pacifist views plunged her into disfavor at home and Wellesley fired her. She was unbowed, however, and helped to found the Women's International League for Peace and Freedom. The rise of fascism and the outbreak of World War II, however, persuaded her—at least temporarily—to choose freedom over peace as an ideal, and she participated in the war effort as an advocate for interred Japanese-Americans and for Jewish refugees arriving in the U.S. Her World War II work earned her the 1946 Nobel Peace Prize.

234. *Eleanor Roosevelt* (1884–1962)

The niece of one president and the wife of another, Eleanor Roosevelt devoted her life to humanitarian causes and liberal ideals. Already revered around the globe, she served as a delegate to the infant United Nations after her husband's death. As the chair of the UN's Human Rights Commission, she fought for two years to convince member nations to agree on a sweeping human rights policy. She overcame opposition from many countries that wanted to retain various prerogatives for themselves, and the Universal Declaration of Human Rights was adopted on December 10, 1948. A fundamental expression of the UN's mission, the declaration has helped define the organization's principles and priorities.

235. *The Good Doctor*

In 1978, Australian-born doctor Helen Caldicott (1938–   ) founded Physicians for Social Responsibility. The American-based organization works to halt nuclear proliferation and the atmospheric testing of nuclear weapons.

Part

THREE

Education and Academia

Eleven Opinions on the Female Intellect

236.

"And if . . . the male and female sex appear to differ in their fitness for any art or pursuit, we should say that such pursuit or art ought to be assigned to one or the other of them; but if the difference consists only in women bearing and men begetting children, this does not amount to a proof that a woman differs from a man in respect of the sort of education she should receive." —Plato, *The Republic*

237.

"The fair sex has just as much understanding as the male, but it is a *beautiful understanding,* whereas ours should be a *deep understanding. . . .* Laborious learning or painful pondering, even if a woman should greatly succeed in it, destroys the merits that are proper to her sex, and because of their rarity they can make of her an object of cold admiration; but at the same time they will weaken the charms with which she exercises her great power over the other sex. . . . Her philosophy is not to reason, but to sense. . . . They will need to know nothing more of the cosmos than is necessary to make the appearance of the heavens on a beautiful evening a stimulating sight to them." —Immanuel Kant, *Observations on the Feeling of the Beautiful and Sublime,* 1764

238.

"Suffer me to ask, in what the minds of females are so notoriously deficient? [And whether] the judgement of a male of two years old is more sage than that of a female's of the same age? But from that period what partiality! How is the one exalted and the other depressed. . . . The one is taught to aspire and the other is early confined and limited." —Judith Sargent Stevens, *Massachusetts Magazine,* 1790

239.

"Business of various kinds, they might likewise pursue, if they were educated in a more orderly manner, which might save many from common and legal prostitution. Women would not then marry for a support . . . nor would an attempt to earn their own subsistence, a most laudable one! sink them almost to the level of those poor abandoned creatures who live by prostitution. For are not milliners and mantua-makers reckoned the next class? The few employments open to women, so far from being liberal, are menial; and when a superiour education enables them to take charge of the education of children as governesses, they are not treated like the tutors of sons." —Mary Wollstonecraft, *A Vindication of the Rights of Woman,* 1792

240.

"Women can, of course, be educated, but their minds are not adapted to the higher sciences, philosophy, or certain areas of the arts. These demand a universal faculty. Women may have happy inspirations, taste, elegance, but they have not the ideal. . . . The education of women goes on one hardly knows how, in the atmosphere of picture-thinking, as it were, more through life than through the acquisition of knowledge. Man attains his position only through stress of thought and much specialized effort." —Georg Hegel, *The Philosophy of Right,* 1821

241.

"You need only look at the way in which she is formed, to see that woman is not meant to undergo great labor, whether of the mind or the body. She pays the debt of life not by what she does, but by what she suffers; by the pains of childbearing and care for the child, and by submission to her husband. . . . In the case of woman, it is only reason of a sort—very niggard in its dimensions. That is why women remain children their whole life long; never seeing anything but what is quite close to them, cleaving to the present moment, taking appearance for reality, and preferring trifles to matters of the first importance. . . . She may, in fact, be described as intellectually short-sighted, because, while she has an intuitive understanding of what lies quite close to her, her field of vision is narrow and does not reach to what is remote; so that things which are absent, or past, or to come, have much less effect upon women than upon men." —Arthur Schopenhauer, "On Women," 1851

242.

"Women can afford to teach for one-half, or even less, the salary which men would ask, because the female teacher has only to sustain herself; she does not look forward to the duty of supporting a family, should she marry, nor has she the ambition to amass a fortune." —Catherine Beecher, address to Congress, 1860

243.

"The chief distinction in the intellectual powers of the two sexes is shewn by man's attaining to higher eminence, in whatever he takes up, than can woman—whether requiring deep thought, reason, or imagination, or merely the use of senses and hands. If two lists were made of the most eminent men and women in poetry, painting, sculpture, music (inclusive both of composition and performance), history, science, and philosophy with half-a-dozen names under each subject, the two lists would not bear comparison. We may also infer, from the law of deviation from averages . . . that if men are capable of a decided pre-eminence over women in many subjects, the average of mental power in man must be above that of woman." —Charles Darwin, *The Descent of Man,* 1871

244.

"With the exception of the tests for arithmetic, mathematics, mechanics and mazes, females achieve significantly and consistently higher scores on the intelligence tests than males. . . . In short, the age-old myth that women are of inferior intelligence to men has, so far as the scientific evidence goes, not a leg to stand upon." —Ashley Montagu, *The Natural Superiority of Women,* 1952

245.

"It has been said time and time again that education has kept American women from 'adjusting' to their role as housewives. But if education, which serves human growth, which distills what the human mind has discovered and created in the past, and gives man the ability to create his own future—if education has made more and more American women feel trapped, frustrated, guilty as housewives, surely this should be seen as a clear signal *that women have outgrown the housewife role."* —Betty Friedan, *The Feminine Mystique,* 1963

246.

"But you see, there's a difference from birth. Now, the male mind thinks in certain attitudes; the female thinks in a little bit other attitudes. . . . But the key in terms of mental—it has nothing to do with physical—is chess. There's never been a woman Grand Master chess player. And if, you know, once you get one, then I'll buy some of the feminism, but until that point . . ." —Pat Robertson, 1994

FIFTEEN FAMOUS MINDS

247. *Aspasia of Miletus*
(c. 470–410 B.C.E.)

Perhaps the first *saloniste* in history, Aspasia mingled with the cultural elite of ancient Greece, influencing famous thinkers such as Socrates and Plato. Born in Asia Minor, she was best known as the wife of Pericles, the Athenian statesman. When Pericles divorced his first wife, Aspasia married him and made their home a center of Greek intellectual life. Plato became part of the circle as a child, after his father died and his mother married Pyrilampes, a colleague

of Pericles. Aspasia's brilliance and education apparently gained her ample sway over her husband, the leader of Athens starting in 461 B.C.E. Pericles made Athens great through internal political reform and expansionist foreign policy, and the resulting prosperity allowed the arts and literature to flourish. In the so-called Age of Pericles, Aspasia had such behind-the-scenes clout that some historians have charged her with igniting the Peloponnesian War in 431 B.C.E.

Aspasia.

Pan Chao.

249. *Anna Comnena* (1083–c. 1148)

This Byzantine princess is best known for *Alexiad,* a history of her father's establishment of the Comnenian dynasty over the eastern Roman Empire. Named for her father, Emperor Alexius I, the book represented a major contribution to medieval Greek history. She wrote it while confined to a convent after conspiring against her brother, Emperor John II, in 1118.

250. *Margaret of Angoulême* (1492–1549)

This queen, the wife of Henry II of Navarre, supported intellectual and cultural progress in France. The writers and humanists she attracted to her court made it Europe's most intellectually vital; John Calvin, Desiderius

Margaret of Angoulême.

248. *Pan Chao* (c. 45–c. 115)

The daughter of a Han dynasty official, Pan Chao was a lady-in-waiting and teacher to China's Empress Teng. She wrote many poems, earning recognition as a poet laureate. Among her numerous essays was *Lessons for Women* (106), in which she describes the qualities of the ideal woman, such as modesty and piety. Historian to the court of Emperor Ho, Pan Chao collaborated with her father and one of her brothers on the *Han shu (History of the Former Han Dynasty),* an archetype for dynastic histories written in ensuing centuries.

Erasmus and François Rabelais were among those who held her progressive imagination in high regard. *Heptaméron,* her collection of stories, raised provocative questions about the place of women in a world ruled by men. With her sponsorship, a foundling school opened in Paris in 1527 and the Collège de France opened in 1539.

251. More Than Frank's Mom

The mother of Sir Francis Bacon was a respected intellectual in her own right. Anne Cooke Bacon (1528–1610), an acquaintance of Queen Elizabeth I, translated a number of important works from Latin into English.

252. Mogul Maven

Jahangir, the fourth emperor of the Mogul empire in India, was greatly influenced by his wife, Mihr-un-Nisa' (c. 1571–1645). Known as Nur Jahan ("Light of the World") and Nur Mahal ("Light of the Palace"), she not only wielded political power but was famed as a great *saloniste.* She filled the court with scholars, artists and writers, promoting the intellectual and cultural development of the empire.

253. Sor Juana Inés de la Cruz
(1646–1695)

In a time and place where women's lives seldom ranged beyond church and family, a Mexican nun became a renowned scholar and the greatest poet of colonial Latin America. Largely self-taught, Juana Inés de Asbaje learned to read in her grandfather's library at the age of three. She longed to study in Mexico City and planned to dress as a boy in order to do so. At nine, already

Sor Juana Inés de la Cruz.

an avid poet, she got her wish and went (dressed as a girl) to live with relatives. Supposedly, she could read and write Latin after only twenty lessons. She became a lady-in-waiting to the wife of New Spain's viceroy, soon gaining celebrity in her own right. At a public exhibition of her genius when she was just seventeen, she correctly answered the questions of forty university professors in topics such as mathematics and history. Two years later, she became a nun at the convent of San Jerónimo, where as Sor Juana Inés de la Cruz she could dedicate herself to scholarship. For twenty years she studied theology, literature, history, music and science, assembling a library of more than four thousand volumes and corresponding with other distinguished scholars. At the same time, the beauty of her allegorical poetry, carols and plays inspired the Mexican literati to call her the Tenth Muse. One of her especially profound theological essays led both to her downfall and to her historical immortality. Published under her own name, it aroused the censure of Roman Catholic authorities, who felt she had transgressed womanly boundaries. Sor Juana's response to that criticism, *Respuesta a Sor Filotea,* endures as a fiercely articulate argument for women's right to intellectual freedom. She fell out of favor with the Church, however, and in 1693 was forced to capitulate and sign a confession of her wrongs in blood. She remained a nun, but her scholarly career came to an end.

254. *Mary Wollstonecraft*
(1759–1797)

The author of the first major feminist tract written in English drew her thinking directly from Enlightenment notions of equality and individual rights. Originally a schoolteacher and governess in England and Ireland, she published her first novel, *Mary, a Fiction,* in 1788. She started working as a translator in London and became friends with Thomas Paine, William Blake and other leading minds of the Enlightenment. During this time, inspired by the French revolutionary "Declaration of the Rights of Man," she wrote her masterpiece, *A Vindication of the Rights of Woman.* Published in 1792, the book attacks social conventions that oppress women, including inequality in

education, and proposes that marriage should be a partnership of intellectual equals. Wollstonecraft lived according to her radical ideals of feminine equality, moving to Paris during the French Revolution, writing *A Vindication of the Rights of Man* (1793) and giving birth out of wedlock to a daughter, Fanny, in 1794. Fanny's father, Gilbert Imlay, abandoned Wollstonecraft, who then attempted suicide. She died in England in 1797, after bearing a daughter by her new husband, English political philosopher William Godwin. As Mary Shelley, that daughter became the author of *Frankenstein* and other novels.

255. *Margaret Fuller* (1810–1850)

One of the greatest minds of her time, Fuller was the author of *Woman in the Nineteenth Century,* a keen examination of women's place in society. As a child she learned Greek and Latin from her father and at a young age was drawn to the transcendentalist movement, which encouraged the cultivation of the female intellect. She taught at Bronson Alcott's Temple School in Boston and Providence from 1836 to 1839, following a curriculum based on transcendentalist principles. Seeking greater intellectual challenges, in 1839 she launched a series of weekly seminars, known as "conversations," for women. Fuller disregarded the ban on paid female public speakers, and soon attracted the leading women of Boston to her brilliant talks on topics such as science, art, ethics and mythology. From 1840 to 1842 she served as the editor of *The Dial,* the journal of the transcendentalist movement, which she started with Ralph Waldo Emerson. She then moved on to

Horace Greeley's *New York Tribune,* where she became a nationally renowned literary critic. During this time she wrote *Woman in the Nineteenth Century,* the 1845 work that remains a vital example of feminist thought. In 1847 Fuller became the first American woman to work as a foreign correspondent, traveling in Europe and meeting luminaries like George Sand, William Wordsworth, Frédéric Chopin and Elizabeth Barrett Browning. Political turmoil in her adopted home of Italy forced her back to the United States in 1850. She died on the trip, in a shipwreck off Fire Island, New York.

256. Mary Ritter Beard
(1876–1958)

The author of *On Understanding Women* (1931) and *Women as a Force in History* (1946), this American historian studied women and their place in history long before the term "women's studies" gained currncy. Among the topics Beard illuminated were coverture—the traditional ownership by a husband of all his wife's property and legal rights—and matriarchy in both prehistoric and later societies. Before writing women's history, Beard participated in it as a suffrage and labor activist. She also contributed to other areas of historical inquiry, writing with her husband (Charles Beard) the classics *History of the United States* (1921), *The Rise of American Civilization* (1927) and *The American Spirit* (1942).

257. Hannah Arendt (1906–1975)

The philosopher who coined the phrase "the banality of evil" derived her theories from direct experience. When the Nazis gained control of Germany in 1933, Arendt fled to Paris with little but her Ph.D. from the University of Heidelberg. She held a job as a social worker until the advance of Nazi troops forced her to flee again in 1940, this time to the United States. Settling in New York City, she worked in the publishing industry and joined a number of Jewish organizations. Politicized by horrors of war, she published *Origins of Totalitarianism* in 1951, the same year she became a U.S. citizen. A highly personal and strikingly original exploration of power and its abuse, her work earned her both acclaim and criticism. Arendt started teaching and published *The Human Condition* in 1958, developing her idiosyncratic yet compelling brand of philosophy. The following year she became the first woman granted a full professorship at Princeton; she later taught at Columbia, the University of Chicago and the New School for Social Research. Arendt continued to write until her death, producing works such as *Eichmann in Jerusalem* (1963) and *On Violence* (1969).

Hannah Arendt.

258. Simone de Beauvoir
(1908–1986)

The product of a conservative French family, De Beauvoir dedicated her life to challenging all the conventions of bourgeois society. She never married her lifelong lover, philosopher Jean-Paul Sartre, with whom she shared a nonmonogamous relationship. She was a leading light of the existential movement, which rejected traditional notions of morality and human purpose. Perhaps most notably, De Beauvoir formulated a feminist theory of women's exclusion from mainstream life that endures as a cornerstone in feminist thought. Her masterpiece, *The Second Sex* (1949), today remains as compelling and provocative as it was when it was first published. She also wrote several memoirs and novels that reflect her progressive outlook.

259. Susan Sontag (1933–)

One of the leading thinkers of twentieth-century America, Sontag has spent her career on the intellectual cutting edge. She honed her skills as a penetrating social observer at some of the world's finest universities and established a name for herself with the 1964 publication of "Camp," an essay in the *Partisan Review*. The article received attention not only within academic circles but from the general public, which was fascinated with her idea of camp as a "love of the unnatural, of artifice and exaggeration." Sontag became an authority on the American experience of the 1960s, publishing the essay collections *Against Interpretation* (1966) and *Styles of Radical Will* (1969) as well as two novels, *The Benefactor* (1963) and *Death*

Kit (1967). During the 1970s she turned her pen to a variety of subjects in the essay "On Photography" (1977) and the short story collection *I, etcetera* (1978). Her battle with cancer precipitated an especially powerful essay, "Illness as Metaphor," in 1978. Since then Sontag has continued to lecture and write, expanding a singular body of work with the essay collection *Under the Sign of Saturn* (1980), the novel *The Volcano Lover* (1992) and other works.

260. Kate Millett (1934–)

A leading exponent of radical feminism, Millett first published her theories in *Sexual Politics* (1970), causing an immediate sensation. Linking Freudian psychology, which she considered anti-woman, with literature by men she perceived as woman-haters, she situated all human adversity in male domination of civilization. She called for the elimination of the family and other social constructs she judged oppressive to women.

261. Camille Paglia (1947–)

In such books as *Sexual Personae* (1990) and *Sex, Art and American Culture* (1992), this college professor attacked the late-twentieth-century trend known as political correctness. Among her targets were modern education techniques, anti-pornography crusades and conventional feminism. Although she declared herself a feminist, she was widely repudiated by established feminists, and conservatives embraced many of her theories. Her controversial views and caustic personality gained her extensive publicity, further irritating her opponents.

Two Womanly Disciplines

262. Home Economics

Founded on persistent notions that women belong at home, domestic science emerged in the nineteenth century as a standard curriculum for girls. Emma Willard started teaching household management at the Troy Female Seminary in 1821, and Catherine Beecher published the field's first text, *Treatise on Domestic Economy,* in 1840. State agricultural colleges first offered formal home economics classes in the 1870s, a practice soon adopted by other colleges and high schools. In the 1890s, the movement found a leader in Ellen Swallow Richards (1842–1911), an alumna of Vassar College and the first woman to graduate from the Massachusetts Institute of Technology. She developed the scientific principles of home economics while teaching at MIT, believing that science and technology could lighten the burdens of keeping house, even as the rapid changes in an industrializing world demanded new skills of homemakers. Richards organized the first conference on home economics in 1899 at Lake Placid, New York, and was elected president of the newly formed American Home Economics Association in 1908. Federal funding

Home economics class, 1943.

promoted the widespread education of girls in nutrition, hygiene and similar subjects early in the twentieth century. The federal government employed home economists during World War I to teach homemakers how to minimize civilian food consumption. But jobs like these were rare, and most girls in public schools sought educations that would help them earn money. Enrollment in home economics classes declined rapidly in the first third of the twentieth century. Schools at all levels still teach the topic today and even offer degrees, but home economics no longer takes center stage in most women's educations.

263. Women's Studies

The women's liberation movement that started in the 1960s inspired the creation of a new academic discipline known as women's studies. Educators and students began to recognize and remedy academia's traditional lack of attention to women's issues and achievements. In 1969 San Diego State University established the first degree program in women's studies. The discovery, analysis and teaching of women's social, cultural, economic, political and historical experience gave rise to an entirely new way of studying virtually any subject from the perspective of gender. The discipline grew rapidly, spawning separate women's studies departments at many universities and introducing the topic to elementary, junior high and high school students. Controversy over whether women's studies should remain a separate discipline or be integrated into other academic areas has given way to the notion that both approaches are valuable.

SEVEN PROPOSALS CONCERNING THE EDUCATION OF WOMEN

264. Adult Subject Matter

In 1250, Philippe de Navarre published an essay on etiquette and morality, in which he warns of the dangers of female literacy. Women should not learn to read, he wrote, because they might be sullied by suggestive love letters.

265. Sacred Subject Matter

Believing that women should be able to read the Bible, the Protestant reformers of the sixteenth century promoted female literacy. In other respects, their interpretation of the proper role of women was at least as oppressive as contemporary Catholic views.

266. Intellectual Inferiority

In 1622, a French woman named Marie de Gournay published *On the Equality of Men and Women,* in which she asserted that women's minds are not "naturally" inferior, as current theory held.

267. A Serious Proposal to the Ladies for the Advancement of their True and Greatest Interest

Published in 1701 by English writer Mary Astell, this daring book almost caused a revolution. It called for the complete and systematic education of women, a proposal that gained widespread attention but which was never adopted. Astell had previously published *In Defense of the Female Sex* (1696) and had recommended that England establish a women's college.

268. Dangerous Instruction

French novelist Choderlos de Laclos, the author of *Les liaisons dangereuses* (1782), in 1785 published a tract entitled *De l'éducation des femmes*, arguing that women should be taught poise and refinement rather than academic topics, which would mar their temperament.

269. Declaration of Women's Rights

By unanimous vote in 1967, the United Nations approved a statement calling for the advancement and protection of women's rights. Article 9 of that declaration reads in part: "All appropriate measures shall be taken to insure to girls and women, married or unmarried, equal rights with men in education at all levels." The document, however, was not binding.

270. Title IX of the 1972 Education Act Amendments

"No person in the United States shall, on the basis of sex, be excluded from participation in, be denied the benefits of, or be subjected to discrimination under any education program or activity receiving Federal financial assistance."

TWELVE PEDAGOGICAL PRACTICES

271. The Early Middle Ages

From the sixth century, when the first abbeys appeared, until the twelfth century, when the first universities were founded, European women of the nobility received much the same kind of education as their brothers. They learned basic reading, genteel manners and feudal administration, usually from nuns. These skills, it was thought, equipped them for aristocratic life; women from lower classes received virtually no education.

Medieval nuns at their studies.

272. The Late Middle Ages

Educational opportunity declined for most European noblewomen after the rise of the universities, from which they were excluded (except in Italy and Spain). Manuals on raising daughters warned against education for girls, except those who were to be nuns. Education of men's supposed intellectual inferiors was considered a waste, and even dangerous. As a result, the vast majority of medieval and early modern women received no real education. If they did, they generally learned at home from parents or, if they were wealthy, from private tutors or in the houses of great ladies. Some noblewomen, however, sought higher learning in the convents. There, nuns and their students could study freely, presumably in the service of God, Latin and other languages, philosophy, the arts and the sciences.

273. Dame Schools

In the eighteenth century, those European and American girls who received any education did so at the hands of their parents, private tutors or local women who conducted classes in their home. These so-called dame schools generally offered only primary education.

274. The Young Republic

The American Revolution not only freed a nation, its goals had a significant impact on educational opportunities for girls. In colonial times, few women were schooled in anything more than rudimentary reading, writing and arithmetic. Their autonomy during the war, when they managed farms and businesses while the men fought, convinced some Americans of the value of educating girls. As early as 1779, Judith Sargent Murray argued that girls should be educated so as not to be completely dependent on marriage for their social identity and economic well-being. Her article "Desultory Thoughts upon the Utility of Encouraging a Degree of Self-Complacency, Especially in Female Bosoms" and subsequent magazine essays helped accustom the public to the idea of female education. The real impetus for education came from evolving notions of women's roles. Girls should attend school to prepare for the most important task of their adult lives: raising their sons to be good citizens of the new republic. Institutions such as the Moravian Young Ladies Seminary, in Bethlehem, Pennsylvania, and Sarah Pierce's School in Litchfield, Connecticut, opened for this purpose before the turn of the century. For the first time, significant numbers of American girls learned geography, history, music and other subjects. Nevertheless, female education advanced only because of its perceived benefits to men.

275. Integration, Part I

In 1793 an integrated school for poor children opened in New York City. Its founder was Katy Ferguson, a slave who had bought her own freedom. For its first class, the Katy Ferguson School for the Poor recruited twenty-eight black students and twenty white students from the city's poorhouses.

276. Birth of the American Schoolteacher

American women's role as teachers of their children paved the way for female domination of the teaching profession in the United States. Early in the nineteenth century, the young democracy sought to broaden literacy among women and men of all classes, spurring the establishment of common schools starting in the 1820s. The proliferation of girls' schools augmented the trend, so that half of American women could read and write by midcentury and a quarter of American schoolteachers were women when the Civil War started. Women steadily replaced men as schoolteachers, extending their duty as women beyond the home. Before long, the education of children became a "women's" profession.

277. American Public Schools

In 1826, the cities of New York and Boston opened America's first public high schools for girls.

278. Free Women and Ex-Slaves

Even before Emancipation, a number of white women worked to bring education to African-Americans. In U.S. Army camps, Charlotte Forten taught reading and writing to slaves freed by the Union forces. Prudence Crandall, a Connecticut schoolteacher, opened the Canterbury Female Boarding School to a local African-American girl in 1831. When the local townspeople protested, she solicited the support of well-to-do African-Americans and launched a segregated school—for blacks only—in 1833. Threats, boycotts and ostracism did not shake her, but Crandall's enemies finally managed to pass a law making her school illegal. The authorities arrested her, sparking a na-

tional outcry among abolitionists. Two trials and an overturned conviction left her free to continue her work, but her white neighbors made life miserable for her and her students. In 1834 she was forced to close the school and move away from Connecticut.

279. Integration, Part II

In 1848, the daughter of abolitionist Frederick Douglass gained admission to a female seminary in Rochester, New York. The female principal, however, barred the African-American girl from attending classes. Even when all but one of the students voted to admit her to class, the principal, a professed abolitionist, refused to allow it.

280. Maverick Teacher

When Myrtilla Miner opened the Miner Normal School in 1851, her neighbors threatened it with arson. The white educator scandalized Washington, D.C., by daring to train African-American women for teaching careers.

281. Native American Schools

First white missionaries and later the federal government took it upon themselves to educate Native Americans who had been forced onto reservations by the advance of white settlers. For girls and boys alike, the aim of these programs was to impart white culture to young Native Americans. But while boys actually attended reading, mathematics and history classes, in practice girls received very little book learning. Instead, they spent most of their time learning white domestic skills. Some did so in white homes, where they served as household servants, while many others were put to work at the Native American schools. Budgetary problems in the 1880s prompted white administrators to assign cooking, cleaning and laundry duties to girl students at the expense of their academic training. Native American girls thus left these schools ill prepared for life in either their own or white culture.

282. *Military Academies*

In 1975 the United States Congress passed legislation requiring the military to admit women to its service academies. Entrenched resistance to the integration of women into the academies and into the military as a whole posed extra challenges to female cadets in an already demanding academic environment. At West Point and Annapolis, official policy toward women initially failed to recognize the problems that might arise from coeducation, essentially ignoring the presence of women and allowing sexist abuses to flourish. Numerous reports of sexual harassment and sexual assault finally forced military educators to take action on behalf of women cadets, especially after the Tailhook Scandal of 1991 and 1992. Things went a little more easily for women at the United States Air Force Academy at Colorado Springs, where the administration from the start made vigorous efforts on their behalf. A program to draw attention to the new cadets and their talents helped establish an atmosphere of mutual respect between the sexes. However, anti-harassment policies at each of the academies have yet to remove the barrier to full gender equality in the armed forces. According to a 1992 Air Force Academy study, 78 percent of female cadets and 52 percent of male cadets reported hearing sexist comments every day. A 1994 survey by the U.S. General Accounting Office showed that half to three quarters of all academy women encountered some form of harassment at least once a month. Despite the ongoing discrimination, women have managed to excel at the military academies. In 1989, Kristin Baker became West Point's first female Captain of the Corps of Cadets, and in 1995, a woman was valedictorian of the graduating class.

TEN NOTABLE INSTITUTIONS

283. *Oberlin College*

In 1833, Oberlin Collegiate Institute opened in Oberlin, Ohio, as the first coeducational college in the United States. Not only was it the first to admit women, but two years after it was established it also opened its doors to students "with-

First Ladies' Hall, Oberlin College.

out respect to color." A hotbed of abolitionist and feminist activity, the college nonetheless maintained a separate "Female Department" with special "Ladies" courses. The first woman to graduate from the men's "Full Course" did so in 1841. Among Oberlin's distinguished early graduates were women's rights activist Lucy Stone, theologian Antoinette Brown Blackwell and African-American educators Fannie Jackson Coppin (a former slave) and Anna Julia Cooper.

284. Mount Holyoke College

In 1837 Mary Lyon opened what many consider to be the first American women's college, in South Hadley, Massachusetts. The product of years of planning and fund raising, the school broke new ground by offering young women a complete education while maintaining high academic standards. To keep tuition expenses down and allow women of lesser means to attend, students paid their way in part by helping run the institution, cooking and cleaning in addition to studying. Originally housed in a single building, the school placed students and teachers in constant contact as they lived and studied together each day. Lyon's intention was that young women would find mentors among the faculty, but her technique also reduced the risk of criticism by outsiders: Many opponents of higher education for women argued that allowing young women the independence to attend college would result in scandal. As Mount Holyoke Seminary, the school first offered a four-year college curriculum in 1861. It became a full-scale college in 1888 and changed its name to Mount Holyoke College in 1893.

285. Spelman College

A noted liberal arts college attended mostly by African-American women, Spelman appeared in embryonic form in 1881. That year, two white missionaries named Sophia Packard and Harriet Giles raised $100 from Baptists in Massachusetts to open a school for black women in the South. With the help of the Woman's American Baptist Home Mission Society and a prominent local African-American preacher, the missionaries found eleven students in Atlanta. Temperance and "right Christian living" formed the basis of the curriculum, which initially emphasized practical skills that would help graduates find employment. The school produced many teachers who in turn helped educate other Southern blacks. Amply funded by John D. Rockefeller, the school took his wife's maiden name, becoming Spelman Seminary and, in 1924, Spelman College.

286. College Sororities

Once American women gained a foothold at colleges and universities, whether single-sex or co-educational, they formed all kinds of clubs and organizations to meet their social and educational needs. Among these were the Greek-letter societies, commonly known as sororities. The first white sorority, Kappa Alpha Theta, was founded at DePauw University in 1870, while the first African-American sorority, Alpha Kappa Alpha, was founded in Washington, D.C. in 1908. Sororities served as a support system for young college women, many of whom were living away from home for the first time.

287. Women at Oxford

Women first took the Oxford University examinations in 1870, eight years before the institution launched its first two women's colleges. Also in 1878, the university established the Association for the Education of Women. In 1901, St. Hilda's College for Women Teachers, founded in 1885 by Dorothy Beale, became an Oxford college. Despite these advances, the university would not confer degrees upon women until 1920.

288. Women at Cambridge

Two English educators dedicated to women's right to higher education established a place for women at Cambridge University. Emily Davies (1830–1921), London school board member and author of such treatises as *The Higher Education of Women* (1866), founded a women's college near Cambridge in 1873. The school, Girton College, became a college of the university that year. Anne Jemima Clough (1820–1892), who as a leader of the women's education movement had persuaded two other colleges to admit women, organized Newnham Hall in 1875. A school for female teachers, it became Newnham College at Cambridge in 1880. The following year, the university allowed women to take the third-year exam for the first time, but it would not confer full degrees upon them until 1948. Cavendish College, a graduate school at the university, allowed women to pursue graduate studies there starting in 1965.

289. Women at Harvard

Women first entered Harvard University in 1893, when Radcliffe College established a formal relationship with the university. Radcliffe rose from the ashes of the Harvard Annex, a school set up in 1879 and incorporated in 1882 as The Society for the Collegiate Instruction of Women. Harvard professors taught all the classes at Harvard Annex, but the university declined to accept it as an affiliate until it took its final shape as Radcliffe College. Harvard Medical College did not accept Radcliffe students until 1917, and Harvard Law School did not admit women until 1950. Radcliffe, however, continued to advance the cause of higher education for women. By 1976, it boasted the largest women's history library in the U.S.

290. Late State College

The last existing state to open a college for women, Delaware established the Women's College at the University of Delaware in 1914.

291. American Association of University Women

Even as educational opportunities for American women expanded rapidly in the late nineteenth and early twentieth centuries, most women with college degrees encountered barriers to applying them in the professions. The Association of Collegiate Alumnae formed in 1881 to address this problem, followed by several regional alumnae groups. Merging in 1921, these groups formed the American Association of University Women. The organization has since worked to improve educational opportunities for women and girls, especially at the university level. Now comprised of more than two thousand local chapters, the AAUW also offers scholarships and sponsors studies of issues relevant to women's education.

292. Long Road to Rhodes

The prestigious Rhodes Scholarship program did not accept applications from women until 1976. The following year, thirteen of its thirty-two honorees were women.

FIVE MEASURES OF SCHOLASTIC STATUS

293. Female Illiteracy

Throughout history and in every culture, women have faced overwhelming discrimination in the field of education. Many of those barriers have fallen in industrialized nations, but progress has been slow for women in the developing world. A United Nations survey published in 1990 shows that the illiteracy rate of non-Western women exceeds that of their male counterparts by 15 to 30 percent. In Africa and Asia, three quarters of women over the age of twenty-five cannot read, compared with 40 percent of women ages fifteen to twenty-four. In Mali, the rate soars to 97.9 percent for women twenty-five and up; the figure is 97.6 percent in Afghanistan.

294. College Students

Within thirty years of the 1963 publication of Betty Friedan's *The Feminine Mystique,* the book that launched the modern feminist movement, the proportion of female college undergraduates soared from 20 percent to 54 percent.

295. University Faculty

A higher percentage—36 percent—of American university faculty members were women in 1880 than in any year before or since. Their growing presence on campus worried many male academics, who sought to keep women out of their profession by blocking their access to graduate school education. Still, Boston University, Syracuse University and other schools began granting graduate degrees to women, and in the 1890s elite institutions such as Yale, Stanford and the University of Chicago followed suit. In response, many academic organizations refused membership and accreditation to women, hindering their efforts to gain a foothold. Women formed their own associations, but segregation effectively limited their advancement as university professors. By 1960, women made up 22 percent of college faculty members nationwide; by 1991, the number had risen to only 31.7 percent. Such gains are largely the result of affirmative action, first initiated at the university level in 1971 by the University of Michigan.

296. Sex Bias at School

When they first enter school, young girls perform at least as well as young boys in every respect. Around sixth or seventh grade, however, their grades often start to fall, especially in science and math, and at the same time they lose much of the self-confidence and self-esteem they once had. A number of recent studies have sought to explain this phenomenon and identify remedies. One, "How Schools Shortchange Girls," a February 1992 report from the American Association of University Women, showed that teachers pay more attention to boys than to girls in the same classroom, encouraging them and listening to them. Many studies have backed up this finding, and a growing number of American school districts have implemented programs to help teachers teach girls better.

297. Sexual Harassment at School

In 1993, *Seventeen* magazine published a poll that showed 89 percent of girls ages nine to nineteen had been pinched, taunted, groped or otherwise sexually harassed at school, 39 percent on a daily basis. The 1993 "Hostile Hallways" survey commissioned by the American Association of University Women corroborated *Seventeen*'s results, finding that 85 percent of girls experienced harassment at school, most often in the sixth through ninth grades. Some instances of at-school harassment have made their way into the courts and the newspapers. In 1992, in a case called *Franklin v. Gwinnett County Public Schools,* the Supreme Court ruled in favor of a high school student who charged a teacher with sexual harassment. In 1993, seven-year-old Cheltzie Hentz of Eden Prairie, Minnesota, won a Title IX lawsuit against her school district, which had failed to discipline boys who had been taunting and teasing her on the school bus. Such problems do not stop with high school graduation: Recent studies show that anywhere from 30 to 80 percent of women experience sexual harassment at college.

ELEVEN EDUCATORS

298. Mothers of Cambridge

In 1342, Marie de Saint Pole established Cambridge's Pembroke College. At the time, she was the widow of the Earl of Pembroke. Margaret of Anjou and Elizabeth Woodville founded Queens College in 1465.

299. Lady Margaret Beaufort
(1443–1509)

This English noblewoman, the politically influential mother of King Henry VII, the first of the Tudors, is best remembered as a patron of learn-

Lady Margaret Beaufort.

ing. A student of medicine and theology, she wrote and spoke on those topics at the courts of Edward IV and Richard III. She sponsored the work of William Caxton and Wynkyn de Worde, England's first printers, and endowed divinity professorships at Oxford and Cambridge universities. Her generosity also led to the founding of two colleges at Cambridge, Christ's College in 1505 and St. John's College in 1508. Today, the Lady Margaret professorship at Cambridge remains the university's oldest.

300. *Radical Teacher*

Early in the sixteenth century, an English nun named Mary Ward saw the need for a women's college along the lines of Jesuit schools. She established the Institute of Mary, but before long Roman Catholic authorities shut down her school, abolished her order and threw her into prison.

301. *The Ursulines*

Known officially as the Order of Saint Ursula, the Ursulines were the first Roman Catholic teaching order. An Italian nun, Saint Angela Merici of Brescia (c. 1470–1540, canonized 1807), founded it as The Company of St. Ursula in 1535. Ursuline nuns took vows, but lived in the community and devoted themselves to the education of young girls. As Church support for the unconventional arrangement waned, the Ursulines began to set up convents, in Milan in 1572 and in Avignon in 1596; the Church finally required complete cloistering in 1612. The nuns continued to teach, though, and the order spread to North America and other parts of the world. The Ursuline schools in Quebec City (Canada), founded 1639, and New Orleans, founded 1727, were among the first girls' schools in the New World.

302. *Mère Marie de l'Incarnation*
(1599–1672)

Born Marie Guyart in Tours, France, Mère Marie was a major figure in early Canadian history. In 1639, she sailed from France and founded an Ursuline school in Quebec City, where she taught young girls and worked among the indigenous local peoples. A student of Native American languages, she translated the Roman Catholic catechism into Iroquois and produced French-Algonquin and French-Iroquois dictionaries. Her extensive writings, which include religious lectures, prayer notes, autobiographies and thousands of letters, vividly record the early history of the colony and remain the primary source for historians of seventeenth-century Canada.

303. *Emma Willard* (1787–1870)

This American educator was the first to give girls the opportunity to study certain subjects previously thought to be beyond a woman's comprehension. A teacher in Connecticut from 1803, she opened the Middlebury Female Academy in 1807 in order to make more money. Her success teaching mathematics, history and other "boys only" subjects allowed her to open a girls' boarding school, also in Middlebury, in 1814. But Willard recognized women would never achieve true educational equity unless their schools gained access to the public funding allotted to men's schools. Failing to convince Connecticut officials to back her plan, Willard moved to New York, which seemed to hold more potential. In 1818 she offered Governor DeWitt Clinton *An Address to the Public: Particularly to the Members of the Legislature of New York, Proposing a Plan for Improving Female Education.* The following year, even before she won public funding, she opened a radically innovative girls' school in Waterford. She taught college-level courses while lobbying government officials for money. In 1821 she finally attained her goal, receiving a grant of $4,000 for a school in Troy. Relocating her Waterford school, Willard founded the Troy Female Seminary, where girls could study mathematics, science and other subjects at an advanced level. The institution, which she ran personally until 1838, is now called the Emma Willard School. Willard remained a force in American education until her death, influencing educators such as Mary Lyon, the founder of Mount Holyoke College.

304. *Catherine Beecher* (1800–1878)

The sister of novelist Harriet Beecher Stowe was one of the nineteenth century's most active exponents of education for women. She did not exactly approach the topic from a feminist perspective, instead emphasizing women's importance as the conscience of society. If women were educated, she argued, they could teach outside as well as inside the home, thereby ensuring the growing nation's moral fortitude and unity. Founder of the Hartford Female Seminary in Connecticut, Beecher traveled and lectured widely, encouraging young women to become teachers. At the same time, the rapid establishment of new communities in the West escalated the demand for teachers. In the 1840s Beecher campaigned for the broad use of women teachers, arguing not only for their moral qualifications but that women would work for half the salary demanded by male teachers. She opened several training schools that produced hundreds of female teachers, many of who found work in the West. Beecher may not have advanced feminist political goals, but she was a major force in opening a new profession to women.

305. *Ellen Key* (1849–1926)

With her book *The Century of the Child* (1900), Swedish feminist and educator Ellen Key stirred controversy and profoundly influenced education in many countries. She proposed that education should serve the promise and problems of individual children rather than the demands of society or religion. Key's liberal thinking also extended to women's rights, pacifism and the relations between the sexes.

306. *Martha Carey Thomas* (1857–1935)

From 1894 to 1922, Bryn Mawr College was led by this tireless and dynamic educator. An English professor and dean at the school, she had already co-founded (in 1885) the Bryn Mawr School for Girls in her hometown of Baltimore. She was an ideal choice to be president of Bryn Mawr College, founded in 1880 to offer women an education equal to that available to men. Thomas raised that standard, determined that on every level the college should exceed the standards of the best men's schools. She inspired students, faculty and staff with her approach, which she described in her 1900 book, *The Higher Education of Women.* In 1910 she inaugurated America's first graduate school of social economy at the college, and in 1921 she launched the Summer School for Women Workers in Industry. That school brought working women to Bryn Mawr for six weeks of higher education designed to prepare them for leadership roles in labor unions.

307. *Maria Montessori* (1870–1952)

This Italian educator, the first woman to receive a medical degree in Italy, became interested in education through her experiences as a doctor. After studying psychiatry and pedagogy, she tested some of her principles at a school she established for handicapped children. She opened the first Montessori school for normal children in 1907, in the slums of Rome. To encourage initiative and physical development in young children, her method allows them to follow their own interests in a controlled environment. Teachers equipped with special games and materials help children get off on the right foot but then leave them to their own devices. Evidence that the Montessori method fosters earlier and better reading skills has captured the attention of educators worldwide, and aspects of the method are used in schools around the world.

308. *Mary McLeod Bethune*
(1875–1955)

The seventeenth child of former slaves, Bethune worked all her life to improve the lot of African-Americans. She saw education as the key to that

Mary McLeod Bethune *(Photo by Gordon Parks)*

goal and started teaching school in Georgia and Florida in 1894. In 1904, armed with only $1.50, five students and a rented house in Daytona Beach, she founded the Daytona Normal and Industrial Institute for Negro Girls. Bethune raised funds from sponsors such as Procter & Gamble and John D. Rockefeller and saw the school grow to three hundred students and twenty acres of campus by 1923. In 1929, the school merged with the all-male Cookman Institute, becoming Bethune-Cookman College in 1936. Even as she oversaw the college's activities, Bethune got involved in dozens of causes and organizations. She fought lynching, racial inequities in insurance and health care, and founded, presided over or served in groups such as the National Association of Colored Women, the National Council of Negro Women, the National Association for the Advancement of Colored People and the National Urban League. Under presidents Hoover, Roosevelt and Truman, Bethune held a number of minority affairs posts. She also organized the Federal Council on Negro Affairs, known as the "Black Cabinet," a group of African-American officials in the Roosevelt administration, to increase government job opportunities for blacks and promote civil rights.

Ten Ideas, Bright and Otherwise

309. The Weaker Vessel

Long-standing attitudes about women's roles and frailties limited their access to education well into the nineteenth—and even the twentieth—century. As the more delicate sex, it was said, women belonged at home. Serious education or employment was thought to impair their natural development, sap their vitality and induce various mental problems. Even by the late 1800s, scientists were lending the stamp of legitimacy to these notions. One, a professor at Harvard Medical School, wrote in 1873 that higher education could cause "neuralgia, uterine disease, hysteria and other derangements of the nervous system" in girls, ruining them for marriage and motherhood.

310. Bluestockings

In the eighteenth century, literary clubs known as Bluestocking societies appeared in England and America. The groups took their name from the signature fashion statement of prominent member Benjamin Stillingfleet, who rejected men's customary white hose for blue hose. Women joined Bluestocking societies in such great numbers that the term bluestocking came to refer to any woman with literary or academic interests. The word became a put-down, connoting a woman who put on intellectual airs.

Nineteenth-century caricature of a bluestocking.

311. Forbidden Fruit

In the 1890s, Elizabeth Cady Stanton voiced her opinion on women's historical exclusion from education. Eve, she commented wryly, tasted the apple in the Garden of Eden in order to slake "that intense thirst for knowledge that the simple pleasures of picking flowers and talking to Adam could not satisfy."

312. Sexism

The modern fight for women's rights has for the most part been a fight against sexism, the collection of male assumptions concerning women's place in the world. The notion that women are somehow inferior, that they should be excluded from certain areas of life and that they are born with certain responsibilities lies at the heart of sexual discrimination. So deeply ingrained as to seem innate, sexism appears in every culture and has colored every era of history. Its pervasiveness has accorded men greater privileges and opportunities than those allowed women by assigning specific sex roles to each gender.

313. Feminism

The theory that women are entitled to enjoy all the rights, privileges, opportunities and respect accorded to men. Feminist theoreticians have formulated numerous interpretations of this basic notion, including liberal feminism, the most widely accepted. Sometimes referred to as mainstream feminists, liberal feminists understand theory as a call to social reform, with the goal of achieving equality for women. By contrast, radical feminists posit that the existing structure of family-based society by its very nature oppresses women, and that social revolution is the path to women's rights. Marxist and socialist feminists, meanwhile, see socialism as the basis of gender equality; lesbian feminists assert that only gay women can practice true feminism. And nationalist feminists state that "the malist society is finished and is taking us and the environment down with him . . . wifism destroys our lives, relations, and organizations."

314. Patriarchy

To varying degrees, feminists of all stripes denounce patriarchy, the systematic political, economic, legal and social domination of women by men. They believe its elimination would benefit not only women but civilization as a whole. Antifeminists, however, point to universal male dominance as evidence of male supremacy, which in turn justifies patriarchy.

315. Matriarchy Theory

The notion that the earliest human societies, which appeared in the Near East and the Mediterranean region, were dominated by women. Various male theorists of the nineteenth and early twentieth centuries, such as Friedrich Engels, located the origin of human civilization and matriarchy in the fourth century B.C.E., finding support for the existence of matriarchy in archaeological and anthropological evidence of goddess worship and other practices. According to one theory, patriarchy replaced prehistoric, matriarchal culture after a great natural disaster or other catastrophic event profoundly disrupted or wiped out the earlier civilizations. There is, however, little hard evidence to support matriarchy.

316. Female Supremacy

A minority of feminist theorists of the late twentieth century have maintained that women's biological or cultural traits make them inherently superior to men. The principle known as essentialism ascribes this superiority to female biology, while cultural feminism holds that women have attained their supremacy by virtue of their cultural identity. Some feminists have translated these theories into a mandate that women separate themselves from male culture and establish an exclusively female society. Others have developed the theory of ecofeminism, which attributes the destruction of the earth's environment to male domination of civilization.

317. The Female Eunuch

In 1970, Australian critic and writer Germaine Greer (1939–) published this book, which encouraged women to repudiate monogamy and marriage as forms of subservience to men. Angering many feminists, Greer postulated that action on the individual level, rather than social reform or revolution, is the route to equality for women.

318. Language Desexing

Because language so defines human attitudes and interactions, some modern feminists have called for the desexing of language. Most languages contain built-in features that establish the masculine as universal and the feminine as specific, thereby underscoring deep-rooted discrimination against women. Accordingly, language desexing discards "mankind" in favor of "humanity," replaces "mailman" with "mail carrier," rejects "man-made" for "artificial" and assigns male names to half of all tropical storms.

FIVE FACTS FROM AROUND THE GLOBE

319. Belize

In 1800, a school for nurses opened in the country then known as British Honduras. An Englishwoman named Marian Edith Beresford taught her students at Belize Hospital.

320. Malaysia

Malaysia's first girls' school opened in 1819, in Penang. Another opened in 1833, in Johore Bahru. The country boasted six schools for girls by 1895.

321. Scandinavia

Swedish women were not permitted to teach until 1853, and Norwegian women until 1869.

322. Russia

Despite 1845 laws that limited the access of women, "as a lower creation," to secondary education, girls' high schools opened in Russia in 1858. In 1862, though, the government blamed female students for university riots and ordered their expulsion from university lectures. Russian women continued to make steady educational gains, but they were forbidden to put their training to use in the professions, including teaching. Those who left the country to study came under suspicion from the Russian police, who considered them potential subversives. Czar Nicholas II broadened women's domestic educational opportunities in 1895, founding a medical school for them and ordering that more women be accepted into universities.

323. *Australia*

In Australia, girls could obtain much the same education as boys in the late nineteenth century. Reflecting this relative equity, the University of Melbourne became the first Australian university to open its doors to women in 1881. Many other institutions soon followed suit.

Three Famous Students

324. *Hellen Keller* (1880–1968)

Although illness left Hellen Keller deaf, mute and blind when she was only nineteen months old, she went on to lead a distinguished life. She learned to communicate via sign language at age ten and subsequently learned to read, write, "hear" and "speak" from her teacher, Anne Sullivan. Graduating cum laude from Radcliffe College in 1904, two years after publishing her first book, *The Story of My Life,* Keller wrote many more books and became an internationally famous lecturer and humanitarian, champi-

oning the causes of the blind and helping to found the American Civil Liberties Union.

325. *Learned Wives*

Soong Ch'ing-ling, the wife of Chinese revolutionary Sun Yat-sen, graduated from Wesleyan Female College in Macon, Georgia, in 1913. A few years later her sister Mei-ling, the wife of Chiang Kai-shek, graduated from Wellesley College in Wellesley, Massachusetts.

One Last Thought

326.

"Public opinion seems to relieve men of any duties toward a woman acknowledged to possess a superior mind: one can be unpleasant, vicious, or mean to her without incurring public wrath. *Is she not an extraordinary woman?* Nothing more needs to be said. She is left to her own devices, left to struggle on in pain. Often she lacks both the interest that a woman inspires and the power that a man guarantees. She carries her singular existence, like the Pariahs of India, among all the classes to which she cannot belong, all the classes that consider her obliged to exist on her own: an object of curiosity, of envy perhaps, and in effect deserving nothing but pity." —Madame de Staël, *De la littérature, 1802*

Part

FOUR

Science, Medicine and Technology

INQUIRING MINDS

327. *Pythagorean Women*

Greek science and discovery began with the Pythagorean community, a political/religious group devoted to the study of cosmology, mathematics, physics, medicine and philosophy. The Pythagoreans settled in Croton (southern Italy) in the sixth century B.C.E. Both women and men belonged to the community and taught at its school. Theano, a student, a teacher and wife of Pythagoras, wrote several treatises on the Pythagorean concept of the "golden mean." Among other female Pythagoreans were Phyntys, Melissa and Tymcha.

328. *Mary the Jewess*

Mary the Jewess worked as an alchemist in Alexandria in the first century B.C.E. Her theories and inventions serve as the practical foundation for modern chemistry. She described how to make copper tubing from sheet metal and invented a prototype of the autoclave, devices for distilling liquids; a reflux apparatus called the *kerotakis* to produce alloys; and the bain-marie, or double boiler, used in laboratories—and kitchens—for more than two thousand years.

329. *Hypatia of Alexandria*
(c. 370–415)

Hypatia was a famous mathematician, eloquent teacher and political force in Hellenic Alexandria. Even in a city of nearly a million people, her fame was so extensive that letters addressed simply to The Muse reached her. A child prodigy and daughter of Theon, a gifted mathematician and astronomer, Hypatia wrote extensively on philosophy, mechanics and mathematics and significantly advanced algebraic theory. Huge audiences came to hear her lectures, including, according to some accounts, Plato and Aristotle. Like other intellectuals, she wore a tattered cloak, but unlike most Alexandrian women, she never married. Her views on respect for women conflicted with the

Hypatia.

anti-feminist doctrine of the early Christian church; moreover, her scientific views threatened religious leaders who preached that the earth was flat. Finally, Archbishop Cyril ordered that her carriage be ambushed as she drove to the university to deliver her weekly lecture. The mob stripped her, scraped the flesh from her bones with oyster shells and threw her remains into a fire. Many scholars mark Hypatia's death as the end of ancient science and the beginning of the Western world's descent into the darkness of the Middle Ages.

330. Queen Sonduk

From 632 to 647, Korea was ruled by a woman with a head for science. At age seven, Sonduk impressed her father, the king, when scientists confirmed her explanation of why peonies have no aroma. During her reign she built Asia's first observatory, known as the Tower of the Moon and Stars.

331. Muslim Model

In the collection *Arabian Nights,* Scheherazade tells of Tawaddud, a young Arab slave girl of exceptional brilliance. Tawaddud answers a long series of questions posed by experts in medicine, mathematics, law, religion and philosophy, dazzling all with her intellect. She exemplifies the many Muslim women scientists of the Middle Ages who either wrote anonymously or had their work incorrectly attributed to men. But the story of Tawaddud has often been left out of the *Arabian Nights;* according to Sir Richard Burton, it is "extremely tiresome to most readers."

332. Saint Hildegard of Bingen
(twelfth century)

This medieval German abbess, known as the "Sibyl of the Rhine," was the earliest female scientist whose writings survived intact. A sickly child, she claimed to have visions throughout her life, which, according to modern researchers, may have been the manifestations of migraines, epilepsy or some other nervous disorder. Both a mystic and a scientist, she produced theological works, an encyclopedia of natural history and several volumes on medicine. She advocated careful hygiene, a balanced diet and regular exercise and recommended that all drinking water be boiled.

333. Herrad of Landsberg
(twelfth century)

The only original manuscript copy of Herrad of Landsberg's encyclopedia, *Hortus Deliciarum* ("Garden of Delights"), was destroyed in 1870, but copied portions of it remain. One of the last of the great medieval abbesses, she created a *computus* table for calculating religious and secular holidays, advanced explanations of world climates and winds, provided information on medicines and herbs and gave an overview of history, geography, astronomy, philosophy and natural history.

UNSEEMLY STUDIES

334. Agnodice

Greek law prohibited women from practicing medicine until Agnodice defied tradition in the fourth century B.C.E. Disguised as a man, she studied medicine with Herophilus, a famous anatomist, then set up a successful practice in Athens. When jealous fellow physicians accused the supposedly male doctor of "corrupting" aristocratic women, Agnodice dropped her disguise and was promptly arrested. Her patients, all noblewomen, threatened to kill themselves if she was executed. Agnodice was freed and allowed to practice medicine. Thenceforward, other freeborn women could also become physicians, provided they treated only women.

335. *Fear and Loathing*

As early as the third century, women herbalists, physicians and midwives were condemned as abortionists. By the Middle Ages male physicians dominated the medical hierarchy, although midwives and predominantly female folk doctors still practiced, often charging less while giving similar advice. Competition for patients became fierce from the thirteenth to fifteenth centuries. Male doctors and university medical facilities sought to increase their power by stamping out ancient traditions. Once again, they labeled their female competitors abortionists and added new epithets: witch, charlatan, heretic.

336. *Margaret Lucas Cavendish*
(1623–1673)

Attended by scholars like Thomas Hobbes and René Descartes, the salons of "Mad Madge" helped to popularize the emerging disciplines of modern science, especially among women. Her own scientific works, written in eccentric prose, were denounced as plagiarism because "no lady could understand so many hard words."

Nevertheless, Cavendish persisted in her study of science, and on May 30, 1667, she was the first woman to attend a lecture of London's Royal Scientific Society. On this symbolic opening of the doors of science to women, diarist Samuel Pepys remarked that Cavendish was "a good comely woman; but her dress so antic and her deportment so unordinary, that I do not like her at all."

337. *Les Hommes Savants (Not)*

In 1672, Molière's play *Les femmes savantes* critiqued bourgeois mannerisms and foibles, including those of pseudo-intellectual women. Other writers followed Molière's lead but lacked his incisive wit and flair for social satire. Edmond and Jules de Goncourt, for instance, wrote, "No science repels her; the most virile sciences seem to exercise a temptation and a fascination . . . Anatomy is the chief feminine fad. Certain women of fashion even dream of having, in a corner of their gardens, a little boudoir containing . . . a glass case filled with corpses!" And Edmonde-Pierre Chanvot de Beauchêne said, "Science seldom renders men amiable; women, never."

338. *Maria Agnesi* (1718–1799)

At age nine, Italian prodigy Maria Agnesi could speak for an hour, in Latin, espousing the rights of women to study science. After publication of her two-volume work on calculus, the French Academy sent her a congratulatory letter, with regrets that they could not offer her academy membership because she was a woman. Agnesi said, "Nature has endowed the female mind with a capacity for all knowledge and . . . in depriving women of an opportunity for acquiring knowledge, men work against the best interests of the public welfare."

339. Here to Stay

During the nineteenth century, many scientific societies and natural history clubs struggled with "the woman question." In 1838, the British Association for the Advancement of Science tried to exclude women from its meetings, especially the natural history lectures, "on account of the nature of some of the papers belonging to the Zoology division." Most women ignored such bans, refused to sit in separate galleries and eventually, by virtue of their numbers and expertise, gained admittance to scientific societies.

WOMEN OF THE SCIENTIFIC REVOLUTION

340. Perrenelle Lethas Flammel

In fourteenth-century France, alchemist Perrenelle Lethas Flammel and her third husband claimed to have changed mercury into pure gold and to have discovered a potion that guaranteed long life. More than three centuries later, the couple was reportedly seen attending the Paris Opéra.

341. Alexandra Giliani

While anatomy professors lectured medical students in fourteenth-century Bologna, Alexandra Giliani, a nineteen-year-old surgical assistant, performed dissections as a visual aid. She developed a method for removing blood from cadavers and refilling the arteries and veins with colored fluids so the circulatory system could be studied.

342. Mining Mind

In 1640, the Baroness Martine de Beausoleil urged the king of France to make use of his country's rich mineral deposits. Her writings centered on geology but also included studies of chemistry, mechanics, mathematics and hydraulics.

343. Lady Anne Conway (1631–1679)

Lady Anne Conway's place in the early scientific revolution was almost lost. Born into the English aristocracy, she studied Euclidian geometry and taught herself mathematics and astronomy. She attracted leading scientists to her ancestral home and energetically pursued the nature of matter despite chronic and painful illnesses. Her central "vitalistic" theory of nature was that matter and spirit are one, comprised of life-force particles called monads. Constrained by the aristocratic mores of the day, she published her work under her editor's name; her own name all but disappeared until recent years.

344. Scientific Sisters and Daughters

Two sisters, Elizabeth of Bohemia (1618–1680) and Sophia of Hanover (1630–1714), were a force in German science not only by virtue of their affiliations with Descartes and Leibniz, but through the work of their descendants. A student of Leibniz, Elizabeth corresponded with her close friend Descartes regarding the relationship between matter and spirit, inspiring his *Treatise on the Passions.* Similarly, Sophia of Hanover was Leibniz's closest colleague and markedly influenced his political and intellectual views. Sophia's daughter, Sophia Charlotte (1668–1705), married Frederick I of Prussia and helped establish the Berlin Academy, a scientific society, in 1700. Raised as the ward of Sophia Charlotte, Queen Caroline of Brandenburg-Ansbach (1683–1737) mediated a famous 1716 feud between Leibniz and a disciple of Newton. She also helped popularize smallpox innoculations, despite opposition from physicians and clerics.

345. *Maria Merian* (1647–?)

After seventeen years of marriage, Maria Merian left her husband, took back her maiden name and went to live in a radical Protestant commune in Holland. Already an accomplished botanical illustrator, she enjoyed the huge collection of South American insects housed in the castle belonging to the sect. Later, with her daughter Dorothea, she traveled to Surinam to paint and collect the insects and plants that became the basis for *Metamorphosis,* the book she published in 1705. It served as a fundamental entomology text for years and helped advance the techniques of biological classification.

346. *Like Mother, Like Daughter*

Astronomers Maria (1670–1720) and Christine Kirch (1696–1782) were mother and daughter. Maria discovered the comet of 1702, which should have been named after her. Because it was not, she is best remembered for her writings on the conjunctions of the Sun with Saturn and Venus, her notes on the aurora borealis and her prediction of a conjunction of Jupiter and Saturn in 1712. Maria trained her son Christfried and daughter Christine as her assistants, but when Christfried became director of the Berlin Observatory, she and Christine became his assistants.

347. *A Womanly Science*

During the eighteenth century, European society encouraged young women to study botany and other "soft sciences," believing that these "modest amusements" would keep women passive and virtuous. Original experimentation in any scientific field by women was considered socially inappropriate and beyond the feminine intellect. Regardless, many women made significant contributions to the study of botany. Anne Worsley Russell, a botanical artist and field botanist, created important plant catalogs; Priscilla Bell Wakefield's *Introduction to Botany* was a runaway bestseller in 1841. Margaretta Riley wrote a monograph on British ferns, but the work, published under her husband's name, established his reputation, not hers. Beatrix Potter, best known as the author and illustrator of children's books such as *Peter Rabbit,* became an expert in the study of mushrooms.

348. *Émilie de Breteuil, Marquise du Châtelet* (1706–1749)

While she was growing up, Breteuil's father described her as "an odd creature destined to become the homeliest of women. Were it not for the low opinion I hold of several bishops, I would prepare her for a religious life and let her hide in a convent." Instead, this mathematical genius disguised herself as a man in the 1730s and frequented Paris cafés to discuss science and philosophy. Her translation of Newton's *Principia,* accompanied by her own commentaries, introduced the Newtonian scientific method to French intellectuals. In papers presented at the French Academy of Science, she also advanced the works of Anne Conway and Leibniz, but her lover, Voltaire, received much of the credit.

349. Celestial Forecaster

On December 25, 1758, when Halley's comet returned, astronomers were prepared for the event because of the steadfast work of a French astronomer, Nicole-Reine Lepaute (1723–1788). Her collaborator mathematician Alexis Clairaut said, "Without her I should never have been able to undertake the enormous labor . . . to calculate the distance of each of the two planets Jupiter and Saturn from the comet, separately for each successive degree for 150 years." He later took full credit for himself, but a crater on the moon is named for Lepaute.

350. Caroline Herschel (1750–1848)

This scientist gave up a singing career to become her brother William's astronomy assistant. One of her jobs was to pound and sieve horse manure in order to make the molds for the great telescope mirrors she and her brother built. William discovered the planet Uranus and together they discovered and cataloged thousands of stars and nebulae. Later, using her own telescopes, Caroline discovered several comets, the first woman ever to do so.

351. Marie Lavoisier (1758–1836)

Married at fourteen to a twenty-eight-year-old chemist, Lavoisier helped develop the law of conservation of matter. She was a gifted artist who studied painting with Jacques-Louis David, and she illustrated her husband's published work. Both her husband and her father were guillotined during the French Revolution, and she was imprisoned for a time.

352. Jane Marcet (1769–1858)

In the early nineteenth century, few books explained science in elementary terms, until 1809, when Jane Marcet published *Conversations on Chemistry, intended more especially for the Female Sex.* Marcet used dialogues between a fictional teacher, Mrs. Bryan, and two students—Emily (who was plodding and serious) and Caroline (who loved explosions)—to create the lively text that became a bestseller in England, France and the United States. The noted chemist and physicist Michael Faraday, who in his youth worked as an apprentice bookbinder, was first introduced to chemistry while binding Marcet's book.

353. Marie-Sophie Germain (1776–1831)

In 1816, Napoleon ordered a branch of the French Academy to award a gold medal worth 3,000 francs for an explanation of the vibrations of elastic surfaces. It had been submitted anonymously by Marie-Sophie Germain. The founder of mathematical physics, she lacked formal training in mathematics yet became the first woman invited to attend lectures at the Institute de France.

354. Mary Somerville

(1780–1872)

Scottish astronomer, scientist and feminist Mary Somerville was the first to sign John Stuart Mill's petition for women's suffrage. She began her scientific work in middle age, still raising a family and fulfilling social commitments. In her autobiography, she commented, "A man can always command his time under the plea of business, a woman is not allowed any such excuse." In 1834, publication of *The Connexion of the Physical Sciences* won her an annual government pension of £300. Another book, *Physical Geography,* published in 1848, became a standard text until the end of the century. Her final book, *On Molecular and Microscopic Science,* was published when Somerville was eighty-nine. When she died, *The London Post* called her the "Queen of 19th Century Science."

MALE SCIENCE

355. Quaint Theory

Aristotle considered a female to be "a male deformed." He thought that semen was the source of the soul and that a male fetus became human forty days after conception, while a female fetus took longer, ninety days. Women were considered weaker, less intelligent creatures with numerous negative personality traits. For centuries, Aristotle's bias against women dominated Western scientific attitudes.

356. Unnatural Birth

Once a royal secret of the French court, forceps were invented by male physicians to speed up the birth process and replace midwives. Their use, however, could result in rupture of the uterus, injury to the child or the deaths of mother and child.

357. Labor Pains

"In the 17th century began a two centuries' plague of puerperal fever which was directly related to the increase in obstetric practice by men. . . . In the French province of Lombardy in one year no single woman survived childbirth." —Adrienne Rich

358. A Delicate Constitution

Upper- and middle-class nineteenth-century women were expected to be ill. A wan, almost tubercular pallor was considered normal. Painful menstruation was often attributed to "uterine congestion," the result of any number of female "weaknesses," including prolonged reading of romance novels.

359. Misdiagnosis

When diagnosing women, nineteenth-century physicians based their reasoning on an assumption of women's mental and physical inferiority. An introductory lecture at the Philadelphia College of Medicine in 1853 declared, "Women's reproductive organs . . . exercise a controlling influence upon her entire system and entail upon her many painful and dangerous diseases. They are the source of her peculiarities, the center of her sympathies and the seat of her diseases. Everything that is peculiar to her springs from her sexual organization."

360. It's All in Her Mind

All the rage in the nineteenth century, hysteria (from the Greek *hystera*, "womb") was a diagnosis applied to a wide variety of disorders suffered by women. A mental illness, it related directly to women's supposed physical weaknesses. Remedies included cold baths; avoidance of coffee, tea, alcohol and snuff; and long ocean voyages. One physician urged the patient's friends to "indulge her whims and caprices, sympathize with her troubles, for it should be recollected that her fanciful notions are realities to her." Often used to treat hysteria, Lydia Pinkham's Vegetable Compound, a common patent medicine of the time, contained 18 percent alcohol. Another contained even more alcohol as well as opium.

361. Sexual Mythology

In 1905, Sigmund Freud wrote that female frigidity is a psychological problem of "sexually immature women," treatable by psychoanalysis. Women, he claimed, are capable of two kinds of orgasm: clitoral—an "adolescent" response—and vaginal, a superior response achieved only through vaginal penetration by the penis.

MODERN MATHEMATICS

362. Ada Augusta Lovelace
(1815–1852)

Lady Lovelace, the sole legitimate daughter of Lord Byron, asked the Royal Society in London to bend their rules barring women and allow her to use their library very early in the mornings. She promised she "would not make it notorious." The society refused, so her husband joined the society and hand-copied information for her. She translated and improved upon an Italian account of mathematician Charles Babbage's calculating machine, a precursor to modern computer technology. She compared the machine's operation to a weaving loom's reliance on patterns dictated by punched cards, saying, "It weaves algebraic patterns just as the Jacquard loom weaves flowers and leaves." Unfortunately, Lady Lovelace and Babbage lost a fortune on an "infallible" system of betting on horse races.

363. Sonya Kovalevsky
(1850–1891)

"A female professor of mathematics is a pernicious and unpleasant phenomenon—even, one might say, a monstrosity": So said the Swedish playwright and novelist August Strindberg. He referred to Sonya Kovalevsky, a summa cum laude graduate in mathematics who arrived at the University of Stockholm after she was not permitted to teach in a Russian university. She became a tenured professor and published a famous theorem on differential equations. When she won the French Academy's Prix Bordin in 1888, the judges were so impressed with her work that they increased the prize by 2,000 francs. The Russian Imperial Academy of Sciences finally changed its rules and granted her membership.

364. Nina Bari (1901–1961)

Moscow changed rapidly in the years following the Russian Revolution, and part of that change—at least in the field of mathematics—was Nina Bari. In 1918, she became the first woman allowed to enroll at Moscow State University. She soon joined a group of eager math students known as "the Luzitania" for their devotion to their mentor, Nikolai Luzin. Bari became a leading mathematician, specializing in the theory of trigonometric series and problems associated with expansion of a function. She lectured throughout Europe and taught as a full professor at Moscow State University.

GEOLOGY, CHEMISTRY, SPACE EXPLORATION

365. Rock Solid

Florence Bascom (1862–1945) became the first woman to receive a doctorate from Johns Hopkins University and the first woman member of the Geological Society of America. Graduating in geology in 1893, she went on to found the geology department at Bryn Mawr College. She also was the first woman to work for the U.S. Geological Survey.

366. Marie Curie (1867–1934)

On December 10, 1903, Marie Curie became the first woman (along with her husband, Pierre) to receive the Nobel prize. The discoverer of radium and polonium coined the term radioactivity to describe the elements' radiation of alpha, beta and gamma rays. In 1911, five years after her husband's death, she became the first person to win a second Nobel prize, for further work on radioactive elements. Curie also invented the mobile X–ray unit. These "Little Curies" were simply Renault cars outfitted with X–ray machines, driven onto the battlefields of World War I. Although she had never driven a car before the war, Curie even drove one herself. A champion of radiation's curative potential, she died of side effects from her years of exposure to radioactive elements.

367. All in the Family

Irène Joliot-Curie, daughter of double-Nobelist Marie Curie, earned her family an unprecedented third Nobel prize in 1935. She shared the prize, for chemistry, with her husband Frédéric, for the synthesis of radioisotopes. However, while Frédéric was elected to the French Academy, Irène was not. Like her mother, she worked until the very end of her life, and she also died of radiation poisoning.

368. Dorothy Crowfoot Hodgkin (1910–1994)

The first scientist to use computer analysis to unravel a biological puzzle, this British chemist used X–ray crystallography to study the molecu-

Mae Jemison.

370. Mae Jemison (1956–   )

When Mae Jemison was selected in 1987 as the first African-American woman astronaut, she already had an impressive résumé. She'd graduated from Stanford with a dual major in chemical engineering and African and Afro-American Studies. She had a medical degree and had worked with Cambodian refugees and served as a Peace Corps medical officer in Africa. As an astronaut, she spent eight days in space in 1992 as part of the crew of the *Endeavour.*

MODERN LIFE SCIENCES

371. Elizabeth Agassiz (1822–1907)

One of the founders and the first president of Radcliffe College, Elizabeth Agassiz was a respected naturalist. The author and co-author of books such as *First Lesson in Natural History* and *Journey in Brazil,* she also wrote articles for the *Atlantic Monthly.* As a young woman she conducted several scientific expeditions, including a steamer trip to survey breeding colonies of seabirds in the Strait of Magellan and the flora and fauna of the Galápagos Islands.

372. Eleanor Ormerod (1828–1901)

In the nineteenth century, the new science of biology gave rise to various subdisciplines, including economic entomology. The first woman to work as a professional entomologist, Eleanor Omerod, specialized in this field. By making observations on her father's English estate, she became an authority on insect infestation, often

lar structure of vitamin B_{12}, penicillin and insulin. In 1960 the Royal Society designated her a research professor. She received the Nobel Prize for Chemistry in 1964 and, the next year, became only the second woman since Florence Nightingale to receive the British Order of Merit.

369. Star Quality

"Ride, Sally Ride!" the headlines shouted in 1983, when Sally Ride became the first American woman in space. She was part of the *Challenger* crew that spent six days in orbit around the Earth. Only 10 percent of American astronauts have been women.

testifying in court as an expert, but unpaid, witness on contaminated food shipments. She devised many methods for pest control, such as pruning, burning and applications of chemicals, oils and kerosene.

373. Martha Maxwell (1831–1881)

Martha Maxwell followed her husband from Pennsylvania to the gold fields of Colorado in 1860. He had no luck as a prospector, but she took to the new territory and became an expert naturalist and taxidermist. A subspecies of Rocky Mountain owl commonly known as Mrs. Maxwell's owl was named in her honor. Maxwell often traveled into the back country alone, collecting specimens of 224 birds and twenty-seven mammals, including the black-footed ferrets described by John James Audubon but previously unknown to other scientists. In 1876, the State of Colorado sent her collection—along with Maxwell, dressed in a frontier woman's leather hunting outfit—to the 1876 Centennial Exhibition in Philadelphia. The star of the celebration, she reminded admirers that "capacity and ability, rather than birth, color, sex or anything else, should determine where individuals belong and what they shall do."

374. Florence Sabin (1871–1953)

One of the highlights of her life, according to Florence Sabin, occurred the night she stayed up to watch blood vessels form in a chick embryo and see its tiny heart beat for the first time. A respected histologist, anatomist and embryologist with the Rockefeller Institute, she began a new career in 1938 when she retired to her native Colorado. Governor John Vivian had been told that Sabin was "a nice little old lady with her hair in a bun . . . who has spent her entire life in a laboratory . . . and won't give any trouble." Instead, when appointed to a public health subcommittee, she advocated—quite successfully—for health reform. She became the first female member of the National Academy of Science.

375. Mary Leakey

This English archaeologist and scientific illustrator enjoyed a lifetime of professional success. Walking near Lake Victoria in 1948, Mary Douglas Leakey discovered the ancient skeleton of a primitive ape. With cameras rolling in 1959, she uncovered the skull of *Australopithecus*, a hominid 1.75 million years old, at Olduvai Gorge. Later, she found jaws and teeth with human characteristics in creatures that were more than 3.75 million years old. Finally, in 1976, a few miles south of Olduvai Gorge, she located the fossilized footprints of human ancestors and asserted that they had walked upright 3.6 million years ago.

376. Rachel Carson (1907–1964)

A marine biologist by training, Rachel Carson began her second career, writing, when she was thirty-four. While she worked for the U.S. Bureau of Fisheries (the first woman scientist to be employed by the agency, she wrote her first book, *Under the Sea-Wind*. Her second book, *The Sea Around Us*, secured her literary reputation. When a friend said that she wondered why birds in a wildlife sanctuary died after aerial spraying with DDT, Carson began four years of investigation that led to her award-winning book, *Silent Spring.* Although ridiculed by the chemical industry, *Silent Spring* heightened the world's awareness of environmental problems in general and of the use of pesticides in particular. Upon her election to the American Academy of Arts and Letters, Carson was cited as "a scientist in the grand literary style of Galileo and Buffon, [who] used her scientific knowledge and moral feeling to deepen our consciousness of living nature and to alert us to the calamitous possibility that our short-sighted technological conquests might destroy the very sources of our being."

377. Barbara McClintock

In 1950, fellow geneticists called Barbara McClintock's theory of jumping genes—genes that can change their positions on plant chromosomes—crazy. But in 1983, McClintock received the Nobel Prize for Physiology and Medicine for her work.

378. Jane Goodall

When Louis Leakey needed someone to study the primates of Africa, he thought women observers might be more patient than men, so he hired Jane Goodall in 1957. She spent fourteen months near Lake Tanganyika tracking chimpanzees and gaining their acceptance so that she could study them. In 1971, she published *In the Shadow of Man,* chronicling the complex social life of chimpanzees. Her research showed that chimpanzees could modify objects into tools, were not strict vegetarians, enjoyed play and communicated with one another through body language, facial expressions and sound.

Jane Goodall.

379. Dian Fossey

Another woman recruited to primate studies by Louis Leakey, Dian Fossey is best known for her 1983 book, *Gorillas in the Mist: A Remarkable Woman's Thirteen-Year Adventure in the African Rain Forest with the Greatest of the Great Apes.* Director of the Karisoke Research Centre in Rwanda, she was murdered there in 1985, probably by poachers angered by her fierce defense of African wildlife and habitat.

380. Women Nobel Prize Winners in Physiology and Medicine

1908: Elie Metchnikoff (U.S.S.R., with Paul Ehrlich of Germany), for an investigation of immunity

1947: Gerty T. Cori (U.S., with Carl F. Cori), for her research in animal starch metabolism

1977: Rosalyn S. Yalow (U.S., with Roger C. L. Guillemin, U.S., and Andrew V. Schally, U.S.), for her work on hormones in body chemistry

1986: Rita Levi-Montalcini (U.S./Italy, with Stanley Cohen, U.S.), for studies of substances that influence cell growth

1988: Gertrude B. Elion (U.S., with George H. Hitchings, U.S., and Sir James Black, U.K.), for developing principles of drug treatment

THE SCIENCE OF HUMAN BEHAVIOR

381. *Karen Horney* (1885–1952)

Trained in Germany, psychoanalyst Karen Horney practiced in the United States and criticized Freud's views of feminine psychology, including the notion of penis envy. The powerful New York Psychoanalytic Society expelled her from its membership because of her outspoken views; in response she founded the Association for the Advancement of Psychoanalysis in 1941. In one of her books she wrote, "Fortunately, analysis is not the only way to resolve inner conflicts. Life itself still remains a very effective therapist."

382. *Ruth Benedict* (1887–1948)

At the age of twenty, Ruth Benedict wrote in her journal, "I long to speak out the intense inspiration that comes to me from the lives of strong women. They have made of their lives a great adventure; they have proved that out of much bewilderment of soul, steadfast aims may [arise]." She studied anthropology with the renowned Franz Boas at Columbia University and in 1936 replaced him as head of the department. Her research on Native American cultures established her as one of the world's leading anthropologists. *Patterns of Culture* is considered a classic in the field of cultural psychology, as is another of her books, *The Chrysanthemum and the Sword: Patterns of Japanese Culture.* The U.S. Army distributed excerpts from her third book, an anti-racism treatise, to soldiers during World War II.

383. *Anna Freud* (1895–1982)

The youngest daughter of Sigmund Freud, Anna became a leading expert on child development and psychoanalysis. In England, she established homes for children orphaned by World War II and published papers about them as well as about childhood survivors of the Holocaust.

384. *Margaret Mead* (1901–1978)

"If we are to achieve a richer culture, rich in contrasting values, we must recognize the whole gamut of human potentialities and so weave a less arbitrary social fabric, one in which each diverse human gift will find a fitting place." So remarked Margaret Mead in her pioneering work, *Coming of Age in Samoa,* which established that "masculine" and "feminine" characteristics are not based on biological differences but rather on cultural conditioning. Noting that she had never heard women in primitive societies describe the pain of childbirth, Mead demanded

Anna Freud.

disease." In ancient Egypt, the word for physician often referred to priestesses, since women who worked as doctors and surgeons usually attributed their skills to the goddess Isis. Some women healers specialized in gynecology, performing cesarean sections and removing cancerous breasts.

386. Another Cleopatra

The ancient Romans gained much of their medical knowledge from the Greeks. Although women generally had low status under Roman law, they were respected as physicians and could treat men, women and children. Cleopatra, a second-century physician, wrote *Geneticis,* a standard reference work on gynecology and obstetrics. After the Roman era, women were gradually restricted from medicine

delivery without anesthesia for the birth of her own child. Her anthropological observations challenged the long-held belief that adolescence had to be a difficult transition and noted that women and children in matrilineal societies enjoyed greater self-esteem and freedom.

MEDICINE WOMEN

385. Ancient Healers

An inscription at the Temple of Sais, near Memphis in Egypt, reads, "I have come from the school of medicine at Heliopolis and have studied at the woman's school at Sais where the divine mothers have taught me how to cure

Traditional herbal healer, early-twentieth-century Bhutia.

and their practices limited first to diseases of women and then to midwifery and herbal medicine.

387. Women and Herbalism

During the Middle Ages, when herbalism was largely the province of women healers, most women learned herbal medicine from their mothers. Female herbalists and healers were often accused of witchcraft, although the same rarely happened to male priests and doctors. Nevertheless, their traditional remedies survived, often in the form of old wives' tales. Many folk remedies were pharmacologically sound. Eastern European folk healers, for example, bound moldy bread over wounds to prevent infection, a peasant version of antibiotic therapy.

388. Trotula and the Ladies of Salerno

In the eleventh century, a group of well-respected women physicians known as the Ladies of Salerno served on the faculty of that southern Italian city's university. Trotula, the best known among them, authored several books on general medicine, including *Passionibus Mulierum Curandorum* ("The Diseases of Women"), a standard text for centuries. She described children's diseases, cures for skin eruptions (including syphilis), causes of infertility, methods of birth control, surgical repair of the perineum torn during childbirth, and a variety of general medical problems including toothaches, worms and obesity.

389. Louyse Bourgeois
(1563–1636)

For a time, Louyse Bourgeois was the most famous midwife in France. She delivered seven of the queen's children (including the future Louis XIII), even reviving some of them from apparent stillbirth. Her techniques included passing warm wine from her mouth into the baby's, rubbing the infant's body to stimulate breathing or bathing it in warm water and wine. She was paid 1,000 ducats at the royal birth of a son and 600 for a daughter. King Henry IV promised her a pension, but after his death it was never paid. Her most famous book was *Observations*, published in 1610 and based on her attendance at over two thousand births. She described the stages of pregnancy, pelvic anatomy, the importance of diet for pregnant women, difficult labors (including detached placentas) and new methods of delivery.

390. Lady Mary Wortley Montagu (1689–1762)

While visiting Turkey in 1717, Lady Mary Wortley Montagu described smallpox immunization as it was practiced by Turkish women: "The old woman comes with a nut-shell full of the matter of the best sort of smallpox, asks what veins you please to have opened. She puts into the vein as much venom as can lie upon the head of her needle and after binds up the little wound with a bit of hollow shell. Every year thousands undergo this operation. There is no example of any one that has died in it. I intend to try it on my dear little son." Back in England, Montagu convinced Caroline, Princess of Wales, to inoculate

Lady Mary Wortley Montagu.

her daughters. Because of this royal connection and Lady Montagu's flair for publicity, the rate of deaths from smallpox greatly decreased. One historian said, "Lady Montagu was not a medical woman, but she probably did more for mankind, medically, than most physicians of her time."

391. Elizabeth Blackwell
(1712–1770)

In the eighteenth century, when most people had to be their own doctors, books identifying plants and listing their uses were in great demand. Elizabeth Blackwell created *A Curious Herbal* in 1737, consisting of two volumes of detailed drawings, engravings and medicinal recipes. The book was so successful that she was able to buy her husband's freedom from

debtors' prison. A genus of plants, *Blackwellia,* is named for her.

392. Modern Midwifery

Beginning with Louyse Bourgeois, a number of midwives made significant contributions to the practice of obstetrics. Marguerite du Tertre de la Marche wrote a text in 1677 that described amniotic fluid and blood serum experiments. Marie Louise Lachapelle was head midwife at the Hôtel Dieu, France's famous school of midwifery. Her work, *Practice of Obstetrics,* made recommendations based on the statistical analysis of over fifty thousand cases. Marie Anne Victorine Boivin (1773–1847) invented the vaginal speculum and a stethoscope to detect fetal heartbeat. In Germany, Justine Dittrichin Siegemundin (1650–1705) wrote about breech births, and in Holland, Aletta Jacobs (1854–1929) made the first systematic study of contraception.

393. Florence Nightingale
(1820–1910)

The founder of modern nursing took three dozen personally trained nurses with her to serve on the battlefields of the Crimean War. Even though male physicians refused their help at first, after just a few months the nurses and their sanitary standards had reduced the hospital death rate from 42 percent to 2 percent. Nightingale was well known to patients not only for her care, but because she nightly walked through the wards carrying a lamp and offering comforting words, accompanied by a pet owl in her dress pocket. Opposed to women physicians, Nightingale founded a nursing school in London where students could study for a year without cost.

394. Elizabeth Blackwell
(1821–1910)

"I stand alone," wrote Elizabeth Blackwell, the first woman to graduate from an American medical school and be licensed as a physician. "A blank wall of social and professional antagonism faces the woman physician and forms a situation of singular and painful loneliness, leaving her without support, respect or professional council." Denied admission by twenty-nine colleges, she was treated badly by her professors and other medical students at Geneva College and at medical schools in London and Europe. When she started practicing, she was shut out of hospital and office space in New York City and insulted by strangers on the street. Blackwell opened her own hospital and later a medical school. New York Infirmary for Women and Children became the first place where women students could train with women physicians and earn the clinical experience they needed. Her Women's Medical College, opened in 1868 in New York City, further improved the training of female physicians.

395. Mary Edwards Walker
(1832–1919)

A nurse and surgeon for the Union Army during the Civil War, this physician received the Congressional Medal of Honor for her service. As a doctor and a feminist, she declared that "The greatest sorrows from which women suffer today are . . . caused by their unhygienic manner of dressing. The want of the ballot is but a toy in comparison!" On the battlefields, she wore "bifurcated garments"—i.e., trousers—and thought them so practical that, after the war, she advocated clothing reform for American women. The fifteen to twenty pounds of petticoats and tightly laced corsets worn by proper ladies of the time restricted motion and breathing. Dr. Walker designed lighter, looser underwear, trousers and dresses, but reform did not come easily. Detractors demanded that she use the men's lounge when she wore "Mary Walker Reform Pants" and, when she went walking in public, some people threw rotten eggs at her or chased her with dogs. Her Congressional Medal was rescinded, but in 1977 it was finally restored.

396. Susan McKinney Steward
(1847–1918)

After graduating first in her class from the Medical College and Hospital for Women in 1870, Susan McKinney Steward was the third female African-American doctor in the United States. (Rebecca Lee was first, followed by Rebecca Cole.) She served on the staffs of several hospitals and had offices in Brooklyn and Manhattan. Steward also practiced frontier medicine as an army physician in Montana and Nebraska.

397. Ida Gray Nelson
(1867–1953)

Born in Clarksville, Tennessee, Ida Gray Nelson received her B.S. degree from Ann Arbor College and attended the University of Michigan's dental school. In 1890, she became the first African-American dentist and opened a practice in Chicago.

FEMININE FACTS

398. The Kinsey Report

According to *Sexual Behavior in the Human Female,* the 1953 study by Alfred C. Kinsey, 50 percent of women surveyed had had sexual intercourse before marriage (one third of them with two or more men), 25 percent had had extramarital intercourse and 22 percent of married respondents had had at least one abortion. Kinsey also observed that "There is no evidence that the vagina is ever the sole source of arousal or even the primary source of erotic arousal, in any female."

399. The DES Disaster

In 1971, the FDA circulated its first warnings concerning the use of the drug DES (diethylstilbestrol) to prevent miscarriages. Studies revealed that the adult daughters of women who took DES during their pregnancy had an increased risk for developing a rare form of vaginal cancer and were often unable to bear children.

400. The Dalkon Shield

In 1974, a contraceptive called the Dalkon Shield was removed from the market because its use was associated with a high rate of pelvic infections, miscarriages, birth defects and infertility—not to mention its 10 percent failure rate. A. H. Robins, manufacturer of the intrauterine device, went into bankruptcy in 1986 to seek protection from related lawsuits. However, public outrage over the Dalkon Shield helped the FDA gain authority to regulate medical devices.

401. Born Famous

Louise Brown, the world's first "test tube baby," was born July 25, 1978, at Oldham Hospital in London.

402. Eating Disorders

Women represent an overwhelming percentage of those afflicted with eating disorders. Anorexia nervosa mainly affects teenage girls and women in their early twenties, generally those who come from the middle and upper classes. Despite treatment, 10 to 15 percent of all cases are fatal. Over 90 percent of bulimics are female, representing all ages and classes. Although seldom fatal, bulimia can severely damage a woman's health by robbing her body of essential nutrients.

403. Silicone Implants

In order to better attract American servicemen stationed in Japan after World War II, some Japanese prostitutes had their breasts enlarged with industrial-grade silicone fluid, a by-product of the manufacture of transformer coolant. Soon exotic dancers on the other side of the Pacific demanded the same procedure, even though silicone sometimes migrated to other parts of the body and could cause gangrene, pneumonia, blindness and death. In 1992, the FDA declared a moratorium on silicone breast implants, which by then were blamed for assorted connective tissue diseases, lupus, arthritis, hepatitis, chronic fatigue syndrome and several forms of cancer. Dow Corning, producer of 80 percent of all the silicone gel used in breast implants, declared bankruptcy on May 15, 1995, halting payment of settlements won by women who had sued.

404. PMS/PDD

At the 1993 meeting of the American Psychiatric Association, debate erupted over whether or not to classify Premenstrual Dysphoric Disorder, a severe form of PMS (Premenstrual Syndrome), as a depressive disorder. While some physicians claimed that recognition of PDD as a disabling depression would improve care, the National Organization for Women believed the classification would lead to increased discrimination against women in insurance, employment and custody cases.

405. Women and AIDS

During heterosexual intercourse, AIDS is more likely to pass from a man to a woman rather than from a woman to a man. Women infected with HIV can pass the virus to their babies while pregnant. Less than 25 percent of children born to HIV-positive women are infected, but by the year 2000 at least eighty thousand children will have been orphaned by AIDS. Some cities, like New York, require anonymous AIDS testing for all newborns, and the possibility has been raised of requiring all pregnant women to receive nonanonymous AIDS tests, a move opposed by women's rights groups.

WOMEN IN THE AGE OF EXPLORATION

406. Sacagawea

This sixteen-year-old Native American woman with a tiny baby probably saved the lives and mission of the Lewis and Clark expedition many times. Clark wrote that "her presence reconciles [sic] all the Indians as to our friendly intentions. A woman with a party of men is a token of peace." A former captive and Shoshoni wife of the fur trader Charbonneau, Sacagawea could translate several tribal languages. Her knowledge of the territory was essential to the success of the first great American expedition of Western exploration. She also foraged for food daily, gathered healing herbs and cared for the sick, and bartered for horses. Once, when a pirogue steered by Charbonneau upset in swift water, Sacagawea saved many irreplaceable pieces of equipment. Lewis wrote in his journal, "The Indian woman to whom I ascribe equal fortitude and resolution, with any person onboard at the time of the accident, caught and preserved most of the light articles which were washed overboard." Contrary to legend, Sacagawea probably died in 1812 of fever. Her son was educated by Clark and then returned to the frontier, where he was known as "the best man on foot on the plains or in the Rocky Mountains."

407. Mary Kingsley (1862–1900)

Mary Henrietta Kingsley's expedition to West Africa led her through country so dangerous that it was called "the white man's grave." She was prepared, however, because she could paddle her own canoe and knew how to live off the land. Still, she always wore long black skirts since, as she remarked, "one would never want to go about in Africa in a way that would embarrass one to be seen in Piccadilly." Kingsley collected beetles, reptiles and fish for the British Museum. Rudyard Kipling noted of the explorer: "Being human, she must have been afraid of something. But one never found out what it was." She died of typhoid fever while caring for soldiers injured in South Africa's Boer War.

408. Ellen Churchill Semple
(1863–1932)

In order to study geography firsthand, Ellen Churchill Semple rode through the Kentucky hills on horseback, meeting people in remote areas and forming theories about how geographic isolation influenced human populations. Her first book discussed how American expansion was the result of a variety of geographic factors. In 1921, she became the first woman elected president of the Association of American Geographers. Her work at Oxford, Wellesley, Columbia and other universities helped earn geography respect within the academic community.

409. Octavie Coudreau
(c. 1870–c. 1910)

Octavie Coudreau explored French Guiana and northern Brazil at the turn of the twentieth century. Her husband died on a trip up a tributary of the Amazon, but she completed the journey and published a book about the expedition,

Voyage au Trombetas. Later, two Brazilian states hired her to continue exploring the territory.

410. Harriet Chalmers Adams
(1874–1937)

This American explorer, a specialist in Latin American culture, wrote for *National Geographic* magazine for twenty-eight years. In 1925 she founded the Society of Women Geographers.

411. Delia Akeley

Delia Akeley went on several scientific expeditions to Africa with her husband. In 1924, working for the Brooklyn Museum, she went without him, setting out to cross Africa on foot. She completed her trek in 1925 and shipped thirty specimens of game animals to the United States, some of them previously unknown species of antelope and birds.

412. Mary Jobe Akeley
(1886–1966)

Mary Jobe Akeley explored the Canadian northwest, becoming first to map the glaciers of Mount Sir Alexander and to trace the headwaters of the Fraser River; Mount Jobe in the Rockies is named for her. Married to the explorer Carl Akeley, the ex-husband of Delia Akeley, she accompanied him on a trip to West Africa, where he died. She took over the expedition, whose mission was to collect mountain gorillas for the American Museum of Natural History.

MOTHERS OF INVENTION

413. Silk Production

Empress Si Ling-chi of China (c. 2640 B.C.E.) discovered how to remove the delicate silk threads from silkworm cocoons. She directed the development of China's massive silk cultivation and weaving industries.

414. Indian Corn and Palmetto Bonnets

Quaker colonist Sibella Righton Masters devised a method for cleaning and airing Indian corn, becoming the first American to receive an English patent—although the patent was issued in her husband's name. She also invented a maize-stamping mill and a device for weaving palmetto leaves into women's bonnets.

415. Elizabeth Pinckney

(1722–1793)

Known as Eliza, this innovator managed a South Carolina plantation at age sixteen, bore four children in five years and was widowed at age thirty-five. She introduced indigo cultivation to South Carolina, came up with a plan to preserve eggs in salt, planted oak trees for future shipbuilding, tutored slave girls and spotted a comet predicted by Newton. When she died, George Washington requested to be one of her pallbearers.

416. Camembert Cheese

Credit for the invention of Camembert cheese goes to Marie Fontaine Harel. Although several stories conflict about just who she was and where exactly she lived, there is a tombstone in the town of Camembert, France, that reads: "Marie Harel, 1791–1845: *Elle inventa le Camembert.*" The industry she set in motion now produces half a million cheeses each day.

417. Paper Bags

Margaret Knight of Springfield, Massachusetts, was called the "Woman Edison" because she had more than twenty-seven inventions to her credit. In 1872, she invented the machine that folded and glued paper sheets together to form the square-bottomed paper bag. Because she exchanged most of her patent rights for cash, her employers and other, later inventors received greater profits. She also invented an emergency stop device for the weaving industry because, at age twelve, she'd seen a shuttle suddenly fly loose from a loom and stab a man. When asked how an uneducated woman with no mechanical training could invent, she replied, "It is only following our nature. As a child I never cared for coddling bits of porcelain with senseless faces: the only things I wanted were a jack-knife, a gimlet and pieces of wood. . . . I'm not surprised at what I've done. I'm only sorry I couldn't have had as good a chance as a boy and have been put to my trade regularly."

418. Circular Saw

Shaker Tabitha Babbit invented the circular saw. Her idea came from watching the action of a spinning wheel.

419. Dairy Technology

Between 1905 and 1921, more than thirty-five patents for dairy equipment were granted to

American women. Some of these patents included: butter churn, cream can, cream dipper, milk-can vacuum, milk-shipping can, milk pail, milk cooler, skimmer, cream separator, cow milker, cow-udder protector and cow-tail holder.

420. Agricultural Techniques

Yekaterina Novgorodova (c. 1930–): Developed several techniques for growing vegetables in Siberia, including hotbeds, ripening shelves and sprinkling systems.

Hsing Yen-tzu (c. 1940–): Worked with a team of women in Hopei to develop a method of planting spring wheat in hard-frozen ground.

Miranda Smith (c. 1943–): Devised rooftop garden projects and other urban agriculture projects in the United States and Canada.

Elizabeth Bokyo (c. 1945–) and Wendy Campbell-Purdie (c. 1947–): Worked in Israel and Algeria to advance desert cultivation techniques.

421. American Ingenuity

Paper dress patterns: An idea of nineteenth-century milliner Ellen Demorest that enabled middle-class women to reproduce fashionable clothes at home.

Liquid paper: Developed by Betty Graham in the 1960s, a Texas secretary and artist.

Hang glider: Conceived and tested by Gertrude Rogallo and her husband, Francis, in 1948. The Rogallos and their children tested the hang glider in a homemade wind tunnel in their attic.

Illuminated writing board: Becky Shroeder, age twelve, became one of the youngest Americans ever to receive a patent when in the 1980s she created a device that allowed her to finish her homework after turning out the bedroom light.

Part

FIVE

Economics, Work and Business

GREAT PROVIDERS

422. Prehistoric Provisions

While the clichéd image of early humanity's struggle for survival is of cavemen hunting down woolly mammoths, Homo sapiens' real defense against starvation was its women. Women spent their days gathering the fruits, nuts, seeds, beans and grains that made up most of their family's diet. But because ancient animal bones and stone weapons resisted decay better than plants, pots and baskets, prehistoric hunting has been more widely studied. However, anthropologists and archaeologists have analyzed fossilized teeth of prehistoric humans and found them to be primarily plant eaters and have determined that the gathering done largely by women was a more productive source of food than hunting.

423. Arctic Hunters

According to *Historia Delle Genti,* published by Olaus Magnus in 1565, the Laplanders of northern Scandinavia "run swiftly after Beasts, with Bowes and Arrows, over Valleys and Snowie Mountain tops, up and down, upon bending downwards broad slippery boards, bound to their feet. The Women shoot their Arrows with their Hairs hanging about their Ears . . . the Women hunt . . . as nimbly and may be more nimbly than the men do."

Lapp huntresses of the Renaissance era.

African farmers, early twentieth century.

424. Breadwinners

The Anglo-Saxon word for lord, *hlaf-ward*, means "guardian of the bread." The word for lady, *hlaf-dige,* means "giver of bread," referring to the times when women supervised communal food storehouses and divided harvest bounty among clan members.

425. Survivors

Into the early 1960s, the people of rural Iran still lived in a hunting-and-gathering economy. As was the case in earlier such societies, women provided the bulk of the food. They collected food in groups on daylong trips, looking for wild plants like acorns, vegetables, roots, fruits and berries.

426. Farmer Jane

In the twentieth century, much of agricultural work around the world is done by women. However, whether in industrialized nations or developing countries, women usually are paid less than men for the same work—and many are not paid at all. In Libya in 1977, women made up about 13 percent of agricultural workers; about 90 percent of them were unpaid family workers. In 1979, 28 percent of farm workers in Denmark were women; of these 81 percent were unpaid family laborers.

Growing an Economy

427. Settling Down

Agricultural civilization began at the end of the Pleistocene era (around 8000 B.C.E.), when women in the Near East invented digging sticks, hoes and plows. The first crops included wheat, barley, millet and other grains. Later, the women planted more crops and bred domesticated animals for their milk, meat and skin. Farming proved a more reliable source of food than hunting and gathering, leading people to abandon their nomadic ways. As they settled in one place, it became easier to start communities, and villages formed.

428. Feudalism

During the Middle Ages, peasants and nobles lived on large estates that operated like small cities, with peasants working for noblemen and noblemen working for kings. While the noblemen fought to protect their estates, their wives ran them. The women supervised the staff and laborers, managed the finances, oversaw the harvest and bought and sold goods. If these fortresses were cities, then the noblewomen were the mayors.

429. Mercantilism

The modern mercantile economy, based on commerce and money rather than trading and bartering, emerged during the thirteenth century, when commercial fairs and markets sprouted across Europe. There, peasant women sold eggs, milk, butter, chickens, wool, vegetables and other products from the livestock and gardens they raised. Their activities thus earned cash for their families and fueled the expansion of mercantilism.

430. Slave Women's Work

Among the myriad tasks performed by Southern slave women were: housecleaning, cooking, raising white children, weeding, chopping sugarcane, picking cotton and plowing. In addition, they had to perform all the tasks of caring for their own families, from tending gardens to splitting firewood. Based as it was on slavery, the economy of the antebellum South thus depended greatly on the work of women.

431. Home Improvement

In the 1970s and 1980s, when international development agencies and governments started efforts to build subsidized housing in Third World countries, women often took the lead. Extending their traditional responsibility for domestic matters, some women built their homes and paid most of the costs. One housing project in Panama was built entirely by women.

Woman as Commodity

432. Wife Swappers

Women have been bought with bride prices and sold with dowries in many cultures throughout history. Marriage almost always has been more beneficial to the man, who had more rights within the marriage and more rights to divorce should he want out. In ancient Jewish custom, the woman called her husband "my master." In early China, men were allowed to sell their wives and children. Wives in Rome had the same legal status as female children; their husbands could even bequeath them to other men in their wills.

433. Getting Ahead in the Oldest Profession

Women enslaved in antiquity were often the wives of men defeated in war, forced to serve the enemy's sexual needs. But slave women also were in a position to use their sexuality to increase their status. If they won their masters' favor, Celtic and Germanic slave women could advance beyond the position of concubine, while Greek and Roman slaves might eventually gain their freedom.

434. Loaners

Under Athenian law, when women married, they were simply "loaned" to the groom's family. Therefore, their fathers and brothers still had authority over them in case something happened to their husbands. As family property, women had little control over their own destiny.

435. Slave Women in the American South

By law, the children of slave women in the antebellum American South were born slaves, even if their fathers were free—or white. They could be sold away from their mothers, just as husbands and wives could be sold separately, and might be included in a sale of livestock, as happened to the young Sojourner Truth. Slave

women were often sold as "good breeders" and mated to the male slave chosen by their white master. They were given short maternity leaves from the fields to ensure a successful birth, but were then required to take their nursing babies with them to work so as not to cost their masters too much in the form of lost labor.

436. Miss Clara Gordon, No. 119 Mercer St.

"We cannot too highly recommend this house, the lady herself is a perfect venus: beautiful, entertaining and supremely seductive. Her aids-de-camp are really charming and irresistible, and altogether honest and honorable. Miss G. is a great belle, and her mansion is patronized by Southern merchants and planters principally. She is highly accomplished, skillful and prudent, and sees her visitors are well entertained. Good Wines of the most elaborate brands, constantly on hand, and in all, a finer resort cannot be found in the city." —from an 1859 guide to brothels in American cities

437. Fame and Fortune

The money to be made on the American frontier attracted women as well as men, although many of the first women to arrive came not as prospectors but as prostitutes. "I went into the sporting life for business reasons and no other," commented one Denver madam. "It was a way for a woman in those days to make money, and I made it." During the mining bonanzas of the late 1860s, prostitution was the most common form of employment for women in boom towns, where they outnumbered other women twenty-five to one. One analysis of California's female population in the 1850s estimates that one in five women living there were prostitutes. Some madams acquired great wealth, such as Doña Gertrudis "La Tules" Barcelo of Santa Fe—worth more than $10,000 in 1852—and Julia Smith, whose Julia's Palace took in $1,000 a night. When Kansas madam Dixie Lee died, her minister father was shocked to learn how much money she'd made, commenting, "The wages of sin are a damned sight better than the wages of virtue." Mattie Silks was the darling of Denver's red-light district and underworld. She even took her girls on vacations—working vacations—to Colorado's mining camps and to the Alaskan Klondike. Ah Toy was a Chinese slave who managed to buy her freedom and then established a brothel in California. She often paid to ship the bodies of dead Chinese workers back home for burial.

438. Wifely Duty

Russian laws at the turn of the twentieth century equated wives with minors and put them under the control of their husbands. All a married woman's earnings, property and inheritance belonged to her husband.

439. Bad Investments

Among the poor in China, India and Latin America, girl babies are sometimes allowed to starve to death on the assumption that sons will become economic assets for the family while daughters will be liabilities. The practice continues today despite laws against it.

440. The Asian Sex-Slave Trade

Kicked into high gear when the U.S. government contracted with Thailand to provide "rest and recreation" for troops fighting in Vietnam, Thailand is home to a booming sex industry. By the late 1990s, sex was estimated to bring in $4 billion a year to the tiny country. In 1995, Human Rights Watch/Asia reported that thousands of young Asian women are tricked into prostitution by sex traders and relatives with promises of jobs or marriage. They are then sold to brothels for as little as $4. In Thailand, the Philippines, India and Sri Lanka, many of the prostitutes—some as young as eight years old—are kidnapped by brothel agents and sold into slavery. Others are traded to brothels by their parents and work until they make back the money given to their parents—or until they contract AIDS.

441. High-Class Call Girls

Descendant of two Pilgrims who landed at Plymouth in 1620, Sidney Biddle Barrows—the Mayflower Madam—merged breeding and business sense to create a thriving prostitution operation in New York City. When she was arrested in a sting operation in 1984, documents revealed that she directed twenty to thirty call girls and brought in over $1 million a year. According to the terms of her plea bargain, Biddle paid a fine and kept her client list. Heidi Fleiss operated a similar prostitution business in Hollywood. When she was arrested in 1993, her client list included many people working in the film industry.

ECONOMIC STATUS

442. Family Finance

Solon, an Athenian lawmaker of the sixth century B.C.E., decreed that women should try to keep their husbands' property in the family. Since they couldn't own property, women were to achieve this by bearing a male heir. Women were even encouraged to get pregnant by one of their husband's kin if their husband wasn't able to have intercourse.

443. Tibet

Tibetan society permitted women to have more than one husband. In a country with little tillable acreage, a group of brothers could marry one woman and their children could inherit the entire family's property.

444. Laws of Inheritance

In some tribes in the early Americas, land was passed from mothers to daughters. In ancient Rome, women were not allowed to inherit their husband's property, but daughters could receive up to half of their father's holdings. In fourth-century Greece, women weren't allowed to own land or homes, but they could own slaves.

445. Left Out

In 18 B.C.E., Roman Emperor Augustus decreed that single women and women with no children could inherit only a certain amount of property, and unmarried women over fifty couldn't inherit at all.

446. Charlotte Perkins Gilman
(1860–1935)

In her 1900 masterwork, *Woman and Economics: A Study of the Economic Relation Between Men and Women as a Factor in Social Evolution,* Gilman probed the disturbing questions surrounding the economic nature of women's oppression. She concluded that women's economic dependence was their chief barrier to progress. A talented writer and fierce feminist, Gilman also penned the short story "The Yellow Wallpaper," which probes the psy-

Charlotte Perkins Gilman.

chological impact of female oppression, and the novel *Herland,* which depicts a utopian society made up of women only.

447. The Impact of Divorce

Even with more women working outside the home, divorce is still likely to be an economic setback for women. In 1991–92, the U.S. Census Bureau found that female-householder families were fifteen times as likely to be poor as families headed by a man and woman. And a 1994 census report showed that 38 percent of divorced or separated women with children live in poverty. On average, the standard of living for mothers raising their children drops by 33 percent following a divorce; the standard of living for divorced fathers rises 13 percent. American fathers owe $24 billion in unpaid child support.

448. Poor Moms

In 1992, the U.S. Census Department reported that 47 percent of families headed by single women live in poverty, as compared with only 8.3 percent of families headed by a woman and a man. The U.S. government defined the poverty line as income below $15,141 a year for a family of four. In 1996, about 31 percent of American babies were born to unwed mothers. While many more single professional and older women were choosing to have children, the majority of single mothers were poor or working class. Almost 50 percent of children born to high-school dropouts were born out of wedlock; only 6 percent of single college graduates had babies. Almost half of single mothers reported their annual household income as less than $10,000.

449. Homeless Women

In 1987, the Urban Institute estimated the number of American homeless to be between 500,000 to 600,000. By the 1990s the fastest-growing homeless population was women and children. Homes for the Homeless reported in 1996 that families with children accounted for 75 percent of U.S. homeless. Worldwide, according to Amnesty International, women and children made up more than 80 percent of the world's 20 million refugees in 1995.

WOMEN'S WORK

450. Spinsters

Making cloth has been "women's work" since ancient times. Spinning, weaving and sewing were assigned to women because they could be performed while watching children. The association of women with textile work shows up in language: the word *gynacea,* meaning "women's places," described places throughout the Roman Empire where garments were woven, spun or dyed; the "distaff side" was a term applied to female family members in European cultures. Textile making as women's work also showed up in Navajo legend, in which Spider Man told women how to make a loom and Spider Woman taught them how to weave on it.

451. Cleaning Ladies

Throughout the ages, one of the duties of wives and daughters was cleaning the house and garments worn by the family. Making soap, doing

Housewife vacuuming, 1942.

452. Silk-Making

After Si Ling-chi, a Chinese empress, developed techniques of silk production in the third millennium B.C.E., women established an enduring position in the silk industry. Close to 200 B.C.E., Chinese women cared for silkworms and made textiles from silk. Later, silk-making as women's work spread to Europe and Japan. In the 1500s, silk-making was a "free trade" in Europe, which meant that anyone could practice it, so it was easier for women to get around restrictions designed to keep them out of business. By the late 1800s, silk thread was Japan's biggest export, produced by young women working in silk mills similar to European and American textile factories.

laundry, scrubbing pots and pans and beating rugs took up long hours in the life of the early housewife. Noblewomen and royalty hired others to conduct these duties for them, but were still expected to supervise their activities. In Victorian times, beating rugs was, according to one columnist, "the hardest torture of the week . . . persecuted until every nerve is throbbing in fierce rebellion at the undue pressure to which it is subjected." Mechanical carpet sweepers and the electric vacuum machines that followed made one woman so happy that she gushed, "I never hesitate to spend money for any labor-saving device."

Silk production, nineteenth-century China.

453. Home Cooking

For centuries women have been taught that preparing food is part of being good wives and mothers. Women have long been responsible for baking, churning and canning, as well as planting and harvesting much of the food. One of the first cookbooks was *The Art of Cooking Made Plain and Simple,* published in England in the 1700s. In 1896, Fannie Farmer wrote her now famous *Fannie Farmer's Boston Cooking-School Cookbook.* Although men have dominated modern professional cookery, one of the best-known twentieth-century cooking authorities is Julia Child, who specialized in French cuisine. She wrote many cookbooks, co-founded a cooking school in Paris in 1951 and started her popular cooking show, *The French Chef,* in 1963.

Nineteenth-century cooking class.

454. Governesses

Governesses tutored and baby-sat the children of Victorian England's upper class, typically living in the home with the family. Usually women from middle-class families, governesses were "above" maids but "beneath" the ladies in the hierarchy of the house. In the early 1800s about 25,000 women worked as governesses in England. The Governesses' Benevolent Institution was set up in 1843 to help these working women find jobs and receive financial support if they became ill or retired.

455. Schoolmarms

In the nineteenth century, many of the educated, single Eastern women who headed to the American West worked as schoolmarms. These rapidly expanding areas desperately needed teachers but generally could not afford to hire men. Qualified women often took charge of entire schools, teaching children of different ages and reading levels in one-room schoolhouses. Because they were responsible for teaching moral values and good behavior as well as academic subjects, schoolmarms became synonymous with fastidiously correct comportment.

456. Nursing

In 1859, through the efforts of Florence Nightingale, the Society for Promoting Employment of Women started to advance nursing as a desirable career for women. The first American nursing schools opened in 1873 in New York, New Haven and Boston; the American Nurses Association formed in 1886. Nursing became an acceptable profession for women because it reflected their prescribed roles as nurturer and caretaker.

457. Piecework

Not all textile work was done in factories. Women with young children and immigrant women often sewed in their homes and were paid by the piece. Though it paid poorly, piecework allowed mothers to be near their children, who often helped. In addition, women working as teachers and in other positions often took in piecework to subsidize meager salaries.

Women doing piecework, early twentieth century.

458. Sweatshops

The growing demand for ready-made clothing, which spawned large department stores during the nineteenth century, created a need for cheap needlework, traditionally done by women. Sweatshops in England, France and the U.S. during the mid-1800s employed young single women working in poor conditions for low wages, although some of the women were married or widowed with children to support. Women often worked as long as they could see—from early in the morning until late in the evening—in generally miserable and often dangerous conditions. Seeking to boost profits by cutting costs, manufacturers frequently decided to ignore the few safety regulations on the law books. They knew public officials seldom decided to enforce the labor laws or punish offenders. The same conditions prevail today, both in the U.S. and overseas.

459. Unseemly Work

In the *Independent* of April 11, 1901, one Henry T. Finck decried the rising presence of women in the American workplace. His essay included the following prophecy: "Having once discovered the charm of the eternal womanly, men will never allow it to be taken away again, to please a lot of half-women who are clamoring for what they illogically call their 'rights.' Men will find a way of making these misguided persons understand that it is as unseemly for them to be—as many of them are now—butchers, hunters, carpenters, barbers, stump speakers, iron and steel workers, miners, etc., as it would be for them to try to take the place of our soldiers, sailors, firemen, mail carriers and policemen. All employments which make women bold, fierce, muscular, brawny in body or mind will be more and more rigidly tabooed as unwomanly. Woman's strength lies in beauty and gentleness, not in muscle."

460. Shop Girls

In England, retail shop assistants often worked more than seventy-five hours a week, taking only one forty-five-minute break per day. Large department stores in the United States around the turn of the century provided company housing for salesgirls in order to control their behavior at all times. Like teachers, typists and other women workers, they were required to be single.

461. Waitresses

From the 1880s to the 1950s, Harvey Girls worked as waitresses in restaurants along the Santa Fe Railway's southwestern route. At a time when there were "no ladies west of Dodge City and no women west of Albuquerque," Harvey Girls led lives regulated by a strict set of rules laid down by restaurateur Fred Harvey. Harvey saw himself and the women—mostly Anglo—as "civilizers." In 1905, the Leavenworth, Kansas, *Times* reported, "The girls at a Fred Harvey place never look dowdy, frowsy, tired, slipshod or overworked. They are expecting you—clean collars, clean aprons, hands and faces washed, nails manicured—there they are, bright, fresh, healthy and expectant."

462. Good Help

This category of employment pays women to do in other people's homes what they do for free in their own. Throughout American and European history, domestic service has been one of the major sources of employment for women, especially for immigrants and women of color. By the early 1900s, roughly 90 percent of African-American women worked as domestics or agricultural workers. More opportunities for work—in industrial settings—opened to them during World War I, but after the war they were forced back into domestic and agricultural work.

463. The Independent Woman

At the beginning of the twentieth century, teachers were seen as feminist role models. The unmarried schoolteacher who provided for herself was held up as an example of women's capabilities. Indeed, many of the early feminists were educators.

464. The Triangle Shirtwaist Company Fire

Late in the afternoon on Saturday, March 25, 1911, a flash fire engulfed the New York City quarters of the Triangle Shirtwaist Company. Within ten minutes, 140 of the six hundred workers—mostly young women between thirteen and twenty-three years old—lay dead across sewing machines, in elevator shafts and on the sidewalk below. Aware that factories were hardly ever inspected for violations, the Triangle Company and its landlord had routinely flouted local fire laws. They took few, if any, safety precautions and crammed as much equipment as possible into the factory, blocking access to fire hoses and fire escapes. The two hall doors and single fire escape door on each floor were locked to prevent employee theft, leaving elevators as the only way out. Only a few dozen passengers reached the street before the fire knocked the elevator out. Some workers pounded on locked exits while many others jumped to their death down the elevator shafts or out the windows. When Triangle's owners were tried on manslaughter charges, the judge directed the jury to acquit them; when the families of the fire victims sued the landlord, they won only $75 per family.

465. *Katherine Gibbs*

In 1911, Gibbs created the first school for women who wanted to be secretaries. "Katie Gibbs girls" learned business law and liberal arts as well as secretarial skills. World War I created a demand for such trained office workers, and the school grew into America's most prestigious secretarial school.

466. *White Shoes*

More than one thousand nursing programs operated at American hospitals by 1909, and nurses such as Lillian Wald and Lavinia Dock pioneered social work and public health efforts. In the 1920s almost two thousand American schools offered nursing training and women flocked to the profession. However, as women were allowed to pursue medicine, law and business, enrollments in nursing schools declined dramatically. Of the more than 2.25 million registered nurses in the U.S. at the end of the twentieth century, more than 95 percent are women.

467. *Secretaries*

The twentieth-century office was set up much like the family, with secretaries supporting male bosses as wives supported their husbands. Like wives, secretaries received their status by the achievements and success of the men they were attached to. If the boss was promoted, his secretary moved up with him; if he was fired, she often lost her job.

468. *Stewardesses*

From 1935, when "air hostesses" first served passengers for TWA, to the 1970s, when "coffee, tea or me" was the catchphrase, being a stewardess was considered an exciting, glamorous job for women. But the hours were long, the work grueling, and the women were often subject to sexual harassment by passengers and pilots. The women's movement encouraged these often mistreated workers to demand better working conditions. They unionized and fought to revoke the airlines' age and weight restrictions, which limited the job to the young and trim. In addition, men entered the field in greater numbers and the gender-neutral "flight attendant" became the job's title, making the skies a little friendlier for women workers.

469. *Role Repair*

As the women's movement affected women's role in the home, so it did in the office.

Airline stewardess, 1970.

Secretaries protested "domestic" duties and stopped making coffee, running errands and handling the personal affairs of their bosses. In the 1980s and 1990s, the workplace saw the rise of the "executive assistant," who, though given less respect and pay than her male or female boss, was treated as a professional.

OFF LIMITS

470. Turf War

In 1835, male printers in Boston organized to force women typesetters out of the profession. They pursued a campaign of intimidation and sexual harassment to achieve this end.

471. When a Woman Becomes a Worker

In 1860, Jules Simon, a French legislator, said that "a woman who becomes a worker is no longer a woman." His statement illustrated the debate over women's roles at home and work, ignoring the fact that women had always worked inside the home and on family land.

472. Post-War Bust

Pleased with the income and independence industrial employment offered, large numbers of American women decided to stay in the workforce after World War II ended. But when discharged veterans came home looking for work and defense plants shut down, many women who had worked so hard during the war found themselves unemployed. Men were given preference by post-war employers while the govern-

ment launched a propaganda campaign to convince women their true place was in the home. Most wartime women workers became homemakers; women who had jobs from the 1950s to the 1970s were kept out of higher-paying, more powerful positions, earning on the average 59 cents for every dollar men made.

473. The Glass Ceiling

In 1984, *Business Week* reported that only about 2 percent of the top U.S. management jobs belonged to women. Twelve years later, the same magazine reported that women in Europe made up 41 percent of the workplace, but only 1 percent of corporate board members.

NEW OPPORTUNITIES

474. Labor Maker I

In 1850, Isaac Merrit Singer invented the Singer sewing machine. Singer advertised his invention as a "mother's machine" and as a great wedding gift. Thirty-seven years later, the I. M. Singer Company introduced the first electric sewing machines and sold a million of them, mostly to sweatshops. As a result, demand for largely female sweatshop workers soared.

475. Go West, Young Woman

The Homestead Act of 1862 allowed American women, even single ones, to own land. Thousands of women (and men) headed West with the hope of staking a claim for themselves. By 1900, about 800,000 women lived west of the Mississippi. Though most worked in traditional female capacities as teachers, cooks, laundresses and prostitutes, they also farmed and ranched and enjoyed a kind of freedom never before dreamed of. Indeed, men in Western states were the first to support women's right to vote.

476. Work During Wartime

During the Civil War, women served as nurses, factory workers and government clerks, gaining greater access to the professions. The war created more than 100,000 new jobs for women, most of which disappeared at war's end. But the war accustomed Americans to working women and eased women's way into the workplace.

Office workers, c. 1905.

477. Rag Trade

The Industrial Revolution didn't create women workers, it simply moved "women's work" from the home to the textile factory. By 1870, 10 percent of American industrial workers were women. Around the same time, the United Kingdom had about 600,000 women working in factories, with half the weaver's union made up of women. Women's involvement in unions, walkouts and strikes helped them combat the abuse they suffered at the hands of mill owners and overseers. They were paid even less than men and were charged for needles, for the use of lockers and chairs and for any clothing that did not turn out right. Sexual harassment was another major abuse, not to mention widespread safety violations.

478. Labor Maker II

In the 1800s, office work was done by men. When the typewriter was introduced in 1873, young women were trained to demonstrate the device, and women seized upon typing as an opportunity to earn a living. By the turn of the century, women were firmly entrenched in clerical work. The telegraph and the telephone opened up many office jobs for women; in these fields about 45 percent of employees were women. By 1900, women made up one third of all office workers.

479. Rosie the Riveter

The American mobilization for World War II involved a massive conversion of private industry to wartime production and created an enormous demand for labor. At the same time, American men joined the army, navy, air force and marines by the millions. The resulting shortage of able-bodied men hit manufacturers hard, for they had long relied on men to meet their labor needs. In the push toward victory, industry turned to the nation's women. Government propaganda urged women to join the industrial workforce for the good of their country. Posters and songs extolled the virtues of "Rosie the Riveter," the patriotic "girl" defense worker. Eager to make a contribution and reap the rewards of high-paying industrial work, women flocked to the factories and shipyards. Married women ignored traditional strictures against employment in record numbers, soon outnumbering single women in the workplace. By 1943, as wartime production peaked, nearly 17 million women worked outside the home, making up a third of the nation's labor force. About 6 million worked in war industries; 40 percent of aircraft workers and 14 percent of shipyard workers were women. Women joined or replaced men in every job, including those formerly off limits to the "weaker sex." They worked as toolmakers, machinists, welders and stevedores, making tanks, bombers, anti-aircraft guns, battleships and anything else the military required. Women built most of the vehicles and equipment used by the men fighting overseas. Rationing severely restricted the consumer goods workers could buy with the money they earned, so millions of Rosie the Riveters bought war bonds instead, thereby multiplying their contribution to national defense.

480. Party Girls

From the 1950s through the 1970s, Tupperware parties were one of the rituals of suburbia. Tupperware hostesses invited friends to their homes, where, after icebreaker games and refreshments, distributors extolled the benefits of their latest polyethylene storage products, such as Snak-Stors, Serve-It-Alls, Square-A-Ways, Tri-Jels and Velveeta Keepers. By the end of the 1970s, a sales force of 100,000 Tupperware salespeople (mostly women) was selling more than $900 million worth of products a year.

481. The Professionals

Between 1963 and 1993, the number of women lawyers in the U.S. leapt from 7,500 to 180,000; seven times as many women were doctors in 1990 as practiced in 1960.

482. Breaking the Mold

The U.S. Congress passed the Non-Traditional Employment for Women (NEW) Act in 1991, requiring all states to increase the number of women trained in traditionally male occupations. The act was designed to open up male-dominated industries to women. Jobs like truck driving, construction work and carpentry tend to pay about 30 percent more than waitressing and secretarial work. In 1992, the Women in Apprenticeship Occupations and Non-Traditional Occupations Act was passed to protect women in nontraditional fields from sexual harassment.

SEX DISCRIMINATION

483. Held Back

As women flocked to careers in education during the twentieth century, they were increasingly relegated to lower-paying elementary school jobs. Principals and professors, who make far higher salaries, were typically men. As women moved into administrative positions and into higher education, they still were likely to be paid less and receive tenure less often, and still are today.

484. Pay Equity—a Long Time Coming

Susan B. Anthony called on women to "Join the union, girls, and together say Equal Pay for Equal Work" in 1869. But it wasn't until 1963 that the U.S. government supported the idea by passing the Equal Pay Act. In 1973, Australia mandated equal pay for women. Three years later, Japan made it illegal to have different pay scales for men and women doing the same job. In 1979, Austria and Sweden followed suit.

485. Married to the Job

In 1967, a Japanese woman fired from her clerical job because she was married sued the company and won back her job. In 1992, a survey of Japanese businesses revealed that some companies were still forcing women to quit if they got married or pregnant.

486. Harassment as Discrimination

In *Meritor Savings Bank* v. *Vinson* (1986), the U.S. Supreme Court ruled that sexual harassment violates federal law. The Court held that sexual harassment is a form of sex discrimination under Title VII of the Civil Rights Act of 1964, which guarantees employees the right to work in an environment that does not discriminate based on sex, race, religion or national origin. In 1992, 10,532 people filed sexual harassment reports with the EEOC; 90 percent of the complaints were from women.

487. Sex and Socialism

In the mid-1990s, China, the most populated country on earth, had a labor force that was 43 percent female; in 1996, 70 percent of Chinese women were employed. However, their salaries tended to be lower than men's, and they had less access to higher education and training.

488. Occupational Hazard

According to recent studies, 40 to 60 percent of American women experience sexual harassment in their lifetime. Fifteen percent have been sexually harassed in the past year alone.

FIGHTING BACK

489. Pulling Together

In the twelfth century, guilds of people working in the same crafts arose in Europe. By the fifteenth century, they had become formal organizations that regulated the professions. Most women became associated with guilds by marrying a craftsman. However, a few earned independent membership, probably taking their husbands' places after they died. Also, women who made cloth and thread formed all-female guilds. To join such a guild, young girls were apprenticed with mistresses to learn their trades.

490. Early Activists

In a preview of the industrial strikes of the late nineteenth and early twentieth centuries, peasant women in the sixteenth, seventeenth and eighteenth centuries fought against unfair taxation and noblemen's privileges. Poor women led revolts against lords who took over common lands, joining in riots and marching in uprisings in England, Germany and France.

491. What Goes Around

Like their male counterparts, female slaves in the American South were subject to severe punishments if they dared resist their white masters or mistresses. Beatings, whippings and even harsher measures were meant to keep them in their place. But some slave women took their revenge, fomenting revolts like the one thousand-slave uprising led by Nancy and Gabriel Prosser in 1800. That revolt was put down, but it established a precedent for later uprisings. Other slaves burned their masters' homes or property, secretly poisoned their owners or conspired to murder them. If caught, such women were summarily executed.

SLAVE-BRANDING.

Slave branding, early nineteenth century.

492. Women on Strike

Women factory workers of the Industrial Revolution were integral to the emergence of the American labor movement. The 1830 shoeworkers' strike in Lynn, Massachusetts, was the largest American labor turnout to date. About five thousand men and one thousand women

Women mill workers on strike, Lynn, Massachusetts.

joined together, carrying banners and chanting slogans in great marches through the streets. The Boston police and state militia were called in to maintain order, bringing national attention to their cause. But women soon saw the need to separate from the male-dominated organizations, which did little to improve women's working conditions, and form their own unions. When cotton mill owners in Lowell, Massachusetts, announced a severe pay cut in 1834, women workers organized a strike. Women in Dover, New Hampshire, also joined the walkout, and the strike was successful.

493. The Lowell Factory Girls

In 1845 Sarah Bagley and other women formed the Lowell Female Labor Reform Association. Branches sprung up in every New England textile center and the association soon had five hundred to six hundred members. In the first investigation into working conditions in U.S. history, Bagley and others brought to light the long hours, low wages and unhealthy working conditions endured by the mill girls.

494. ILGWU

The International Ladies' Garment Workers' Union was established in 1900 by cloakmakers in New York. Starting with more than two thousand workers in New York, Baltimore, Newark and Philadelphia, within four years membership had doubled and spread to twenty-seven cities. In 1909, the union's garment workers, some twenty thousand women, went on strike and won. By 1913, ILGWU was one of the largest affiliates of the American Federation of Labor.

495. The Bread and Roses Strike

In 1912, labor leader Elizabeth Gurley Flynn helped organize a two-month strike of twenty thousand textile workers in Lawrence, Massachusetts. The strike was known as the "bread and roses" strike because the women complained both that they received less pay than men and that they still had to do the housework. The strike was violent, with men and women smashing sewing machines; one woman was killed in a fight with police. Flynn tried to send the children of female strikers to foster homes in New York to keep them safe, but police blocked the move. Police attacks on mothers and children swayed public opinion in favor of the workers, forcing mill owners to settle the strike and meet most of the strikers' demands.

496. Elizabeth Gurley Flynn
(1890–1964)

A leader of the International Workers of the World, labor organizer Elizabeth Gurley Flynn created the Workers' Defense Union to protect immigrants from being deported and to give them financial and legal help. She joined the Communist Party in 1936, believing that "the full opportunity for women to become free and equal citizens with access to all spheres of human endeavor cannot come under capitalism,

Elizabeth Gurley Flynn.

although many demands have been won by organized struggle." She became leader of the American Communist Party and was jailed in 1952 for her political views.

497. *Business Associates*

One product of the World War I increase in women's job opportunities was the National Federation of Business and Professional Women's Clubs. Founded in 1919 by Lena Madeson Phillips, the organization started as a means to help women who were running businesses involved in war work. Other groups, such as the Association of Business and Professional Women and Zonta, cropped up in the 1920s to support women trying to move into the professions. Founded in 1921, Soroptimist International of the Americas is an international association of executive and professional women that focuses on economic and social development, education, human rights and women's status. Members work in twenty-one countries in North America, South America and Asia. In 1935, the National Association of Negro Business and Professional Women's Clubs was founded. The Association of Women Business Owners, the first association for women entrepreneurs, was created in 1972 by thirteen women in Washington, D.C.

498. *Dorothy Day*
(1897–1980)

Dorothy Day was an activist for civil rights, pacifism and the rights of Jews and migrant workers. She was probably best known for founding the *Catholic Worker* in 1933. The publication's goal was to bring together workers and intellectuals to improve education, farming and social

conditions. Within three years, the publication established itself as a voice for social justice and generated a circulation of 150,000.

499. *Dolores Huerta*

In the mid-1960s, Dolores Huerta, who was pregnant with her seventh child, organized the United Farm Workers with Cesar Chavez. The union protested against the use of dangerous pesticides, poor wages and living conditions in the California grape-growing industry, which mainly employed Hispanic migrant workers. The union's successful national boycott of California grapes led the industry to increase wages and improve working and housing conditions.

500. *Not Good Enough*

Responding to the demands of civil rights proponents, Congress enacted the Equal Pay Act in 1963 and the Civil Rights Act of 1964, whose Title VII included provisions banning discrimination in employment. Both laws extended wage and job protection to women, but in the years following their passage, federal officials made little effort to enforce this aspect of the legislation. The budding women's movement made this failing the target of its first organized action on the national level. In 1965 feminist author Betty Friedan and others went to Washington, D.C., to pressure the government to enforce its own laws, but they made no headway with the male officials they met. This thwarted labor effort led directly to the formation of the National Organization for Women (NOW).

MOVERS AND SHAKERS

501. Madame Tussaud
(1760–1850)

During the French Revolution, Swiss artist Marie Gresholtz Tussaud became famous for her gruesome work making wax death masks of famous Parisian guillotine victims. She opened her wax museum in London in 1802, and in 1833 she added a chamber of horrors.

502. Lydia Pinkham
(1810–1883)

In 1876, Lydia Pinkham patented her "vegetable compound," which she promoted as a cure for "women's complaints." According to Mrs. Pinkham, three spoonfuls a day would help with

a host of female illnesses, including painful menstrual cycles. Her claims may well have been true, for the tonic of herbs and roots was 18 percent alcohol. By 1925, her company had made almost $4 million.

503. The "Witch of Wall Street"

Henrietta Howland Green (1834–1916) parlayed a $10 million inheritance into an exponentially larger fortune by making shrewd investments in stocks, bonds and real estate and by being exceptionally frugal. Known for her stinginess, she died in 1916 at the age of 81. She left an estate of $100 million, making her the richest woman in America at the time.

504. Harriet Hubbard Ayer
(1849–1903)

Ayer was a beauty reporter for the *New York World* and author of *Harriet Hubbard Ayer's Book of Health and Beauty*. She bought the formula for a skin cream from a chemist who swore it was the cream that his grandfather had invented for a legendary French beauty. While entertainers and socialites helped spread the word about her cream, Ayer grew rich but then fell on tough times. Her ex-husband, her daughter and her financial backers turned on her. Her daughter even sued her and had her committed to an insane asylum.

505. Pioneer Entrepreneur

Outside each military garrison on the American frontier stood a line of houses, known as Soapsuds Row, where the laundresses lived.

Madame Tussaud.

Though mostly uneducated, these laundresses helped found many frontier towns. Clara Brown, a freed slave who charged 50 cents a shirt at her Colorado laundry, had Horace Greeley as one of her customers. By working hard, saving money and investing in land, she earned enough money to help other ex-slaves establish themselves. She also financed a successful search for her daughter, who had been sold away from her years before.

506. Madame C. J. Walker
(1867–1919)

If Madame C. J. Walker (born Sarah Breedlove) wasn't the first female American millionaire, she was one of the first. She was definitely the first African-American woman to become a millionaire. She got rich by inventing and selling products that straightened black women's hair. By 1910, she had factories in Denver, Indianapolis and Pittsburgh; her sales force of "beauty analysts" dressed in tasteful uniforms to sell her products door-to-door throughout the U.S. and Caribbean. A role model for black women, she opened beauty schools and taught them that they too could abandon domestic work and become successful. Her firm was the largest black-owned company of its time.

Madame C. J. Walker.

507. Coco Chanel
(1883–1971)

French fashion designer Gabrielle Chanel got her nickname "Coco" when she was twenty, while entertaining the 10th Light Horse Regiment. Mistress to rich businessmen and British royalty, she opened a millinery shop in 1913 and went on to command the world of haute couture. Chanel dressed princesses and duchesses in simple yet elegant chemise dresses. She pioneered the "sweater look," developed a line of women's sportswear and costume jewelry and in 1921 introduced her perfume Chanel No. 5, which went on to become one of the most popular perfumes of all time. In 1954 Chanel produced the first of her classic suits, still admired and emulated today.

508. More than Skin Deep

Elizabeth Arden (Florence Nightingale Graham) started her chain of beauty salons in New York in 1910. By 1938, she had twenty-nine salons, ten in foreign countries. In 1914, Helena Rubinstein joined the fledgling cosmetics industry after making a small fortune selling skin cream in Australia. She opened England's first beauty salon and one in Paris, and became a beauty adviser to society women. She pioneered the makeover by sending saleswomen on tours to show women how to properly apply makeup. By the time she died in 1965, her business was valued at $60 million. Estee Lauder (Josephine Esther Mentzer) came on the scene in 1946 and created a cosmetics company that went on to outsell Revlon, Arden and Rubinstein.

509. Mary Kay Ash

Mary Kay Ash started her cosmetics company in 1963. Thirty years later the company charted $163 million in sales and boasted a sales force of 300,000 women. Mary Kay Cosmetics is unique in its recruitment, training and support of women. The company gives pink Cadillacs and other trophies to women who achieve high sales. While some of the "beauty consultants" who work for the company are housewives, many are women trying to "escape" corporate America.

510. Runway Rulers

Anne Klein created the popular A-line dress in 1949 and founded her own company in 1968. Donna Karan, Klein's protégée, kept the Anne Klein label alive when Klein died in 1974. In 1984, Karan struck out on her own and has since become one of the world's most successful fashion designers.

511. Martha Stewart

Called the "diva of domesticity," Martha Stewart went from modeling to selling stocks to running a multimillion-dollar company. Her good looks, business acumen and sense of style made the perfect combination for pitching the "beautiful life" to media-savvy women in the 1980s and 1990s. Her many books on cooking, gardening, entertaining and decorating have sold millions of copies. In addition, her magazine, *Martha Stewart Living,* and television show of the same name brought her thousands of followers.

Part

SIX

Daily Life

Fear and Fantasy

512. The Virgin and the Whore

For thousands of years, societies have seen women's sexuality as a chaotic force to be tamed. "Good" women were docile, virginal and free from sexual desire. "Bad" women enjoyed sex and were considered evil and dangerous. According to the Old Testament (Isaiah 3:16–17), "Because the daughters of Zion are haughty and walk with outstretched necks, glancing wantonly with their eyes mincing along as they go, tinkling with their feet; the Lord will smite with a scab the heads of the daughters of Zion and the Lord will lay bare their secret parts."

513. Virgin Territory

Throughout history, the best way for a man to ensure that his offspring belonged to him was to marry a young virgin who had been secluded from society. Or, in the words of an ancient Athenian wedding ceremony, "I give you this woman for the ploughing of legitimate children."

514. Faking It

So highly has virginity been prized by husbands that women developed a number of ways to feign deflowering on their wedding night. They might insert tiny pieces of broken glass into the vagina prior to intercourse; insert sponges or fish bladders soaked with pigeon blood into the vagina; apply leeches to the labia. Alternately, they could pack a poultice of tissue-tightening herbs around the vagina, a practice described in the lyrics of a seventeenth-century song:

The already Cuckold getts a Maidenhead,
Which (is) a toyle, made of restringent aide.
Cunt wash't with Allom makes a
Whore a Maid.

515. Watch Out

"Three things are insatiable: the desert, the grave and a woman's vulva." —MUSLIM PROVERB

516. Be Afraid

Male fear of female sexuality has been expressed via a wide range of symbolism over the ages. *Vagina dentatas,* or toothed vaginas, along with terrifying images of women castrating and then consuming their partners, surface in art, legend and psychology. The Sheila-na-gig, however, is a more benevolent representation of female genitalia. It shows a naked woman, knees apart, displaying her vulva. Ancient Celts placed such carvings over their doorways for good luck and as reminders of the pathway of each person's birth. Some people believe that placing horseshoes over doorways is a modern version of invoking the blessings of the Sheila-na-gig.

517. The Double Standard

Societies around the globe reward men but punish women for sexual behavior. Men are studs; women are sluts. While a young man may be encouraged to "sow his wild oats," a young woman is warned that a future mate "won't buy the cow if he can get the milk for free." Perhaps the reasoning behind this behavior is biological. Women produce one egg a month during their sexual lifetimes. Men produce around 200 million sperm per ejaculation. For a woman to succeed biologically, she benefits from having a faithful partner who is willing to help her and her children over a long period of time. For a man to succeed biologically, he needs to sow his genetic seed with as many females as possible.

518. Machismo vs. Marianismo

In Hispanic cultures, young men demonstrate their machismo by being sexually active and exerting authority over women. Young women are expected to follow the ideal of marianismo and be selfless, subservient, pure and chaste—like the Virgin Mary.

519. Cheaters

Ancient Hebrew women found guilty of adultery were stoned to death. An Egyptian woman who protested her innocence was spared—provided she and her lover had not been caught in the act. Emperor Augustus declared that adulterous Roman wives should be divorced, lose half their dowries and a third of their properties, be banished and be forbidden to remarry. Men, on the other hand, rarely received punishment for adultery. In England, a husband's adultery was not considered grounds for divorce until 1923, and until the early 1970s only women could be charged with adultery in Italy.

520. Crimes of Passion

A legal defense for killing one's spouse existed in some European countries, particularly France, until the twentieth century. *Crime passionnel* stated that a husband or wife had the right to kill their spouse if he or she was discovered *in flagrante delicto*. Regardless of the equality of the statutes, juries acquitted husbands more frequently than wives.

Violence Against Women

521. The Dawn of Civilization

Legend says that the male founders of Rome—Romulus and Remus—and their followers kidnapped and raped the female founders of Rome, the Sabine women; the Romans invited their neighbors to a feast and then attacked them. In the fifth century B.C.E., the son of King Tarquin raped Lucretia, an honorable Roman wife. She told her father, husband and uncle about the rape and then killed herself "rather than be an example of unchastity to other wives." Outrage over the violation of the laws of hospitality (raping the wife of one's host) helped lead to the downfall of the Etruscans and establishment of the Roman Republic.

522. Prima Nocta

King Ewan III of Scotland decreed in 875 that "the Lords of the ground shall have the maidenheads of all the virgins dwelling in the same." Laws proclaiming the right of noble lords to be the first to have sex with the bride on her wedding night—before the groom—existed all over Europe during the Middle Ages and persisted for centuries.

523. Great White Fathers

"Like the patriarchs of old, our men live all in one house with their wives and their concubines; and the mulattoes one sees in every family partly resemble the white children. Any lady is ready to tell you who is the father of all the mulatto children in everybody's household but her own. Those, she seems to think, drop from the clouds." —Mary Chesnut (1823–1886), South Carolina

524. White Slavery

The first attempts to prohibit "white slavery," or the international traffic in women for the purpose of prostitution, began in the last part of the nineteenth century. The Mann Act, also called the White Slave Traffic Act, was passed in the U.S. in 1910 to forbid the transport of women across state lines or international boundaries for immoral purposes.

525. Regimented Rape

The German High Command directed mobile brothels during World War I, where prostitutes sometimes averaged ten customers in less than two hours.

526. Women in the Holocaust

Some Nazi concentration camps, such as Ravensbrüch, held only women. Some were Jews, some had worked actively for reforms for the working class, some were imprisoned in order to coerce their relatives into confessions. Many prisoners were compelled to be prostitutes for the German army. Some women led defiant protests inside the camps. Olga Benario and Charlotte Eisenblettermen formed the Women's Resistance at Ravensbrüch.

527. Korean Comfort Women

During World War II, the Japanese military had seventy thousand Japanese camp followers when it conscripted eighty thousand additional Korean women to work as prostitutes. The hor-

rendous treatment of these "comfort women" by the Japanese army remains a major diplomatic issue between the two countries. When they returned to their homes after the war, the surviving Korean women suffered persecution and ridicule. Many committed suicide.

528. Genital Mutilation

As late as the 1940s, clitoridectomies were performed in the United States as a "cure" for female masturbation. Clitoridectomy, the excision of the clitoris and sometimes the adjacent labia, has been done for centuries in other countries, especially in Africa and the Middle East. Infibulation, another form of genital mutilation, joins the sides of the vulva across the vagina, leaving only a small outlet for urine and menstrual flow; the seal is cut open when the husband desires intercourse. Clitoridectomies and infibulation are performed—usually without anesthetic—on babies, young girls or girls nearing puberty. Reasons for performing these procedures are religious and cultural. Resulting medical problems may include hemorrhages, septicemia, incontinence, abscesses, infertility and a number of obstetric, sexual and psychological complications. Although many countries have passed laws against female genital mutilation, the practice continues.

529. Macho Men

In 1979, a Brazilian judge acquitted playboy Doca Street of killing his millionaire lover, Angela Diniz. Street shot Diniz four times in the face because she had flirted with another man while walking along the beach. The jury acquitted Street on the grounds of "defense of honor."

Huge protests by Brazilian feminists helped reverse the acquittal. Prior to that, Brazilian men who murdered their wives or lovers in "crimes of passion" seldom faced sanction. Today, Brazil has eighty-four all-female police stations devoted to assisting victims of violence.

530. Female Infanticide

For centuries, many societies have prized male offspring far above female offspring. Even though China's government denounced female infanticide in 1983, the practice has persisted in response to the country's one child–one family law. Girls have been killed in astonishing numbers and female fetuses are often aborted.

531. Childhood Sexual Abuse

Every thirteen seconds, a child—most often a girl—is abused in the United States. Ninety-five percent of the victims know their abusers. Child sex offenders—most often men—molest, on average, 117 children over their "career." Most of those children do not report the abuse. Ninety-five percent of all teenage prostitutes were sexually abused as children.

532. Domestic Violence

A woman is battered every fifteen seconds in the United States. Every five years, domestic violence kills as many American women as the total number of Americans who died in Vietnam. Over 50 percent of all married women will experience some type of violence during their marriage. About one quarter of all pregnant women are physically abused. Half of all homeless women and their children are fleeing domestic violence.

533. Dowry Death

Many cultures continue the practice of presenting dowries to one's in-laws at the time of marriage. The groom's family, in effect, purchases a wife through the dowry and the bride's family offers money or goods to make their daughter more acceptable as a marriage partner. In reality, dowries often turn into a form of extortion. Brides are harassed, beaten, starved, forced to work as virtual slaves within their in-laws' households and even murdered when dowry demands continue. In India, dowry deaths often are made to look accidental. A bride is doused with kerosene, set on fire and the incident is labeled a "cooking accident."

534. War Crimes

Under the Serbian policy of "ethnic cleansing," thousands of Muslim women in Bosnia-Herzegovina were raped. Many became pregnant. Rather than allow their sisters to bear Serbian children, Muslim brothers often killed their sisters. Sometimes, the women killed themselves.

535. Date Rape

In the United States, one out of eight women has been the victim of rape. A woman is more likely to be raped by someone she knows than by a stranger. Ten percent of all rapes are committed by boyfriends or ex-boyfriends, 29 percent are committed by friends or neighbors, 9 percent are committed by husbands or ex-husbands. The median time served in prison for rape is forty-one months.

536. Stalked

In 1960, Linda Pugach's former boyfriend, Burton, hired men to throw lye in her face and blind her so other men would not desire her. Burton went to prison, Linda later married him and together they authored a book about their lives. In 1992, several states in the U.S. passed anti-stalking laws that made it illegal for abusers to relentlessly pursue their victims. Nevertheless, women who leave their battering husbands or boyfriends are at a 75 percent greater risk of being killed than women who choose to stay with their abusers.

EVERYTHING A WOMAN SHOULD BE

537. Defining Femininity

Studies of gender stereotyping have compared the characteristics considered "typical" or "desirable" in males and females. College students surveyed in 1983 described the "typical man" as independent, aggressive, active, skilled in business, liking math and science, self-confident, ambitious, dominant, having mechanical aptitude, acting like a leader, adventurous. The "typical woman," meanwhile, is emotional, gentle, grateful, home-oriented, enjoys art and music, considerate, devoted to others, in need of approval, likes children, cries easily, needs security.

538. The Cult of Domesticity

Colonial women performed their chores in order to help their husbands and families; American women in the nineteenth century were charged with helping to produce good citizens. For middle-class white women, "the cult of domesticity," or "cult of true womanhood," decreed that the ideal woman concentrate on home life, be untainted by the crass concerns of commercial and political life and remain spiritually superior to their husbands, all in the name of safeguarding the nation's morality. Including these responsibilities within "women's sphere" actually broadened women's educational opportunities and helped to foster a sense of solidarity among them. Because its focus was women's role in nation building, the cult of domesticity helped set the stage for later feminist movements.

539. Tough Love

A successful Spartan woman fulfilled her civic duty by raising warriors. Future mothers learned wrestling, javelin throwing and running. Sons had to be fierce in battle, so fierce that Plutarch described one mother handing a shield to her son with the warning, "Either with this or on this." Husbands in Sparta did not "own" wives as in other ancient Greek cities. They might even introduce stronger, younger men to their wives in hopes of helping to create, through eugenic selection, biologically superior children.

540. In Check

Passed by Rome in 215 B.C.E., the Oppian Law stated that "No woman might own more than half an ounce of gold or wear clothes of various colors or ride in a horse-drawn carriage in any town or city or within a mile of its confines, except on the occasion of some public religious ceremony." The law had been passed as a wartime austerity measure, but it took twenty years—and women's protests in the streets—to repeal it. Cato argued against repeal, saying, "Woman is a headstrong and uncontrolled animal. . . . What [they] want is complete freedom. . . . If you allow them one right after another, so that in the end they have complete equality with men, do you think you will find them bearable? Nonsense!"

541. *Pretty Little Heads*

Too many participants in the first Miss America contests were, according to one official, "Dumb Doras"—beautiful but vapid young women. In 1925, contest sponsors promised that the event would be "on a higher plane than ever and its fair participants will represent pastors' daughters, schoolteachers, college girls and femininity generally of the most desirable type." Nevertheless, the image of the Dumb Dora, or bimbo or airhead, lived on in American culture. The assumption was that a woman could not be both intelligent and attractive.

542. *Playing Dumb*

Some successful actresses were known more for their figures than for their intelligence or their acting abilities. Jayne Mansfield, who had a 163 IQ, became the epitome of the 1950s sex kitten. She squealed and purred as she balanced (at her biggest) a 46-24-36 figure over stiletto heels. Squeaky-voiced Judy Holliday made the character of the dumb blonde a Hollywood staple. "Valley Girl" roles of the early 1980s—which de-

picted giggling, spoiled teenagers—continued the tradition of stereotyping women and girls as silly and vacuous.

543. *Ladylike Behavior*

Advice to ladies from nineteenth- and early-twentieth-century etiquette books included the following admonishments on achieving the feminine ideal:

"A lady in society must, if she would not grow utterly wearing in company, know how to dance. . . . It is one of the most healthful and elegant amusements and cannot be too highly recommended.

"The chaperone must . . . watch the characters of the men who approach her charge and endeavor to save the inexperienced girl from the dangers of bad marriage, if possible.

"Even if his kiss would be acceptable, let him make the first move. The reputation of being a 'hot number' is anything but complimentary."

544. *Emily Post* (1873–1960)

"She must not swing her arms as though they were dangling ropes; she must not switch herself this way and that; she must not shout and she must not, while wearing her bridal veil, smoke a cigarette." So sayeth Emily Price Post, author of the bestselling *Etiquette: The Blue Book of Social Usage.* Post's books, articles and magazine columns codified social rules for the changing world of twentieth-century America. She drew upon her finishing school upbringing to demystify both formal and informal rules of etiquette and did so with great wit. To arbitrate marriage customs, dress codes and table settings, Post used fictional characters jauntily named Mrs. Toplofty, Gloria Gorgeous, Miss Elizabeth Orphan, Mary Neighbor, Mrs. Oncewere and Her Grace the Duchess of Overthere.

545. *Plastic Perfection*

The bestselling doll in history is Barbie, a curvaceous clotheshorse with unnaturally large breasts and long limbs. In one of Barbie's latest computer games, the goal is to help the doll become the top supermodel. In another game, Barbie has to find her way through a mall in order to meet Ken for a date.

FASHION VICTIMS

546. *Engineered Beauty*

Bustles and hoopskirts offered the illusion of a large pelvis, enhancing sexual attractiveness by subliminally projecting a womanly image of complication-free childbirth. In reality, wearing as much as thirty pounds of skirt fabric (all suspended from the corset or from the waist) often displaced a woman's internal organs. The original crinolines and hoopskirts consisted of horsehair petticoats and wire cages with fabric draped over them. Many women burned to death by misjudging their distance from a fireplace and thus ignited their crinolines.

547. *Cinched Waists*

Corsets deformed the female body while providing the illusion of large breasts, a narrow waist and sturdy, good-for-childbearing hips. Complications from wearing corsets included skin welts, broken ribs, collapsed lungs, prolapsed uterus, neurasthenia and weakened abdominal walls. Women in corsets needed servants because it was difficult to bend or stoop while tightly laced and banded with steel or whalebone.

548. *Masculine Attire*

The Napoleonic Code of France forbade women to dress like men. Writer George Sand noted that, while wearing women's clothing, "I was like a boat on ice. My delicate shoes cracked open in two days, my pattens sent me spilling and I always forgot to lift my dress. I was muddy,

Women in corsets, late nineteenth century.

tired and runny-nosed." On the other hand, when she adopted trousers, vest, hat and boots, she said, "I was solid on the sidewalk at last. I dashed back and forth across Paris and felt I was going around the world. I was out and about in all weather, came home at all hours, was in the pit of all the theatres."

549. High Heels

In 1874, health reformers were already warning about the dangers of wearing high heels: "The Chinese shock our moral sense when they deform the feet of their women by merciless compression in infancy . . . [but] high heels . . . are one of the most fruitful sources of disease. They not only cause contractions of the muscles of the legs . . . [but also] induce the corns and bunions that alone suffice to make locomotion very painful."

550. Bloomers

Amelia Jenks Bloomer copied the design for pants for women from her friend Elizabeth Smith Miller. Miller's original design for Turkish-style trousers was inspired by her visit to a convalescent home where she saw women wearing comfortable garments as they recuperated from the effects of corset-related injuries. Early advocates of "bloomers" included many feminists and women who worked in the Lowell, Massachusetts, mills. During World War II, "slacks" finally became acceptable workplace clothing for women factory workers.

551. Hemlines

Skirt lengths for women remained at the ankles from the thirteenth century until 1914. Then

they rose—as much as ten inches in two years. In World War II, women wore short skirts as a way of conserving national resources. After the war, hemlines plummeted, a symbol of postwar prosperity. Mary Quant, a London fashion designer, pioneered the miniskirt—which has been called "less an article of clothing than a flag of revolution"—in the early 1960s. When asked to explain the significance of the short-short-short skirt, Quant replied simply, "Sex."

552. Panty Hose

So great was the demand that riots broke out on May 15, 1940, when Du Pont's first nylon stock-

Bloomers.

ings went on sale, but their 1959 successor, panty hose, created less stir. However, as technology moved ahead, panty hose sales skyrocketed. Women enjoyed being freed from tight girdles and awkward garter belts. Panty hose camouflaged cellulite, body hair and skin blotches. Support hose and tummy control innovations added to the product's popularity. American women now buy over 100 billion pairs of panty hose a year.

553. *Bikinis*

Nineteenth-century bathing suits for women were made from heavy fabric and featured high-necked bodices, knee-length skirts, bloomers and stockings. In 1946, Paris designer Louis Réard revealed a new two-piece swimming suit and named it after the first U.S. peacetime nuclear tests (conducted four days before the introduction of the swimwear) at Bikini Atoll in the Marshall Islands.

554. *Hot Pants*

When Bloomingdale's department store put the first hot pants on sale in 1970, customers mobbed the cash registers to buy the high-cut, low-waisted, skintight short shorts. Women in hot pants—unlike those in miniskirts—could sit down, bend over and cross their legs without embarrassment and without sacrificing sex appeal. Jackie Onassis wore Halston hot pants while yachting; innovative California brides paired white lace hot pants with go-go boots, and Liberace twirled a drum majorette's baton while dressed in red, white and blue hot pants.

SEX OBJECTS

555. *Good Enough to Eat*

Food and love have always gone hand in hand. The design for tortellini mimics the belly button of Venus. So that Louis XIV might always drink from her bosom, the king had a sculptor make the mold of one of his mistress's breasts. Voila! The champagne glass was created.

556. *Sexy Scrimshaw*

While at sea, nineteenth-century sailors sometimes incised whalebones or walrus ivory to pass the time. Scrimshaw art that depicted the sailors' erotic fantasies, scenes of visits to bordellos or images of female genitalia was usually destroyed by order of the captain before the ship returned to port.

557. *Pinup Girls*

For generations, soldiers and sailors pasted images of female celebrities onto their lockers, inside their helmets and above their beds. During the 1940s, Betty Grable, a twenty-nine-year-old movie star with "the world's best legs," earned $300,000 in one year for the photograph of her dressed in a white swimsuit and high heels. Stylized pinup images decorated the fuselages of combat aircraft during World War II and the Korean War, communicating, according to one scholar, "a double message of sex and war, eroticism and courage and pleasure and human destruction." Supposedly, a photo of pinup girl Rita Hayworth decorated the first atomic bomb dropped on Hiroshima.

558. Early Start

The average age when a boy first sees an issue of *Playboy* is eleven.

559. Rape as Entertainment

"I look as though I'm really enjoying myself. No one ever asked me how those bruises got on my body.... Every time someone sees *Deep Throat*, they're seeing me being raped." —Linda "Lovelace" Marchiano

560. Terms of Endearment?

Dolly and *tootsie* originated as expressions of affection, but eventually came to mean mistress or prostitute. Nicknames such as *pussy, chick, fox, honey, cupcake* and *cookie* equate women with animals and emphasize edibility.

Rugged Individualists

561. Soul Mates

Missionaries Narcissa Prentiss Whitman and Eliza Hart Spalding accompanied their husbands to the American West in 1836. The women traveled most of the way riding sidesaddle and became the first white women to cross the Rocky Mountains. After settling 120 miles apart, the women, each lonely for sisterly friendship, agreed to meditate every morning at 9 A.M. in order to "contact" one another and pray for guidance in their work as mothers and missionaries. In 1847, a group of Cayuse Indians who had fallen prey to white people's diseases and resisted the missionary efforts to change their culture killed Narcissa Whitman and thirteen others.

562. Hard Times

"The West was kind to men and dogs but hell on women and horses." —Old pioneer saying

563. Martha Martin

In the 1950s, Martha Martin lived in southeastern Alaska, married to a gold prospector. One year an avalanche trapped her while her husband was away. She dug herself out from under rocks and snow, splinted her broken arm, made a cast for her broken leg and prepared to spend the coming winter alone—and pregnant. A portion of her journal recalled, "I killed a sea otter today . . . with an ax, dragged him home and skinned him. I took his liver out and ate part of it." She chopped extra wood, baked more bread and boiled the string from a flour sack to use to tie the umbilical cord. Martin delivered her child herself, wrapped her in the otter's skin and christened her with seawater. After months alone, Martin and her child were rescued by Indians.

Visions of Loveliness

564. Windows to the Soul

Queen Cleopatra of Egypt, lover of both Julius Caesar and Marc Antony, accentuated her eyes with kohl, a black paste made from burned almonds, copper oxide, powdered antimony and brown clay ocher, moistened by saliva. Some

Egyptians sprinkled an iridescent powder made from crushed beetle shells over their eyelids. Others applied powdered malachite to make green eye shadow. Both Greeks and Egyptians favored eyebrows that met in the middle, using kohl pencils when necessary to connect the brows.

565. Hair Care

Making one's toilette has never been a simple matter. Throughout history, people have lightened their hair color with harsh chemicals and bleaches or dusted dark hair with gold dust, pollen or flour. To conceal gray hair, Mesopotamian women mixed the heads of ravens and storks with oxen galls, opium and scorpions. Egyptians mixed laudanum, raven's eggs and the uterus from a cat into hair dye. In the 1600s, Italian women bleached their hair a fashionable reddish blond. By the time of Marie Antoinette, elaborate hairpieces and wigs added inches—and drama—to court dress. Wire frames balanced cascades of curls and included ornaments like feathers, jewels, artificial birds or scale models of sailing ships.

566. Ouch

Powdered lead has been used since the time of the Greeks to make women's faces appear white. Fifteenth-century Italian women spent hours plucking their foreheads and eyebrows to give the illusion of a high forehead. They whitened their skin with lead cosmetics and rubbed their cheeks with abrasives to achieve a refined pallor. Seventeenth-century beauties used ceruse, a material that hardened like enamel and made it difficult to move the facial muscles. Arsenic was the active ingredient in a popular Greek and Roman depilatory. Egyptian women painted their nipples gold and the veins on their breasts blue. Egyptians also concocted wrinkle creams from milk, wax, olive oil and crocodile dung. In the eighteenth century, women ate Arsenic Complexion Wafers, a product that produced a pale complexion by poisoning the blood. Ladies wearing low-cut gowns in the 1890s sometimes pierced their nipples and inserted jeweled pins.

567. Foot Binding

Chinese mothers began binding their daughters' feet during the tenth century in order to create "lotus blossoms," a mark of beauty and refinement. Girls between ages five and twelve had their arches broken and their toes bent beneath their feet. Tight linen wrappings forced the feet to stop growing. Complications included constant pain and infection, including gangrene. Ideal bound feet were only three inches long and fit into the palm of a man's hand. A woman with unbound feet was considered unmarriage-

Bound feet.

able in all but the poorest classes. Women with bound feet, if they could walk at all, needed assistance and became status symbols for husbands who could afford to support wives incapable of physical labor.

568. Bob

Women began to cut their "crowning glory" short in the early twentieth century, a boon especially for working women, who were sometimes injured when their long hair became tangled in factory machinery. Bobbed hair became a symbol of the Jazz Age and a new era of freedom. Nevertheless, judges at the second Miss America contest, in 1922, decided that bobbed hair was simply too radical for their pageant.

569. Here She Comes

High school sophomore Margaret Gorman was the first Miss America in 1921. Gorman did not receive any scholarship money. Years later she and her husband, in need of cash during the Great Depression, melted down one of her

Margaret Gorman, Miss America, 1921.

prizes for its silver. Today, the Miss America Pageant is the largest private endower of scholarships for women.

570. The White Standard

"Black is beautiful!" proclaimed the African-American community of the 1960s. Despite efforts to diversify standards, the dominant beauty image marketed around the world continues to be a young, thin, small-nosed, fair-haired, Caucasian woman. The result, according to social scientists, devastates the self-esteem of women of color when they try to transform themselves. Asian women may undergo eyelid surgery to Westernize their appearance. Black women may buy contact lenses to alter their eye color or use harsh chemicals to straighten their hair and bleach their skin. In some communities, marrying a lighter-skinned partner may be seen as a move up the social scale.

571. Distinguishing Features

"The middle-aged man's wrinkles and gray hair are seen as evidence of character and distinction, while the middle-aged woman is exhorted to conceal all signs of the process of growing older with makeup, hair dye and cosmetic surgery. The ideal woman's face shows no signs that she has lived a life of experience and emotion; it is supposed to remain unblemished and child-like." —Susan Sontag, "The Double Standard of Aging," 1979

572. Impossible Dream

Fashion photographers use rail-thin models as living coat hangers, equating female thinness with beauty. In the 1960s, model Leslie Hornby, aka Twiggy, was five feet six inches tall and weighed ninety-two pounds. The supermodels of the 1990s are much taller, but continue to be proportionately quite thin. Camera angles accentuate their leg length even more. However, long, lithe legs are only typical of girls during the early stages of puberty, a fact that raises questions about male ideals of beauty.

573. Dieting

Girls suffer from eating disorders more frequently than boys, by a ratio of nine to one. Two million Americans, most of them women, use diet pills. Fifty percent of fourth-grade girls are dieting because they think they are too fat. Although only about 10 percent of them are overweight, 90 percent of all high school junior and senior girls diet. Fourteen percent of all college women vomit occasionally in order to control their weight.

BAD GIRLS

574. In Their Place

"We have hetaerae for our pleasure, concubines for our daily needs and wives to give us legitimate children and look after the housekeeping."
—Demosthenes

575. Hetaerae

The very best ancient Greek courtesans, a class of educated and astute businesswomen known as hetaerae, retained property rights and participated in the intellectual and political debates of their male-dominated culture. Some hetaerae

became quite successful. Aspasia, besides being a skilled healer, directed an influential literary and political salon. Thaïs, the mistress of Alexander the Great, later became the consort of Egypt's king. The word *heter*, or "companion," comes from the Egyptian *glyph* for "friendship," which shows two women holding hands.

576. Concubines

To enter the royal bed, Chinese concubines had to slip under the blanket at its foot and crawl toward the emperor. After a night with the ruler during the T'ang period (618–907), women were stamped with an indelible, cinnamon-based ointment that read, "Wind and moon are forever new."

577. Harems

Records report that one Chinese emperor had a queen, three consorts, nine second-rank wives, twenty-seven third-rank wives and eighty-one concubines. Keeping track of so many women was a logistical nightmare and required creation of special quarters designed to keep them distanced from other men. Indian maharajas, Arab caliphs, Byzantine sultans, Ottoman Turks and others also set up similar women's quarters or harems. The stories in *The Thousand and One Nights* offered western Europeans romantic glimpses into harem life. In reality, while concubines who bore sons often gained elevated rank, they also engaged in endless intrigues in order to guarantee their sons' claims to succession.

578. Mistresses

History contains numerous accounts of famous mistresses. Nell Gwynne (1650–1687) sold or-

A harem.

anges outside theaters before she became an actress and, later, the mistress of Charles II and mother of his son. Once, her coach was attacked by a mob in Hyde Park who mistook her for one of the king's Catholic mistresses. "Desist, good people," she called out. "I'm the *Protestant* whore!" French society was scandalized when Louis XV took Madame de Pompadour (1721–1764), a member of the bourgeoisie, for his mistress. The famous high hairdo, rolled back from the forehead and sometimes padded with "rats of balled wool" was named for her. Daughter of a blacksmith, Emma Hamilton (1765–1815) was mistress to one man and then to his uncle before taking up with Admiral

Horatio Nelson. Their affair and the birth of their child scandalized England. After Nelson died at the Battle of Trafalgar, Hamilton spent a year in debtor's prison and later died penniless in France. To keep her skin young, Lillie Langtry (1853–1929), mistress of England's King Edward VII, rolled naked in the morning dew. When she died at age seventy-six, she owned jewels worth $40,000, including one of the world's largest rubies.

579. *Agnès Sorel* (1422–1450)

"La belle Agnès," widely considered the most beautiful woman in France, became Charles

VII's official mistress in 1443 and was the first in a long line of influential women who exerted power over weak French rulers. Her diplomatic skills helped France expel the English from French territory and establish itself as a world power. When Sorel died following childbirth, Queen Marie mourned her as much as King Charles did.

580. *Madame du Barry* (1743–1793)

Louis XV's *maîtresse-en-titre* wielded so much power that she functioned as an uncrowned queen. Following his death in 1774, she was held as a state prisoner, but later released. She gave aid to the poor and supported a number of artists. Later, she became the mistress of other powerful men, but was never friends with Queen Marie Antoinette.

581. *Devotees and Detractors*

When prostitute Julia Bulette of Virginia City, Nevada, was murdered in 1867, many men in town attended her funeral. The local "respectable" women, meanwhile, lavished attention on her killer, providing him with wine and omelettes in the days before his execution.

582. *Free Love*

"A girl who gives herself to a man in free love stands morally way above the woman who, for pecuniary reasons or out of a desire for a home, marries a man she does not love. . . ."
—Karen Horney, age seventeen, 1903

583. *Flappers*

Flappers have been called "women's Trojan horse on the battlefield of the sexes." Scandalously free of corsets, brassieres and petticoats, their "boyish" figures and behavior allowed them greater entry into the world of men. They were free spirits of the Jazz Age. Flappers smoked, drank, caroused in speakeasies and made love freely, redefining what it meant to be a woman. Silent-screen actress Clara Bow became the "It Girl" of the 1920s, epitomizing the freewheeling flapper and helping to advance the female sexual prerogative.

584. *The Blond Bombshell*

At midcentury, a co-star described Marilyn Monroe's walk as "like Jell-O on springs." Monroe embodied Hollywood's fantasy of the breathy, baby-voiced child-woman. Lavishly endowed by today's standards, Monroe's buxom figure and physical radiance helped make her a star. Women have sought to emulate her, bleaching their hair blond and cultivating the appearance of large breasts.

LOVE AND ROMANCE

585. *The Science of Love*

"Romantic love is a biological ballet. . . . Denial, repression and inhibition all feed romantic love, because people obsess about satisfying their biological drives, yet cannot avoid the confines of morality. . . . 'Falling in love,' we call it, as if into a pothole." —Diane Ackerman, *A Natural History of Love*

586. Knights in Shining Armor

Knights of the Middle Ages and Renaissance were charged with protecting the chastity and good name of their vulnerable lady and honoring her with brave deeds. Chivalry was a code of exaggerated gestures and mannered rituals performed by the knight for his lady. A knight might tip his lance toward the lady at a jousting tournament, hoping to win her favor.

587. Courtly Love

Courtly love flourished during the Middle Ages among the upper classes. Gallant lovers venerated their ladies much as religious people worshiped the Virgin Mary, and remained loyal to their ladies despite all obstacles. Erotic passion between husband and wife could be considered a sin, but passion could exist between a married lady and her hero lover. Conquering lust—while delighting in the intricate, courtly gestures of adulterous affection—became the goal of many knights and ladies. Some famous couples, like Guinevere and Lancelot, and Tristan and Isolde, did not succeed in quashing their desires.

588. Flute Pursuit

Young Cheyenne men once carved courting flutes in order to impress the women they loved. The flute represented all the man's best characteristics: his strength, artistic ability and admi-ration for his beloved. At night, the man concealed himself outside the tepee and serenaded the woman. Because each flute's "voice" sounded different, the woman could choose which suitor to accept.

589. Bundling

Various communities, especially reform-minded American and European religious groups in the late eighteenth century, practiced a courtship ritual known as bundling. To accustom themselves to marital intimacy, engaged couples spent the night together in bed, fully clothed and chaste.

590. Think of England

In 1912, fifty-five-year-old Lady Alice Hillingdon wrote, "I am happy now that Charles calls on my bedchamber less frequently than of old. As it is, I now endure but two calls a week and when I hear his steps outside my door I lie down on my bed, close my eyes, open my legs and think of England."

591. One Hour Mama

In the 1920s, blues artist Ida Cox recorded Porter Grainger's song about sexual gratification:

"I'm a one hour mama, so no one minute papa
Ain't the kind of man for me,
Set your alarm clock, papa, one hour
that's proper,
Then love me like I like to be"

THE TIES THAT BIND

592. The Laws of Manu

In the second and third centuries, Vedic scriptures known as the Laws of Manu established the Indian practice of marrying very young brides, eliminated most education for women and supplanted matrilineal structures with patriarchal ones. An ideal wife was to be one-third her husband's age, and she could be as young as eight years old. The bride would not live with her husband until she reached puberty, however, and then she would be introduced to sex over a period of days because "If a woman is forced to submit to rough handling from a man she scarcely knows, she may come to hate sexual intercourse, even to hate the whole male sex." Child-bride marriages served several purposes: They brought new workers to needy households, they safeguarded the virtue of young girls and they reinforced a woman's intellectual, emotional, economic and physical dependence on her husband.

593. Pre-Columbian In-Laws

In Aztec culture, weddings were preceded with a mock abduction and ritual denigration of the bride's potential as a weaver, cook and mother. During the wedding ceremony, however, women were not handed from the care of their fathers into the care of their husbands. Instead, the care of the young man was transferred from mother to bride. In Mayan culture, women could hold property and daughters could inherit from their mothers. Children added a *naal*, or house name, derived from that of their mothers to their fathers' lineage surname.

594. Arranged Marriage

Many traditionally nomadic groups, including Arabs, Mongols and Gypsies, practiced arranged marriages. Nobles the world over united their families through arranged marriages. Such marriages strengthened political connections, increased fortunes and landholdings, and secured rankings within royal bloodlines. Dowries passed between aristocratic families could be immense. When the daughter of the Duke of Milan, Caterina Sforza, married the King of Poland in the late sixteenth century, her dowry

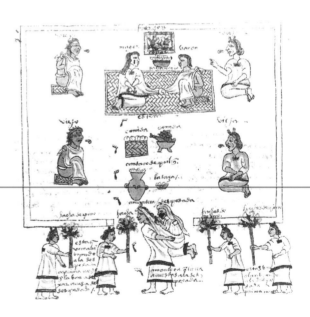

Aztec wedding, from *Codex Mendozo*, fifteenth century.

was large enough to pay off the Swedish national debt. Arranged marriage is still practiced within some cultures today.

595. *Modern Love*

The average engagement lasts fourteen months in the U.S. The fastest-growing age group for brides is thirty to thirty-five. Thirty-eight percent of the respondents in a *Woman's Day* poll said that they would not marry the same spouse if they had it to do over again.

596. *Breaking Up, American Style*

The United States has one of the highest rates of divorce in the world. Only one in four U.S. families is a traditional, nuclear family consisting of two married, heterosexual parents and their children.

597. *The Biology of Boredom*

Anthropologist Helen Fisher concluded that there might be a chemical basis for adultery and divorce. Couples meet, fall in love, get married and have one child, on average, within four years. Then the attachment chemicals begin to falter—and couples begin to look elsewhere for romance. The phenomenon of the "four-year itch" coincides with the end of most first marriages throughout the world.

THE PROBLEM OF PROCREATION

598. *Primordial Prophylactics*

Ancient Egyptian methods of birth control, including coitus interruptus, were described in a series of papyrus writings. While the Egyptians may not have completely understood the biology of contraception, devices they developed did absorb some seminal fluid. One recipe involved inserting a mixture of honey and sodium carbonate or a mixture containing crocodile dung into the vagina. Later writings suggested inserting a pad of lint coated with acacia and honey. These mixtures acted as both cervical caps and spermicides.

599. *French Letters*

Condoms were invented by Gabriel Fallopius, an Italian physician, who was seeking to halt an epidemic of venereal disease in sixteenth-century Europe. Condoms made of vulcanized rubber became available in the 1870s. Some of these early condoms featured colored portraits of Queen Victoria and Prime Minister Gladstone. Much thicker than modern latex condoms, "rubbers" could be washed and reused. They were employed more often for the man's protection from venereal disease than to prevent pregnancy.

600. Gatekeepers

Greek women used empty pomegranate shells as cervical caps. Aristotle recommended anointing the cervix with oil of cedar, lead ointment or frankincense and olive oil. Casanova recommended that his lovers place lemon halves near the opening of their cervixes to prevent conception. In 1870, a German physician, Wilhelm Mensinga, developed a rubber barrier with a watch spring to hold it in place. The "Dutch cap" was 98 percent effective—about the same rate as the modern diaphragm.

601. The IUD

Arab nomads inserted stones into their camels' uteruses to prevent conception during long journeys. To achieve the same result, a variety of foreign objects were placed into women's uteruses: buttons, spools, horsehair and beads of ebony, glass, ivory, pewter, silver or gold. Not until the late 1970s was the scientific action of the IUD understood.

602. Margaret Sanger (1879–1966)

Margaret Sanger saw her mother weakened by multiple pregnancies and, while working as a nurse, witnessed the effects of backstreet abortions. In an effort to help working-class women avoid unwanted pregnancy, she distributed literature about douches, condoms and other forms of contraception. She was jailed several times, but she proclaimed that "women should look the world in the face with a go-to-hell look in the eyes; have an idea; speak and act in defiance of convention." Sanger coined the term birth control and eventually helped establish a network of over three hundred clinics, staffed largely by women physicians, to distribute contraceptives and record their effectiveness. Sanger said that, for women, ". . . without the right to control their own bodies, all other rights are meaningless."

603. The Pill

The birth control pill originated in the 1930s with research into a traditional Mexican contraceptive made of extracts from wild yams. Wild yams produce sapogenins, from which progesterone, the female sex hormone, could be manufactured and used to inhibit reproduction. In 1962, one year after oral contraceptives became available in the United States, more than a million women were taking them.

Margaret Sanger.

604. *Teen Motherhood*

According to Planned Parenthood, one third of all teenage women use no contraceptive during their first sexual encounter. Forty thousand teenage girls drop out of school each year because of pregnancy. The rate of pregnancy among nonwhite teens is twice that of white teens. Ninety percent of teen mothers keep their babies. Almost 20 percent of unmarried teen mothers will become pregnant again within a year. Overall, teen mothers face far greater socioeconomic challenges over their lifetime than women who wait to have children.

LOVING EACH OTHER

605. *The Ladies of Llangolen*

Eleanor Butler and Sarah Ponsonby, upper-class Irish girls from titled families, fell in love while at school in the late 1700s. Both families tried to discourage their relationship. Over time, the pair convinced their families that they should be together. The families agreed, provided that the couple move away. Their home in Wales became a meeting place for intellectuals and artists, where, according to Eleanor's journal, Eleanor and Sarah lived happily.

606. *Boston Marriages*

It was not uncommon, during the nineteenth century, for women to write intimate letters to one another, make extended visits to each other's homes and sleep in the same beds.

Society did not label the friendships perverse and, although the women may have been emotionally committed to one another, they were not sexually involved. In "Boston marriages," women throughout history lived together in committed relationships. Although unmarried, they led conventional lives of domestic partnership and shared a great deal of emotional intimacy. Most often, Boston marriages—so called in the nineteenth century for the relationships among certain upper-class Boston ladies—did not involve sexual relations.

607. *Coming Out*

If, as some historians assert, Gertrude "Ma" Rainey was a lesbian, her 1928 release of "Prove It On Me Blues" was the first public avowal of homosexuality by an American celebrity.

Went out last night,
With a crowd of my friends,
They must bin womens
Cause I don't like no mens.
It's true I wear a collar and tie,
Make all the women-folk
Go all wild.

They all say I do it,
Ain't nobody caught me,
You all got to prove it on me.

608. *Gertrude Stein and Alice B. Toklas*

Gertrude Stein had to publish her first literary works—some of which described lesbian rela-

Alice B. Toklas.

Gertrude Stein.

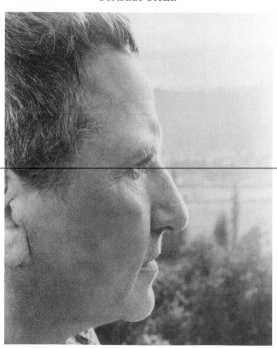

tionships—herself. Then, in 1933, publication of her biography of her longtime companion, Alice B. Toklas, became a bestseller and made her a celebrity.

609. Gay Pride

"My sexuality is a very important part of my life, a very important part of my being, but it is still a very small part of my makeup, a very small part of what creates a whole human being. In any case, being a lesbian is not an accomplishment, it is not something I had to learn, study for or graduate in. It is what I am, nothing more and nothing less." —Martina Navratilova

LEISURE PURSUITS

610. Chatterboxes

Queen Elizabeth I of England was "gossip"—meaning godmother or wise woman—at the baptism of James VI of Scotland. Originally a sign of respect, the term came to refer to the conversations of older women, or gossips.

611. Tea Time

Catherine of Braganza, the Portuguese princess who married King Charles II, introduced tea to England in the seventeenth century. Tea drinking evolved into a polite, at-home social activity and became a customary afternoon practice after the Duchess of Bedford complained she felt faint late every day. She started the tradition of serving tea, sandwiches and tiny cakes at elaborate social teas.

612. Calling Cards

Middle-class women in post-centennial America paid ritual visits to one another each afternoon, leaving distinctive calling cards on silver trays in the front halls of their friends' homes. Calling cards offered a graceful way to be a social climber. A woman could approach a social better, leave her card and, if she proved acceptable, be favored with a return visit. Not returning a visit indicated disapproval while avoiding unpleasant face-to-face confrontations.

Victorian woman serving tea.

613. Shop 'til You Drop

An urban innovation after the Civil War, the department store made shopping as a social activity both possible and acceptable. Department stores had ornate furnishings, art galleries and ladies' lunchrooms. They provided the security of a homelike environment and freed women from the burden of complicated rules of etiquette, but reinforced women's roles as consumers.

614. Quilting Bees

American pioneer women and Depression-era women created quilts out of necessity. They transformed scraps of fabric into functional bedcoverings that were also beautiful works of art. The quilting bee was, according to one woman, "always my time to get off and get some relief. I ain't happy doin' nothin'. But if I can take my relaxation with a needle and have some fun talkin', then I think it's all right . . . to visit the girls there, catch up on all the news and quilt a bit."

615. Racy Bicyclists

When bicycles came into wide use in the 1880s, every family wanted one, but every family also wondered, what to do about the ladies? Ladies needed chaperones when they rode bicycles and they could never share a tandem bicycle with another woman. If they wore full skirts, women could only ride tricycles. Critics said that bicycles threatened a woman's morality and health—especially if she adopted bloomers and shorter skirts in order to ride a two-wheeler. Others said that the angle of the bicycle seat itself could "beget or foster the habit of masturbation."

616. *The DAR*

In 1890, refused membership in the all-male Sons of the American Revolution, four women formed their own group, the Daughters of the American Revolution, in Washington, D.C. Membership in the group was based on heritage, restricted to descendants of those who fought in the War for Independence. The group's conservative politics cost it some members over the years. Because of her pacifist activities during World War I, the DAR revoked the membership of Jane Addams, social reformer and winner of the Nobel Peace Prize. First Lady Eleanor Roosevelt resigned from the DAR in 1939 when the organization refused to allow African-American vocalist Marian Anderson to sing at Constitutional Hall.

617. *Volunteers*

Post-deb Mary Harriman organized her upper-class friends into the Junior League of New York in 1900. By 1920, thirty-nine other cities had Junior Leagues, women's groups dedicated to civic improvement. The Association of Junior Leagues of America continues to promote volunteerism and community improvement in areas such as parent-child relations, domestic vio-

DAR meeting, 1913.

lence awareness, mental health and homelessness.

618. *Girl Scouts*

Juliette Gordon Low met Sir Robert Baden-Powell, founder of the Boy Scouts, while in England. She was eager to give girls the same opportunity at self-reliance, nature appreciation and service to the community. In 1912, she started two patrols of sixteen girls in Savannah, Georgia. Girl Scout badges included cooking and housekeeping as well as knot tying, campfire building and more exotic survival tips, such as "How to Secure a Burglar with Eight Inches of Cord." The organization was open to girls of all races and economic backgrounds. The Girl Scouts grew to be the largest female volunteer organization in the world today.

SEVEN

Literature and Journalism

LITERARY LEGACY

619. *Bookmakers*

In medieval Europe before the invention of the printing press, nuns did much of the manuscript copying and illuminating by which literary works were preserved and disseminated. The biography of Ida von Leuwen, one such copyist in the thirteenth century, notes that "at all times were all her faculties engaged in writing, carefully copying books for the Church."

620. *Words of Devotion*

Almost all the surviving literary efforts of medieval European women are the often anonymous lives of saints written by nuns. The first noted women writers who are known by name also chose spiritual topics. In the thirteenth and fourteenth centuries, for instance, Beatrice of Nazareth wrote *Seven Degrees of Love,* Mechthild of Magdeburg offered *Streaming Light of the Deity* and Marguerite Porete composed *Mirror of Simple and Devastated Souls.* Their religious focus reflected the tenor of the times and partially excused their audacity in taking up the pen. Although their widely read works equaled or exceeded the literary merit of works by their male contemporaries, each piece was accompanied by an apology for the writer's lack of skill.

621. *Christine de Pisan*
(1364–c. 1430)

When her husband died in 1389, this Italian-born French woman went to work as a copyist and writer to support her three children, a niece and her aging mother. She was well edu-cated and socially well situated, but her choice of career was controversial if not shocking, the more so because she addressed secular rather than religious topics. Criticized for daring, as a woman, to write, she dismissed the notion that she—or any woman—could not or should not express herself on paper. Her genius was indisputable, prompting a noted male scholar of the time to call her *"insignis femina, virilis femina"* ("remarkable woman, virile woman"). A brilliant pioneer, she found a way to communicate a woman's point of view within traditional male forms. She sought the advantages of a "man's" education, yet believed her sex gave her work its real meaning. Writing politics and philosophy as well as poetry, she voiced a potent feminism. She came to the defense of her sex in works such as *Epistle to the God of Love* (1399), *The Book of Three Virtues* (1406) and most notably *The Book of the City of Women* (1405), a refutation of traditional male representations of women. She was also appointed to write the official biography of Charles V.

622. *The Art of the Book*

During its first century, printing was the province of men. Some early printers, however, were succeeded in their businesses by wives and daughters. In sixteenth-century Paris, twenty-five women practiced the printer's art. Among them was Charlotte Guillard, whose twenty-two-year career included the publication of numerous volumes of history, philosophy and theology.

623. *Nobel Prize Winners*

Since the annual Nobel Prize for Literature was first awarded in 1901, only eight women have received it:

1909 Selma Lagerlöf (Sweden)
1926 Grazia Deledda (Italy)
1928 Sigrid Undset (Norway)
1938 Pearl S. Buck (U.S.)
1945 Gabriela Mistral (Chile)
1966 Nelly Sachs (Sweden)
1991 Nadine Gordimer (South Africa)
1994 Toni Morrison (U.S.)

THE POETS

624. *Sappho* (c. 610–c. 580 B.C.E.)

Sappho was so highly regarded among Greek poets of her time that Plato dubbed her the Tenth Muse. She wrote nine books of lyric poetry and influenced many later Greek poets, but only one of her poems and a few fragments survive. Among other achievements, she created the verse form called Sapphics. She lived on Lesbos, an island in the Aegean, where her writings suggest she had a devoted following of female students. Her intensely erotic poems show she had passionate relationships with, or at least feelings for, other women. As a result, scholars have speculated that she led a virtual cult of young girls, and that sex among members was rampant. According to another legend, she jumped to her death from a cliff because of her unrequited love for a sailor. Wherever the truth lies, her name and that of her home have evolved into terms for female homosexuality.

625. *Al-Khansa* (600–675)

Along with her daughter Amra, this contemporary of the prophet Muhammad composed elegiac verse. Her poetry, written in Arabic, memorialized her father and brothers, killed in war.

626. *Renaissance Poets*

The sixteenth century saw a flowering of poetry—especially love poetry—by women, earning a respected place in literary history for a number of them. Among the most celebrated were: from England, the two Mary Sidneys, Lady Wroth and the Countess of Pembroke; from France, Marguerite d'Angoulême, Madeleine and Catherine des Roches and Loise Labé; from

Sappho.

Italy, Vittoria Colonna, Isabella di Morra, Veronica Gambara and the Venetian courtesans Veronica Franco and Gaspara Stampa; from Mexico, the nun Sor Juana Inés de la Cruz.

627. Anne Bradstreet (1612–1672)

The daughter of a prosperous English family, Anne Bradstreet moved to New England in 1630. She dedicated herself to raising a family in Puritan Massachusetts, but she could not quell the urge to write poetry. In 1650 her collected work was published in England as *The Tenth Muse, Lately Sprung Up in America,* the first volume of poetry produced in the New World. The poems in this book reveal Bradstreet's struggle to come to terms with Puritan strictures on women's duties and education, but her later works—*Meditations Divine and Moral* and *Upon the Burning of Our House*—express a profound and tranquil piety. Her poetry has since been viewed critically, but Bradstreet's stature as America's first woman poet remains uncontested.

628. Anna Seward (1747–1809)

Known as the "Swan of Lichfield," this English poet wrote elegies, sonnets and a poetic novel, *Louisa* (1782). She was a good friend of the famous Dr. Samuel Johnson, whose idiosyncratic literary style she imitated in a collection of letters published in 1811. Her familiarity with Johnson lent some of the color to James Boswell's famous biography of the man, as Boswell mined her for details about her townsman's life. Sir Walter Scott published Seward's poetry along with a memoir of her life in *Lady of the Lake* (1810).

629. Charlotte Smith (1749–1806)

The mother of ten children, Smith took up a literary career to support her family when her husband was sent to debtor's prison. She became one of the most prolific English writers of her time, publishing more than twenty novels and poetry collections. Her work is most significant for its tremendous impact on Romantic poets such as William Wordsworth, Samuel Coleridge and Elizabeth Barrett Browning.

Phillis Wheatley.

630. Phillis Wheatley (c. 1753–1784)

The African-born Wheatley arrived in Boston via slave ship in 1761, at the age of about seven. She was purchased to serve as the personal servant to a local tailor's wife, who recognized the young girl's potential and allowed her to acquire an education. Wheatley's poise and wit soon dazzled prominent colonists such as George Washington and John Hancock, and before she was twenty she published her first poem. Moving to England with the son of her mistress, she so impressed society figures that she was able to publish a book, *Poems on Various Subjects, Religious and Moral.* Returning to Boston, she was eventually freed, but her influential patrons forgot her and she died in poverty. The only book by the first African-American woman poet appeared posthumously in America in 1786.

631. Elizabeth Barrett Browning
(1806–1861)

More famous in her time than her husband, poet Robert Browning, Elizabeth Barrett Browning was the highly educated and intellectually gifted product of a prosperous English family. By the time she eloped with Browning from under the thumb of a tyrannical father, in 1845, she had published essays, Greek translations and poetry, including *The Seraphim* (1838). Forbidden by her father to marry at all, she fell in love with the brilliant but as yet little known Robert Browning, six years her junior, married him secretly and fled to France and Italy. There she met luminaries such as George Sand, Harriet Beecher Stowe and Margaret Fuller. Her work flourished and she published increasingly ambitious and successful works, political as well as Romantic in content. The collection *Poems* (1850) was followed in 1851 by her famous *Sonnets from the Portuguese, Casa Guidi Windows* and other works. Her epic

Elizabeth Barrett Browning.

Aurora Leigh appeared in 1856 and *Poems before Congress* in 1860, shortly before her death. Robert Browning published her *Last Poems* posthumously. Although she was one of the nineteenth century's greatest poets, Elizabeth Barrett Browning is today more widely known for her romance with Robert Browning and her lifelong addiction to drugs.

632. Emily Dickinson (1830–1886)

One of the most fabled figures in American literature, the "Myth of Amherst" is as famous for her eccentric life as for her matchless poetry. Quirky and engaging as a child, she had an apparently normal upbringing and attended Mount Holyoke for a year. From that point on, however, she became increasingly withdrawn, started dressing entirely in white and ventured off her father's Amherst, Massachusetts, property less and less often. Finally, she stopped leaving the house altogether, refused to see visitors and spent almost all her time in her room. Even in her final illness, she allowed a doctor to "examine" her only from a distance as she passed once behind a partly open doorway. Publishing only eight poems during her lifetime, Dickinson left behind a total of 1,776, neatly written out and hand-bound in little books hidden in her room. This verse came to be recognized as some of the most brilliant ever produced in the English language. Phrased and metered with tremendous economy and art, Dickinson's poetry reveals towering intellect, singular wit and searing passion all the more startling for the seemingly confined life she led. She was undeniably agoraphobic, a condition many scholars blamed on a failed love affair with an unidentified man. But hints dropped to friends and family indicate Dickinson viewed her isolation as a form of freedom and consciously used her idiosyncrasies to construct a literary persona that would long outlive her.

633. Christina Rossetti (1830–1894)

The English-born daughter of Italian émigrés, Christina Rossetti associated with a sophisticated London community of writers, political theorists and artists that included Algernon Swinburne and Edith Sitwell. Privately publishing her first volume of poetry when she was seventeen, she lived at home throughout her adulthood, working for various charitable causes. Rossetti was a fervently pious Anglican, yet she conducted a series of feverish and frustrated love affairs. This duality shows up in her poetry, which reflects both deep religious devotion and seething sensuality. Her seven volumes of verse received an enthusiastic critical response, most notably *Goblin Market* (1862), *The Prince's Progress* (1866) and *A Pageant* (1881).

634. Amy Lowell (1874–1925)

The Boston family into which Amy Lowell was born might more accurately be called an institution: Among other distinguished members it included a president of Harvard University, a board member of MIT and the poet James Russell Lowell (her cousin). Talented but troubled, Lowell was largely self-educated and went through the motions of Boston Brahmin ladyhood. Then, in 1902, she attended a performance by the celebrated Italian actress Eleanora Duse that inspired her to follow her literary ambitions. Ten years later she published a mediocre book of verse, but she did not achieve poetical distinction until she encountered Ezra Pound, H.D., Robert Frost and other Imagist poets. Her *Can Grande's Castle* (1918) and *Pictures of the Floating World* (1919) secured her place among the leading Imagists, while *Tendencies in Modern American Poetry* (1917) revealed her import as a critic. Many of her love poems were addressed to Ada Russell, her lifetime companion.

635. H. D. (1886–1972)

Pennsylvania-born Hilda Doolittle failed English at Bryn Mawr College and became engaged to Ezra Pound before moving to London with him and publishing her first poems in 1912. It was Pound who first dubbed her "H.D. Imagiste," for her word-association brand of poetry, before their relationship deteriorated. Under her initials she published her first collection, *Sea Garden,* in 1916, whose poems voiced disgust at the manly art of war and insistence on the need for spiritual renewal. Marrying, bearing a child, divorcing, losing friends and family to war, and carrying on a variety of relationships with men and women, H.D. published *Hymen* (1921), *Heliodora and Other Poems* (1924), *Collected Poems* (1925) and *Red Roses for Bronze* (1931). She also wrote a number of novels and short stories, including the autobiographical *HERmione* (1923). Her personal conflicts landed her on Freud's psychoanalytic couch in 1933 and 1934, spawning the verse *Tribute to Freud* (1944). She continued to fall in and out of love, struggle with emotional problems and compose verse until her death, notably two epic poems, *Trilogy* (1944–1946) and *Helen in Egypt* (1961), both written in reaction to the horrors of World War II.

636. *Marianne Moore* (1887–1972)

Living most of her life with her mother and working as a secretary and librarian, Marianne Moore wrote striking verse that revolutionized American poetry. Alongside her quiet domestic existence she mingled with the creative elite of New York's Greenwich Village. Her first collection, *Poems* (1921), was published by fellow poet H.D. without the modest Moore's knowledge, but Moore soon jumped into the literary world with both feet, publishing *Observations* in 1924 and serving as editor of the literary magazine *The Dial* from 1925 to 1929. It was not until 1935 that she published another book, *Selected Poems,* which remains among the most highly respected of her works. Her compressed, oddly metered verse, often filled with obscure quotations, won her the Pulitzer prize in 1951. By that time Moore had become an American institution, known for her tricornered hat and her passion for baseball.

637. *Anna Akhmatova* (1888–1966)

Born Anna Andreyevna Gorenko, this lyric poet ranks among Russia's best. In the first decades of the twentieth century she was a leader of the Acmeist movement that promoted realism over symbolism in poetry. Works such as her *Vecher* (1912) and *Chetki* (1914) reflect this point of view, expressing romantic scenes and feelings in precise detail. The movement rankled Communist authorities, who saw Acmeist works as too individualistic, prompting Akhmatova to generate patriotic poems such as *Anno domini MXMXXI* (1922). The poem commemorated the formation of the Soviet Union, but Joseph Stalin's government viewed Akhmatova as a threat nonetheless. In an attempt to silence her, Stalin had her son imprisoned; she continued to write, producing *Requiem,* her masterpiece, and *Iva* during this period. Her last poems, works of stunning visual beauty, included the autobiographical *Poema bez geroya* (1962).

638. *Nelly Sachs* (1891–1970)

The literary fascism and ruthless oppression practiced by the Nazis forced many German writers to leave their homeland during World War II. Among the expatriates was Nelly Sachs, who settled permanently in Sweden in 1940. Writing in German, she produced a major body of lyrical verse including the collections *In den Wohnungen des Todes* (1946) and *Flucht und Verwandlung* (1959). Poems such as "O the Chimneys," a poignant commemoration of the Jewish Holocaust, made her a co-winner of the Nobel Prize in Literature in 1966.

639. Edna St. Vincent Millay
(1892–1950)

Even before she entered Vassar College, Millay had won wide popularity as a poet, publishing *Renascence,* one of the best-known poems of her career, in 1912. She became a prominent citizen of Jazz Age Greenwich Village and continued to write lyrical poetry characterized by readily accessible content and meter. Her celebrity peaked in 1923, when she won the Pulitzer prize for *The Harp-Weaver,* but in the 1930s her career waned. Millay continued to write and became active in various political causes, but she never again achieved the kind of fame that had come to her so early. In the decades to come, young poets distanced themselves from her work, which seemed conventional and even commercial, yet Millay remains the poet most familiar to the general public.

640. Elizabeth Bishop (1911–1979)

This American poet, winner of a 1955 Pulitzer prize and a 1969 National Book Award, earned the admiration of critics and writers both during her life and after her death. Her work blends precise contemplations on emotional and spiritual matters with meticulous descriptions of the physical world. She started publishing while still a student at Vassar College and became a protégée of Marianne Moore. After her graduation she took up a life of almost perpetual travel, settling in Brazil from 1951 to 1966. Her work—volumes such as *North & South* (1946), *Questions of Travel* (1965) and *Geography III* (1976)—display Bishop's preoccupation with places and their meaning.

641. Anne Sexton (1928–1974) and Sylvia Plath (1932–1963)

Although their work is quite different in terms of style, these two poets sounded similar themes. Born four years apart, both grew up in middle-class Massachusetts families. Sexton's childhood was marked by emotional problems and Plath's by the death of her father, but where Sexton displayed no particular talent and dropped out of junior college after a year, Plath started writing and publishing very young and excelled in her studies at Smith College. Marrying in 1948, Sexton settled in suburban Boston and had two daughters—as well as several nervous breakdowns that repeatedly landed her in the hospital. Showered with honors and awards, Plath had her own breakdown and attempted suicide in 1954, an experience she later fictionalized in the novel *The Bell Jar* (1963). She graduated from Smith in 1955, went to Cambridge on a Fullbright and there married English poet Ted Hughes before returning to Smith as a teacher. About this time, Sexton started taking poetry workshops in Boston and met Plath in a class taught by Robert Lowell. The two became friends as each worked to perfect her own brand of "confessional" poetry based on the agony of her personal life. Both published their first books in 1960, Sexton *To Bedlam and Part Way Back* and Plath *The Colossus.* Returning to England, Plath had two children before her marriage ended in 1962. Her poetry became even more intense as she struggled with single motherhood and inner demons. Finally, in February 1963, she killed herself in the gas oven of her London flat. Her late, and most famous, verse was published later that year in the collection *Ariel.* Equally troubled, Sexton wrote at a furious pace even as she sank into alcoholism and drug addiction and fought the stupor induced by the Thorazine prescribed by her psychiatrist. Between 1962 and 1972 she published five volumes of poetry, including the Pulitzer prize–winning *Live or Die* (1966), arousing criticism for her explicit treatment of masturbation, incest and other taboo subjects. Sexton succumbed to despair in the fall of 1974, gassing herself in her car. Two books, *The Awful Rowing Toward God* (1975) and *45 Mercy Street* (1976), appeared after her death. Linked by their tormented lives and outspoken, introspective work, Sexton and Plath exposed harsh truths about women's lives in the twentieth century.

642. Adrienne Rich (1929–)

Highly respected as a poet, Adrienne Rich has also written important essays and books on feminist topics. She graduated from Radcliffe in 1951 and published her first collection of poems, *A Change of World,* as a winner of the Yale Younger Poets award before marrying a Harvard professor in 1953. In the ensuing decade she had three sons and published two more collections of precise, carefully metered verse. Rich moved to New York City with her family in 1966 and got involved with the anti-war, civil rights and women's movements. Like her politics, her poetry became freer; it also started to focus on political concerns, as in *The Will to Change* (1971). She divorced in 1970 and in 1973 published *Diving into the Wreck,* a personal and political collection that won the National Book Award. Rich started teaching and immersed herself in lesbian feminism, producing her groundbreaking prose work, *Of Woman Born: Motherhood as Experience and Institution,* and her bold *Twenty-one Love Poems* in 1976. Moving to Massachusetts to edit the journal *Sinister Wisdom,* Rich penned the books *The Dream of a Common Language* (1978) and *Your Native Land, Your Life* (1986). Her most recent work is *An Atlas of the Difficult World* (1992). One of her generations most gifted poets, Rich has used her work to explore the politics of gender and oppression.

643. Audre Lorde (1934–1990)

This African-American poet used her work to cry out against racism, homophobia, sexism and classism. A teacher of creative writing at Tougaloo College in Mississippi and John Jay and Hunter colleges in New York City, she wrote verse that combined mythical imagery and everyday reality. She published nearly a dozen collections of poetry, including *Cables to Rage* (1970) and *The Black Unicorn* (1978), and the autobiographical *The Cancer Journals* (1980) and *Zami: A New Spelling of My Name* (1982).

AN APPETITE FOR WORDS

644. *Renaissance Readers*

The vast majority of literate Renaissance women did not read or write Latin, the traditional language of learning. Instead, they were fluent in the languages used in daily life. These readers created a demand for books in the vernacular, which before the 1450 invention of Western printing included devotional, how-to, poetry and romance titles. After 1450, women represented a large market for the emerging publishing industry. Printers produced hundreds of titles specifically for female audiences in the next two centuries, most of them how-to texts on childbirth, household management and other practical topics. Works of romance, biography and history rounded out the list of vernacular books, with religious books rapidly waning in importance.

645. *Autobiography and Memoir*

Excluded from formal education and worldly pursuits, most women writers of the Middle Ages turned inward for their subject matter. Women's writing assumed a highly personal character, couching self-reflection in everyday language. This character permeates the earliest known example of autobiography, Margery Kempe's *The Book of Margery Kempe,* published about 1436. From the fifteenth century to the present day, the female sensibility has generated many distinguished works of autobiography and memoir, such as George Sand's *My Life,* Linda Brent's *Incidents in the Life of a Slave Girl,* Gertrude Stein's *The Autobiography of Alice B. Toklas* and Janet Frame's *An Angel at My Table.*

646. *Alice James* (1848–1892)

The sister of novelist Henry James faced intense sibling rivalry in pursuit of her literary ambitions, but this did not dampen her enthusiasm. A towering figure in American letters, Henry revealed an unusual sensitivity to women's emotions in works such as *Daisy Miller* (1879), *The Portrait of a Lady* (1881) and *The Bostonians* (1886). When it came to his memoirist sister, however, he apparently shed this empathy. He dismissed Alice's journals as worthless and prevented them from being published until more than forty years after her death. *Alice James, Her Brothers—Her Journal* finally appeared in 1934.

647. *Letter Writing*

The art of letter writing has traditionally been a woman's art, largely because it was for many centuries one of the few acceptable forms of literary expression open to women. Women such as Queen Isabella, Madame de Staël and Virginia Woolf rank among the greatest letter writers in history. Many letters elegantly served practical, informative purposes, while others were composed as literature and published in collections. The medium allowed women to experiment with the writer's tools and become highly skilled in their use, enticing them to try their hand in different forms. One product of women's wide experience as correspondents is the epistolary novel, one of the earliest manifestations of the novel. Aphra Behn's *Love Letters*

Alice Walker.

Between a Nobleman and His Sister, published around 1683, is recognized as the first novel written in English. It established the epistolary genre, which has been carried on by women from Fanny Burney (1752–1840) to Jane Austen (1775–1817) to Alice Walker (1944–   ).

648. Reading Rage

At the start of the nineteenth century, educated women took up secular reading as never before. Reading provided women a much-needed escape from the confines of daily life and unhappy marriages, in some cases replacing reality altogether. Fed by their appetite, the publishing industry thrived, especially when it came to novels of every description. As the century progressed, the quest for knowledge replaced the desire to escape as women's main motivation for reading. Women took up periodicals and books of nonfiction to learn about the world around them, and reading groups formed in European and American cities, towns and villages.

649. Godey's Lady's Book

In 1828, *Ladies' Magazine* started publication, bringing American women articles on motherhood, fashion and homemaking as well as bland features and innocuous short stories. Purchased by Louis Godey in 1837, the magazine changed its name to *Godey's Lady's Book.* For several decades it remained the preeminent women's magazine in America, helping to shape the attitudes and values of the nation's women. Its first serious competition emerged in 1883, when *Ladies' Home Journal* began printing advice columns and articles by well-known authors. *Good Housekeeping* appeared in 1885 and *Vogue* in 1893, and in 1898 *Godey's* went out of business.

650. Women of Mystery

Women have figured prominently in the development of the mystery novel from its origins in the nineteenth century, both as creators and as audience. In 1878 Anna Katharine Green wrote *The Leavenworth Case,* the first American detective novel. Looming large in the early fiction of murder and mayhem were the English writer Dorothy Sayers, creator of the detective Lord Peter Wimsey, and the Americans Mary Roberts Rinehart and Carolyn Wells. Perhaps the most famous of all mystery writers was Agatha Christie, whose career lasted from 1920 to her death in 1976. Creator of the fictional detectives Hercule Poirot and Miss Marple, Christie wrote seventy-five books that have sold over 100 million copies and have been turned into movies and television series. She also wrote plays such as *The Mousetrap* (1952) and *Witness for the Prosecution* (1953), best known via its 1957 film version. The other reigning English mystery writer is P. D. James, whose stories are known for their subtlety and literary distinction. In the last two decades of the twentieth century, American women such as Sue Grafton, Sara Paretsky, Patricia Cornwell and Mary Higgins Clark have burst on the scene with blockbuster bestsellers. Their female protagonists share an intrepid self-assurance that has won a loyal female—as well as male—readership.

651. Steamy Stories

Love, perhaps the first and almost a universal topic of literature, has inspired many magnificent novels since the form was invented. In the second half of the twentieth century the romance novel has taken a decidedly prosaic turn, appealing to the escapist fantasies of millions of women worldwide. Not only does the vast female readership for mass-market romance represent a phenomenon in itself, it has opened opportunities for women writers interested in commercial success. From Jacqueline Susann, pioneering author of the racy *Valley of the Dolls,* to the scores of formula contributors to the mild Harlequin Romance series, women have produced the lion's share of titles in this genre. Indeed, some of the bestselling authors of all time are women who write fat volumes of fast-paced fiction filled with gorgeous heroes, ravishing heroines, glamorous settings and breathless quasi-sex. Danielle Steel, author of more than thirty such confections, has sold 175 million copies of her work worldwide and has seen a number of her stories translated into television miniseries. Judith Krantz, Jackie Collins, Barbara Taylor Bradford and a cadre of others

have enjoyed similar popularity, generating large revenues for the publishing industry.

THE JOURNALISTS

652. Ida Wells Barnett

This journalist championed the cause of African-American civil rights in the post–Civil War period and helped advance the interests of African-Americans into the twentieth century. The daughter of former slaves, she obtained her elementary teaching license by the time she was twenty. But she found her true calling in 1884, while traveling on a first-class railroad ticket. Refusing to move to the smoking car when white passengers objected to her presence, she was forcibly removed by several conductors. She sued the railroad and won her case, then wrote a newspaper piece about her experience. Before long, her articles were appearing in African-American newspapers nationwide. Never hesitating to express her outrage about racism, Wells Barnett made it known she packed a pistol. In 1892, when a close friend was brutally lynched, she used her pen to condemn the culprits and to castigate unresponsive local officials. She then made an exhaustive study of 728 lynchings that had occurred over the past decade and published her findings along with a call for national action on the issue. Her relentless drive to publicize the atrocities faced by African-Americans soon forced reluctant white officials to take a public stand against lynching. At the same time, she

leading politicians and entertainers of her day. She did not join the staff of any one newspaper or magazine, preferring instead to choose the best freelance assignments that came her way. Likewise, she maintained a free-spirited skepticism about women's conventional roles, an attitude that helped shape her fifty-year career.

Ida Wells Barnett.

Frances Benjamin Johnston.

helped organize the National Association of Colored Women to work for racial equality and women's rights, and in 1909 she attended the founding conference of the NAACP, where she was named one of forty founding members. Today, Wells Barnett is viewed as a major figure in the birth of the civil rights movement.

653. *Frances Benjamin Johnston* (1864–1952)

Perhaps America's first photojournalist, Johnston went to work as a news and features photographer in 1888. Her photographs addressed various social issues and portrayed the

654. *Nellie Bly* (1867–1922)

Under this pseudonym, Elizabeth Cochrane Seaman helped invent the provocative, reform-oriented journalistic form known as muckraking. Her biting exposés on prison conditions, political corruption, slum squalor and factory abuses appeared in the *Pittsburgh Dispatch*,

the *New York World* and the *New York Journal.*
Two stunts earned her international fame: In
1888 she went undercover as a patient for ten
days at the infamous mental hospital on New
York City's Blackwell's Island, and in 1889 to
1890 she broke all records by completing a
round-the-world trip by sea, rail and auto in sev-
enty-two days, six hours and eleven minutes.
Her books *Ten Days in a Madhouse* (1888) and
*Nellie Bly's Book: Around the World in Seventy-
two Days* (1890) became bestsellers.

655. *Dorothy Thompson* (1893–1961)

As a radio, newspaper and magazine journalist,
Thompson covered the major issues of international politics from the 1920s through the 1950s.
An American, she spent the first decade of her
career in Europe, writing from Vienna and
Berlin for the Independent News Service, the
Philadelphia Public Ledger and the *New York
Evening Post.* It was in Berlin that she broke
the biggest story of her career. In 1931 she in-
terviewed politician-on-the-make Adolf Hitler
for *Cosmopolitan* magazine, writing him off as
"inconsequent and voluble . . . ill-poised, inse-
cure." However, the rapid mutation of the
German political scene soon convinced her that
Hitler posed a serious threat to world peace.
She filled her articles with warnings to the rest
of the world, for which she was expelled from
Germany in 1934. Back home, she continued to
campaign for American intervention in Europe
via a column in the *New York Herald Tribune*
and as a commentator on NBC radio. Once the
U.S. entered World War II, Thompson's career
started to decline; her post-war support of
Palestinian Arabs diminished her popularity
even more.

656. *The Divas of Dish*

Perhaps the hottest media rivalry of golden-age
Hollywood involved not actresses or directors
but two journalists. From the 1920s to the
1960s, gossip columnists Louella Parsons and
Hedda Hopper documented the private lives and
peccadilloes of the stars for movie fans nationwide. Originally a film writer for the *Chicago
Record-Herald,* Parsons launched her column in
1922; the Hearst publishing empire syndicated
it to more than four hundred newspapers.
Hopper, who started out as a film actress, inaugurated a radio show in 1936 and her column in
1938. The alliances and antagonisms each
formed in the film industry, as well as their
fierce competition for influence, made the two
columnists as famous as the celebrities they
covered.

657. *Barbara Tuchman* (1912–1989)

This Pulitzer prize–winning American author
and journalist wrote on politics and history. As a
correspondent for *The Nation,* she covered the
Spanish Civil War from 1936 to 1939, and during
World War II she worked as an editor at the U.S.
Office of War Information. Although she had no
formal training, she then turned to writing history. *The Guns of August,* her account of the beginnings of World War I, won the 1960 Pulitzer
prize, and in 1971 she received the prize again,
for *Stilwell and the American Experience in
China: 1911–45.* Her work not only received
critical acclaim but enjoyed great popularity
with the reading public. She died while *The
First Salute,* a history of the American
Revolution, was on the *New York Times*'s bestseller list.

658. Katharine Graham
(1917–   )

Since 1963, when she took over as chairman and chief executive officer of the Washington Post Company, Katharine Graham has established herself as one of the most powerful women in the U.S. Her media empire includes not only the highly regarded newspaper but *Newsweek* magazine, a number of other publishing concerns and at least half a dozen television stations scattered across the country. Known as an astute businesswoman with keen journalistic senses, Graham has guided her company to success by maintaining close control over its daily operations.

659. Sisterly Advice

As Ann Landers and Abigail "Dear Abby" Van Buren, a pair of identical twin sisters have reigned as twentieth-century America's most celebrated confidantes. Esther "Eppie" Pauline Friedman Lederer (Ann) and Pauline Esther Friedman Phillips (Abby) collaborated on high

Katharine Graham.

school and college gossip columns and went into the advice business as friendly rivals in the mid-1950s. In 1955 Eppie took over the "Ann Landers" advice column at the *Chicago Sun-Times,* while Pauline inaugurated "Dear Abby" in 1956. "Ann Landers" took a good-humored, common-sense approach to life's problems and was ultimately carried by about a thousand newspapers worldwide. Somewhat spicier but equally down to earth, "Dear Abby" reached more than eighty newspapers within a year and five hundred by 1960. Both sisters have also published a number of advice books.

660. TV News Pioneers

Today, women are highly visible in the field of television reporting, in part because since the mid-1970s news divisions have responded to pressure to hire more women. But women journalists have been a part of television from the start. Pauline Frederick started reporting on television in the early 1950s, first at ABC and then at NBC, where she was a prominent UN correspondent until her retirement in 1975. Nancy Dickerson, the first woman reporter at *CBS Evening News,* signed on in 1962 and became the first woman to report for television from the floor of a national party convention. At ABC, Marlene Sanders substituted for a sick colleague in 1964, becoming the first woman ever to anchor a network newscast; she later served as a war correspondent in Vietnam and in 1976 became the industry's first network news vice president. Also in 1976, Angela Rippon joined the BBC as its first female newscaster and first female anchor.

661. Barbara Walters (1931–)

The first woman hired as a permanent anchor for a network television news show, Walters has achieved fame as a skillful interviewer who elicits startlingly candid revelations from her subjects. Starting out as a producer of women's and public-affairs programming with various stations, she joined NBC in 1961 as a writer and reporter for the *Today* show. She started appearing on the show in 1963 and rose to the co-host chair opposite Jim Hartz in 1974. Her coverage of events such as President Richard Nixon's historic visit to China added to her growing reputation, and in 1976 she became a household name when first ABC and then NBC offered her a salary of $1 million a year. She accepted ABC's offer because of the opportunity to co-anchor the evening news with Harry Reasoner, but the arrangement did not work out and she moved to ABC's *20/20*. While serving as a correspondent and then as co-host with Hugh Downs, she launched her occasional series of interview shows, the *Barbara Walters Specials.* Her subjects have included President Jimmy Carter and First Lady Rosalynn Carter, Fidel Castro, the Shah of Iran and Muammar Qaddafi, as well as numerous Hollywood and media celebrities.

662. TV News Producers

Particularly when it comes to producing, the world of television news has always been dominated by men. A number of women, however, have made significant inroads into the field: *NBC News* documentary producer Lucy Jarvis, creator of news specials such as *Khrushchev in Exile: His Opinions and Revelations* (1967) and *Dr. Barnard's Heart Transplant Operations* (1968); Joan Konner, dean of the Graduate School of Journalism at Columbia University since 1988 and former producer of WNET's *Bill Moyers' Journal* and various Moyers specials; Pam Hill, vice president and executive producer of CNN's investigative news division, who built her reputation as producer and director of controversial documentaries for the ABC series *White Paper, Comment* and *ABC Close-Up;* and Trina McQueen, Canadian Broadcasting Company's (CBC) first woman vice president and head of network news operations.

663. The Women of 60 Minutes

On the air since 1968, the influential weekly television news program *60 Minutes* did not hire a female correspondent until 1984. That year, Diane Sawyer joined the show from the *CBS Morning News,* where she had worked as a reporter and co-anchor since 1978. A former press secretary to President Richard Nixon, Sawyer garnered praise for her *60 Minutes* segments on various world leaders and on Velma Barfield, the first American woman executed in over twenty years; the stepchildren of murder suspect Claus von Bulow; and U.S. Navy Admiral Hyman Rickover. She left the show in 1989 to become co-host with Sam Donaldson of ABC's *Prime Time Live. 60 Minutes* replaced her with Meredith Viera, a dynamic young reporter from CBS's cutting-edge news magazine *West 57th.* Her 1991 departure from *60 Minutes* was precipitated by her pregnancy. With Viera's exit, Lesley Stahl joined the show from her post as moderator of the network's *Face the Nation.* A former White House correspondent, Stahl has interviews with Margaret Thatcher, President George Bush, Boris Yeltsin and other political leaders to her credit. She has distinguished herself as a tough and incisive reporter, bringing new life to a show weakened by an aging and increasingly toothless staff.

664. Connie Chung (1946–)

The first Asian-American to work as permanent anchor on a national newscast at a major network, Chung has had a distinguished television journalism career. Getting her start at a local Washington, D.C., station in 1969, she moved to CBS in 1971. Until 1983 she served as anchor at the network's Los Angeles affiliate, subsequently spending six years on national news programs at NBC. When Diane Sawyer left CBS for ABC in 1989, CBS hired Chung back at close to $1 million a year. She anchored several magazine-style news shows as well as the Sunday edition of the *Evening News* until joining Dan Rather as co-anchor of the broadcast's daily edition in 1994. Partly as the result of poor chemistry between the two anchors and partly as the result of Chung's desire to start a family, she soon left that post.

GLOBAL EXPRESSION

665. China

A number of women figure prominently in China's literary history. From the third to the seventh centuries, the political upheaval surrounding the fall of the Han dynasty, the brief reign of the Sui dynasty and the rise of the T'ang dynasty produced a martial climate reflected in the work of Tzu-yeh. The author of some of China's finest folk lyrics, she wrote the *Ballad of Mulan,* the heroic tale of a woman soldier who passed as a man, and *The Peacock Flew to the Southeast,* an epic of family tragedy. Another of China's leading poets, Li Ch'ing-chao (1081–c. 1141), also worked in a musically based form, the *tz'u,* which developed with the flowering of Chinese culture during the T'ang period (618–907). She wrote exceptionally moving *tz'u* on the subject of her own widowhood.

666. Japan

Besides Murasaki Shikibu (author of *The Tale of Genji,* c. 1020), several other women made important contributions to Japanese literature. In the ninth century, the work of Princess Irge won wide acclaim, while Sei Shonagon, an aristocratic contemporary of Shikibu, wrote a witty account of courtly life. Published before *The Tale of Genji,* Shonagon's *Makura-no-soshi* ("The Pillow-Book") presents the less exalted side of Heian society in a series of sketches. A nonfiction glimpse into patrician life appeared in the mid-eleventh century: *Sarashima Nikki,* a memoir by Lady Sarashima (c. 1008–1060), also known as Takasue-no-Musume. Two centuries later, a nun named Abutsu published a literary memoir, *Diary of the Waning Moon* (1277), which includes both prose and striking poetry. After Japan ended its isolation from the Western world, writers started to blend Western techniques with traditional Japanese forms. Among these experimenters was Higuchi Ichiyo, who wrote collections of short stories, such as *Growing Up* (1896), on psychological themes.

667. India

India's long and rich literary heritage includes relatively few renowned works by women. Before the modern day, when significant numbers of Indian women first attained literacy, only the highly privileged had access to the written word. One such woman, the sixteenth-century Rajasthani princess and poet Mira Bai, wrote lyric poetry to the god Krishna. Her work is suffused with bhakti, a ritualized form of ecstatic love and personal devotion to a deity. In the eighteenth century, Gauribai of Gujarat also wrote religious poetry, expressing the passions of Hindu mysticism. British colonialism completely changed the face of Indian culture and literature. Many poets, such as Sarojini Naidu (1879–1949), started to write in English. Known as the "nightingale of India," Naidu published *The Golden Threshold*, *The Broken Wing* and other popular works. Today, some Indian authors address themes of nostalgia for the past. The novelist Anita Desai, for instance, explores these feelings in *Clear Light of Day* (1980) and *In Custody* (1984), a tragedy about a teacher obsessed with poetry.

668. Scandinavian Trio

The literary pantheon of twentieth-century Scandinavia includes three prominent women, all of them novelists. In Sweden the neoromantic movement of the late nineteenth century produced Selma Lagerlöf, whose works reflect the era's renewed interest in Swedish history and country living. Best known among them are the historical novel *The Story of Gösta Berling* (1891) and the children's story *The Wonderful Adventures of Nils* (1901–1902). A similar appreciation for history showed up in *Kristin Lavransdatter* (1920–1922), the Nobel prize–winning trilogy by Norwegian Sigrid Undset. Its depiction of medieval Norway transports readers back in time by way of psychological realism. By contrast, Denmark's most famous novelist employed symbolism and fable in much of her work. Isak Dinesen (Karen Blixen) gained international recognition with *Seven Gothic Tales* (1934); she took a completely different tack in the even more famous *Out of Africa* (1937), an autobiographical work.

669. Down Under

Women have had a tremendous impact on Australian literature, especially with regard to the novel. Writing under the pseudonym Miles Franklin, Stella Maria Sarah Miles Franklin portrayed the hard life of a woman in the outback in *My Brilliant Career* (1901). Another pseudonymous writer, Henry Handel Richardson (Ethel Florence Lindesay Richardson), greatly advanced Australian fiction via her trilogy, *The Fortunes of Richard Mahony* (1917–1929). A genius of psychological realism, Richardson tells the story of a disaffected Irish doctor against the backdrop of the Australian gold rushes of the 1850s. Equally unsparing in her view of her homeland was Katharine Susannah Prichard, a Communist whose fiction addressed class struggle in Australia. The labor saga *Working Bullocks* (1926) and the racially charged *Coonardoo* (1930) earned wide acclaim, but her goldfields trilogy (1946–1950), a work of historical realism with a strong feminist message, is viewed as her best effort. A writer with a more inward perspective, Eleanor Dark wrote both historical and contemporary mid-century novels of keen emotional insight. Kylie Tennant, meanwhile, vividly depicted the seamier side of Australian life from a comic point of view, in such works as *The Joyful Condemned* (1953) and *The Battlers* (1954). Also renowned worldwide are Christina Stead, author of *The Man Who Loved Children* (1940) and *The Little Hotel* (1973), and Elizabeth Jolley, author of *Miss Peabody's Inheritance* (1984) and *Foxybaby* (1985).

670. South Africa

From its beginning, the literature of white South Africa—written mainly in English—has concerned itself mainly with that country's racial problems. Several women have produced significant works on the topic, including Olive Schreiner, who wrote a daring early treatment of racial and sexual relations in *The Story of an African Farm* (1883). In the twentieth century, the focus shifted to apartheid's impact on individual people. Doris Lessing's *Children of Violence* novels (1950–1969) follows a protagonist, Martha Quest, as she struggles to cope with the conflicts between races and classes. In novels and short stories that were at times banned in South Africa, Nadine Gordimer fearlessly exposed the horrors of apartheid. Praised for novels such as *A Guest of Honour* (1970) and

Burger's Daughter (1979), she won the 1991 Nobel Prize for Literature.

671. The Canadians

Canada's literary scene has produced a number of noted women writers. One of the best-known works of Canadian literature is *Anne of Green Gables* (1908), an idyllic rendering of life on Prince Edward Island written for children by Lucy Maud Montgomery. Setting her novels in British Columbia, Ethel Wilson explored women's quest for fulfillment in *The Equations of Love* (1952) and *Swamp Angel* (1954). Addressing similar themes, Margaret Laurence ranked among the best novelists of the 1960s and 1970s. Her works include *The Stone Angel* (1964), *A Jest of God* (1966) and *The Diviners* (1974). Emotions and relationships—especially those between women—are the province of Alice Munro, whose short-story collections include *Lives of Girls and Women* (1971). The later poetry of Dorothy Livesay also covers intimate territory, leaving behind her earlier political preoccupation for themes of love, marriage and motherhood. Her works include *The Unquiet Bed* (1967), *Collected Poems* (1972) and *The Phases of Love* (1982). Another Canadian poet has achieved international fame as a novelist: Margaret Atwood brings a distinctly feminist sensibility to widely varied stories about women in search of themselves. Her novels include *Surfacing* (1972), *Bodily Harm* (1981), *The Handmaid's Tale* (1986) and *The Robber Bride* (1995).

WRITERS OF MANY TALENTS

672. Gertrude Stein
(1874–1946)

Endowed with nicknames such as "the Mama of Dada," Gertrude Stein might well be called the mother of modernism. She was born in Oakland, California, and educated at the Harvard Annex (a precursor of Radcliffe College) and at Johns Hopkins University before dropping her medical education and moving to Paris with her brother Leo in 1902. The siblings soon met and started collecting the works of radical painters such as Cézanne, Matisse and Picasso. Stein sought a way to apply the principles of cubism to language, yielding the trilogy *Three Lives* in 1909. About that time she met Alice B. Toklas, who would become her lover and lifetime companion. The Stein-Toklas salon became the center of the Parisian avant-garde, the literary version of which Stein continued to pioneer. A massive history (*The Making of Americans*, 1911), a collection of prose poetry (*Tender Buttons*, 1914) and a play (*Four Saints in Three Acts*, 1927) made bold steps forward in English literature, but proved intimidating to mass audiences. She had her first commercial triumph with a portrait of her Parisian community, *The Autobiography of Alice B. Toklas* (1933), and earned further celebrity when composer Virgil Thomson turned *Four Saints* into an opera. Stein wrote several more books, including *Ida, a Novel* (1941), before her death, but she always regretted that "the American public were more interested in me than in my work."

673. Dorothy Parker
(1893–1967)

The empress of the famed Algonquin Round Table, the literary lunch group that met at New York's Algonquin Hotel in the 1920s and 1930s, Parker remains notable for her scorching wit. A writer for *Vogue* in 1916 and for *Vanity Fair* from 1917 to 1920, she served as a book reviewer for the *New Yorker* from 1927 to 1933. She also wrote poetry (*Enough Rope*, 1926; *Death and Taxes*, 1931; etc.) and short fiction (*After Such Pleasures*, 1933; *Here Lies*, 1939; etc.) that satirized modern mores. Parker had a talent for hilariously nasty one-liners made up on the spur of the moment, as well as for darkly humorous writing. In the poem "Résumé," for instance, she reflected: "Guns aren't lawful/Nooses give/Gas smells awful/You might as well live." Her wit camouflaged a stormy personal life that included a suicide attempt in 1923, and she embraced political causes that resulted in her Hollywood blacklisting in the 1940s. Still, she successfully collaborated on screenplays such as *A Star Is Born* (released 1955). Severely alcoholic in her later years, she suggested for her own epitaph: "Excuse my dust."

674. Stevie Smith (1902–1971)

The poetry and fiction of Stevie Smith (born Florence Margaret Smith) radiate a sometimes sharp but always humorous cynicism about English society in the twentieth century. Smith did not start writing until her early thirties, but she became widely read during her lifetime in her homeland. Her first book, one of three novels, was *Novel on Yellow Paper; or, Work It Out for Yourself* (1936), and her first of about a dozen books of poetry was *A Good Time Was Had by All* (1937). Smith's work is often dark, even morbid, but even at its bleakest it has an ironic edge that rescues it from misery.

675. *Lorraine Hansberry*
(1930–1965)

Essayist and playwright Lorraine Hansberry is most famous for her play *A Raisin in the Sun* (1959), the tale of a black family that moves to a white suburb. Produced when she was only twenty-nine, the play won the New York Drama Critics Award for Best Play of the Year. She continued working at *Freedom,* a progressive newspaper, and wrote about racism and sexism in works such as her 1959 speech, *The Negro Writer and His Roots: Toward a New Romanticism,* and her 1961 essay, *In Defense of the Equality of Men.* Her second play, *The Sign in Sidney Brustein's Window,* appeared in 1965, the year Hansberry died of cancer. Three plays and the biographical *To Be Young, Gifted and Black: Lorraine Hansberry in Her Own Words* (1969) were published posthumously.

676. *Ama Ata Aidoo* (1942–   )

One of Africa's finest contemporary writers, Ama Ata Aidoo has produced novels, short stories, plays and poetry that explore the evolution of African culture since the end of colonization. A teacher of English and African literature at the University of Ghana, Aidoo completed her first major work, a play called *Dilemma of a Ghost,* in 1965. Since then, her works have included the novel *Our Sister Killjoy, or Reflections from a Black-Eyed Squint* (1966), a collection of short stories called *No Sweetness*

Here (1969) and her second play, *Anowa* (1970). Each of her works reflects a poignancy and wry wit that allow her to delve into sometimes dark subject matter with compassion and hope. In the conflict between Western culture and the emerging civilization of modern Africa, she sees the potential for a promising future for African women.

MEN OF LETTERS ON WOMEN

677.

"Do not let a woman with a sexy rump deceive you with wheedling and coaxing words; she is after your barn. The man who trusts a woman trusts deceivers." —Hesiod (poet, eighth century B.C.E.)

678.

"Women, women! Cherished and deadly objects that nature has embellished to torture us . . . whose hatred and love are equally harmful, and whom we cannot either seek or flee with impunity!" —Jean-Jacques Rousseau (1712–1778)

679.

"Woman is a slave whom we must be clever enough to set upon a throne." —Honoré de Balzac (1799–1850)

680.

"The woman author does not exist. She is a contradiction in terms. The role of the woman in letters is the same as in manufacturing: she is of use when genius is no longer required." —Pierre-Joseph Proudhon (1809–1865)

681.

"Woman is natural, that is, abominable."
—Charles-Pierre Baudelaire (1821–1867)

Fictional Femmes

682. Classic Cases

Women are prominent in classical poetry, drama and prose written by men, much of which reflected a distinct bias. The literature depicts the good woman as submissive and the bad woman as assertive, that is, masculine. Composing the *Iliad* and the *Odyssey* in the eighth century B.C.E., Homer unjustly blamed the beautiful Helen for the protracted war between Greece and Troy. Three hundred years later Aeschylus depicted Helen's sister Clytemnestra—who cheated on and then murdered her husband—as a manipulative, devious woman who brazenly pursues political power and sexual freedom. In the *Eumenides,* the last play in the *Oresteia* trilogy, her son metes out justice by murdering her.

683. Pallas Athena/Minerva

One of the twelve great Olympians of Greek and Roman mythology, this daughter of Zeus/Jupiter had no mother but sprang from her father's head full grown. The guardian of civilized life, she appears in classical poetry as the personification of reason and wisdom; she was symbolized by the owl. She is also credited with the creation of the Greek alphabet, thereby endowing the people with literacy.

684. Antigone

The notion that women of action are essentially masculine dates back at least as far as ancient Greece. Sophocles created one such woman in his play *Antigone* (produced 441 B.C.E.), which depicts a power struggle between the title character and a tyrant. King Creon will not allow Antigone to bury her brother Polynices, who has betrayed his country. Rejecting her sister Ismene's counsel that women are born to be ruled by men, Antigone secretly buries Polynices. Creon assumes that only a man could have done the deed, provoking Antigone to claim responsibility. Denouncing her for acting like a man, Creon demands that she now behave as a woman. He has her entombed alive, where she grieves over her failure as a woman and, in the end, commits suicide.

685. A Truly Dark Age

Most European literature written before the Renaissance depicts women in a distinctly unflattering light. The Anglo-Saxon epic *Beowulf,* probably written in the eighth century, simply ignores women, except to depict them as servants, possessions or monsters. With the rise of Christianity, European literary misogyny found a new justification in the tale of Eve, whose original sin had sullied all humanity and doomed Christ to the cross. Largely religious in focus, the poetry of the Middle Ages recasts the story again and again, depicting women as temptresses who endanger men's virtue. Allegorical characters such as Hypocrisy, Fraud, Sacrilege and Pride were female; if not kept in check, women had voracious and perverse sexual appetites. Secular works have long depicted good women as silent and submissive, evil women as gossipy and overbearing.

686. *The Wife of Bath*

Chaucer's *Canterbury Tales* (c. 1390) include the tale of a feisty woman who declaims on the war between the sexes and scoffs at men's claims of superiority. At one point angered by the odious image of women conveyed by male-authored literature, the Wife of Bath declares, "By God, if wommen hadde writen stories/As clerkes han withinne hir oratories/They wolde han writen of men more wikkednesse/Than all the mark of Adam may redresse."

687. *Scheherazade*

A fabled queen both narrates and stars in *Arabian Nights,* or *The Thousand and One Nights,* a collection of traditional Persian, Arabian, Indian and Egyptian folk tales completed in the late fifteenth century. Incensed by the infidelity of his wife, the Sultan Schahriar executes her and decrees that he will marry a new woman each night and kill her the next day. Scheherazade marries Schahriar and captivates him with her stories, guaranteeing her survival by starting one each night and saving the conclusion until the next. Won over by a thousand and one nights of storytelling, the sultan ultimately abandons his murderous plot.

688. *Hester Prynne*

The protagonist in Nathaniel Hawthorne's *The Scarlet Letter* (1850) embodies the indecency of American society's insistence on sexual chastity for "decent" women. Abused and ostracized for having an extramarital affair, Hester Prynne faces every indignity that her Puritan community believes she deserves. In the end, however, it is her neighbors who are degraded, while she achieves a kind of personal nobility.

689. *Emma Bovary*

One of literature's most compelling characters, the protagonist of Gustave Flaubert's *Madame Bovary* (1857) rebels against the bourgeois life that bores and stifles her. Seeking romantic fulfillment, she becomes an adulteress; when each affair proves more disillusioning than the last,

Scheherazade.

she commits suicide. Emma Bovary could symbolize the fallen woman who gets her just deserts, but Flaubert himself proclaimed, "Madame Bovary, *c'est moi.*" His novel is an indictment of the mediocrity of modern life, his protagonist, an emblem of individualism.

690. *Nana*

Émile Zola perfected a misogynist stereotype in the eponymous protagonist of *Nana,* his 1880 novel. Controlled by carnal desire, Nana embodies the hedonism of the society around her, a hedonism that dooms that society—and Nana herself. Her fate is a warning to women who would pursue sexual pleasure for its own sake rather than for the sake of procreation.

691. *Tess of the d'Urbervilles*

In an 1891 novel named for its protagonist, Thomas Hardy depicts the tragic fate of a woman who dares to defy social convention. The idealistic Tess flees the life she is expected to lead, briefly finding freedom in the arms of her lover. Ultimately, however, she runs up against the brick wall of conformity and is executed for her transgressions.

MUSES AND SALONISTES

692. *Patrons of the Renaissance*

Even before women established themselves as writers, they promoted literature as the patrons of male writers. Among the notable patrons whose funds helped kindle the Renaissance were Margaret of Burgundy (1290–1315),

Caterina Cornaro (1454–1510), Isabella d'Este (1474–1539), Anne of Brittany (1477–1514), Catherine of Aragon (1485–1536) and Anne of Cleves (1515–1557).

693. *The Salon of the Marquise de Rambouillet*

Immortalized in Molière's satire *Les précieuses ridicules* ("The Pretentious Young Ladies," 1659), the salon of the Marquise de Rambouillet was the birthplace of preciosity, a mode of conversation, etiquette and wit that flourished in seventeenth-century France. At times ridiculously stilted, this style of deportment eventually gave way to the more genuine refinements of aristocratic French culture. Credited—or blamed—as an originator of the form, the Marquise de Rambouillet attracted most of the era's literary figures to her salon. One of her guests was Comtesse Marie Madeleine de La Fayette, author of *La princesse de Clèves* (1678), who today is generally recognized as the finest novelist of her time.

694. *Madame de Staël*
(1766–1817)

Anne Louise Germaine, Baronne de Staël-Holstein, known simply as Madame de Staël, conducted one of the most celebrated salons in history. She started it while living in Switzerland to escape the turmoil of the French Revolution and reconvened it in Paris upon her return in 1794. In the interim, she wrote a commentary on the work of Jean-Jacques Rousseau. At home and abroad, her brilliance attracted famous literary and intellectual figures, making her salon a center of Enlightenment thought. Her progressive ideas, voiced in political commentary, literary criticism and the novels *Delphine* (1802) and *Corinne, ou l'Italie* (1807), aroused the ire of Napoleon, who exiled her. She did not return to France until 1815, but she became a prolific and celebrated letter writer. Her work, including a study of German culture and a treatise on exile, became highly influential throughout Europe.

695. *Natalie Barney* (1876–1972)

The reigning *saloniste* of the modernist period, Natalie Barney was one of many American bohemians in Paris in the first half of the twentieth century. She came from a well-to-do family and conducted weekly salons that attracted the leading artists, musicians and writers of the time, including Mata Hari and Janet Flanner. Her gatherings were also renowned as a center of lesbian life, and Barney was christened L'Amazone. Barney did some writing herself but was more important as an inspiration to others: Djuna Barnes, Radclyffe Hall, Anaïs Nin and others used Barney as a character in their works. Living to the ripe old age of ninety-five, she had countless affairs with women, including a notorious liaison with the French poet Renée Vivien and a fifty-three-year relationship with the painter Romaine Brooks.

696. *Sylvia Beach* (1887–1962)

Proprietor of Shakespeare and Company, a Paris bookstore, Baltimore-born Sylvia Beach was a central figure on the avant-garde literary scene between the wars. Among other accomplishments, she published James Joyce's *Ulysses* (1922) before the Nazi occupation forced her to close down her business. She recounted her ex-periences with literary greats in her 1959 autobiography, *Shakespeare and Company.*

WOMEN ON WRITING

697.

*"Although they are
Only breath, words
which I command
are immortal."*
—Sappho

698.

"By men's words we know them." —Marie de France, twelfth century

699.

*"I have been warned about this book,
And this is what I was told:
That if I did not bury it,
it would be fed to the flames!"*
—Mechthild of Magdeburg (thirteenth century), in *Streaming Light of the Deity*

700.

"Let no one accuse me of unreason, of arrogance or presumption, for daring, I, a woman, to challenge and answer back . . . when he, one man on his own, has dared to slander and reproach the entire female sex without exception." —Christine de Pisan (fourteenth century)

701.

"And if any of us excel to that degree that she can express her thoughts in writing, let her do so proudly and not resist the glory that she will win, greater than that won by necklaces, rings and fine fashions. For these are ours only because we have used them, but the honor which we win through study is truly ours." —Louise Labé (c. 1524–1566)

702.

*"I cannot grant you a greater gift
Than to urge you to do your duty
Toward the Muse and divine learning. . . .
You may become immortal some day through
your virtue,
It is thus that I have always wished you to be."*
—Madeleine des Roches to her daughter
Catherine (sixteenth century)

703.

*"They shut me up in Prose—
As when a little Girl
They put me in the Closet—
Because they liked me 'still' "*
—Emily Dickinson

704.

"The world did not say to her as it said to [men], Write if you choose; it makes no difference to me. The world said with a guffaw, Write? What's the good of your writing?" —Virginia Woolf, *A Room of One's Own,* 1929

705.

"Women have always been poor, not for two hundred years merely, but from the beginning of time. . . . Women, then, have not had a dog's chance of writing poetry. That is why I have laid so much stress on money and a room of one's own." —Virginia Woolf, *A Room of One's Own,* 1929

706.

"Besides Shakespeare and me, who do you think there is?" —Gertrude Stein

707.

"There is no agony like bearing an untold story inside you." —Zora Neale Hurston, *Dust Tracks on a Road,* 1942

708.

"But not until I was seven or more, did I begin to pray every night, 'O God, let me write books! Please God, let me write books!' " —Ellen Glasgow, *The Woman Within,* 1954

709.

"As a writer you are free. . . . You are in the country where *you* make up the rules, the laws. You are both dictator and obedient populace. It is a country nobody has ever explored before. It is up to you to make the maps, to build the cities. Nobody else in the world can do it, or ever could do it, or ever will be able to do it again." —Ursula K. LeGuin, *Language of the Night,* 1979

GREAT NOVELS

710. The Tale of Genji

Widely regarded as the first novel written in any language, *Genji monogatari* ("The Tale of Genji") has also been called the single greatest work of Japanese literature. It first appeared in about 1010, making it one of the earliest works of note by a Japanese woman. Its author, Lady Murasaki Shikibu, filled its fifty-four lengthy chapters with a sweeping and intricate portrait of life in the Heian court of her time. The novel narrates the story of Prince Genji and his son, Kaoru, growing more and more keenly insightful as it progresses. A masterwork of fiction, *The Tale of Genji* also features numerous *tanka*—a uniquely Japanese verse form—composed by the novel's characters.

711. Northanger Abbey

Published in 1818, two decades after Jane Austen wrote it, this parody of a Gothic romance delivers a stinging condemnation of patriarchy. Set in the rarefied atmosphere of prosperous English country life, the novel narrates the disillusionment of Catherine Morland as she enters fashionable society. The subdued behavior expected of proper ladies clashes with Catherine's natural, tomboyish exuberance. She learns, as do all Austen's female characters, that to be a woman (as defined by male-dominated society) is to be dependent, confined and untrue to oneself. Women who make the grade as good daughters and wives are doomed to a suffocating life

Jane Austen.

under the thumb of a family patriarch with absolute power.

712. Frankenstein

Mary Shelley's monstrous tale of creation and fall from grace, published in England in 1818, reworks Milton's *Paradise Lost* from the female perspective. Victor Frankenstein's warped attempt at procreation, which he compares to the creation of Eve from Adam's rib, has equally disastrous results. Like Eve, the monster embodies perversity: His hell on earth mirrors Eve's eternal damnation.

713. Jane Eyre

Charlotte Brontë's portrait of an orphan who endures all manner of tribulation on her path to self-realization first appeared in 1847. Unlike the sentimental fables popular in Britain at the time, *Jane Eyre* depicts an angry young woman who refuses to accept the constraints of conventional femininity. From the stifling Gateshead, her foster home, to the abusive Lowood school to the labyrinthine Thornfield, where she works for Edward Rochester, to the fulfillment of their romance at Ferndean, Jane successfully journeys through the swamps of societal expectation to become her own woman. Along the way she encounters the tragic and elusive Bertha Rochester, Edward's first wife, whose madness suggests one possible result of society's expectations of the "lady." (See *Wide Sargasso Sea*, page 201.)

714. Uncle Tom's Cabin

Published in two parts from 1851 to 1852, Harriet Beecher Stowe's anti-slavery classic appealed to antebellum American readers' emotions as a means of promoting abolition. The hugely successful bestseller inflamed social and political tensions in the U.S., helping to ignite the war that led to the emancipation of African-American slaves. Nevertheless, revisionist historians and critics later dismissed the novel as racist melodrama; the docile Uncle Tom became an emblem of racist complicity. Debate still rages around the book a century and a half after its publication.

715. Little Women

Although by her own admission Louisa May Alcott "never liked girls or knew many," she wrote one of the best-loved girl's stories of all time. Since 1869, when it first appeared in the U.S., *Little Women* has drawn generation after generation of young readers into the world of the virtually all-female March household. The story revolves around the ambitious and independent Jo, who lives with her beloved Marmee and three sisters: serene Meg, frail Beth and obstinate Amy. A departure in children's literature, which until then had been relentlessly didactic and moralistic, *Little Women* gave girls a new kind of role model in energetic, self-confident Jo.

716. Middlemarch

George Eliot already enjoyed renown as an important and popular novelist when she published her masterpiece in 1871. In *Middlemarch,* as in all her work, she addressed universal issues of human uncertainty and hopelessness by exploring the lives of middle-class townspeople in rural England. The failed, colorless Mr. Casaubon, briefly resuscitated by marriage to the naïve Dorothea Brooke, inevitably subjects her to a walking death of housebound tedium relieved only by a romance with the puerile Will Ladislaw. The cynical, pompous Dr. Lydgate ignores and humiliates his willful wife, Rosamond, who sinks into bitter silence. Meanwhile, the miserly Featherstone, the opportunistic Rigg and the weak Bulstrode live in bondage to money. Numerous other characters further illustrate the moral ills besetting modern society.

717. The Awakening

In the last year of the nineteenth century, American writer Kate Chopin published a novel shockingly ahead of its time. It is the story of Edna Pontellier, a woman who comes to realize both that her marriage is suffocating her and that she possesses sexual passions strong enough to draw her into adultery. The frank, feminist book outraged polite society, leading to a ban on its sale and to Chopin's banishment from respectable circles. Her career in ruins and her confidence as a writer ravaged, Chopin sank into oblivion. Not until cultural mores caught up with her work was *The Awakening* recognized as the seminal masterpiece it truly is.

718. *The House of Mirth*

Edith Wharton's first novel, which came out in 1905, outlined the themes that would pervade her later—and more famous—fictions. A scathing indictment of the hypocrisy of American high society, the story follows the tragic fall of a woman who refuses to obey the rules. When blue-blooded Lily Bart falls on hard financial times, she is expected to marry a wealthy acquaintance; in return for a life of comfort she is to serve as a sort of decorative trophy. She balks at selling herself on the marriage market and ends up wretchedly poor, an outcast from the world of privilege. Under Wharton's pen, however, it is society that is condemned for its mistreatment of women.

719. *My Ántonia*

Willa Cather's 1918 novel celebrates a truly heroic heroine, a woman stronger than cruel circumstance and braver than the men around her. A male narrator—almost unheard of in books by women of that time—follows the fortunes of Ántonia, a Bohemian immigrant who grows up on the prairies of nineteenth-century Nebraska. In addition to the hardships suffered by all pioneer farmers on the prairie, Ántonia endures the suicide of her father and illegitimate motherhood at the hands of an unscrupulous railroad man. But nothing breaks her spirit, and she transcends time and place to become an archetypal character in American literature.

720. *Mrs. Dalloway*

Tracing one day in the life of Clarissa Dalloway, Virginia Woolf's 1925 work represented a daring experiment in the novel. The book shifts between the thoughts of Mrs. Dalloway, a well-to-do society matron, and Septimus Warren Smith, a shell-shocked soldier. The similarities and contrasts of the two figures offer a biting analysis of class and consciousness in British culture, even as the novel forges an entirely original literary form.

721. *The Well of Loneliness*

Although, in literary terms, it does not rank among the great novels of history, English writer Radclyffe Hall's 1928 work remains one of the most socially significant works of its era. The tale of Stephen Gordon, an unapologetic (for the time) "invert," was the first serious—and sympathetic—fictional portrait of lesbianism. Seized by authorities and banned in England and the U.S. as obscene, *The Well of Loneliness* was the center of sensational court battles in both countries. The bans eventually fell, but controversy continued to surround the book. To this day, conservatives object to its subject matter, while liberals debate its sociopolitical merits and flaws.

722. Nightwood

In 1936 the American Djuna Barnes published a work of fiction so remarkably revolutionary that it prompted critics to compare her with James Joyce. *Nightwood* follows Robin Vote as she meanders about bohemian Paris encountering, captivating and destroying a roster of startling and peculiar characters. Its prose represented an enormous stride forward for English-language literature, prompting T. S. Eliot to rhapsodize on "the great achievement of style, the beauty of phrasing, the brilliance of wit and characterisation, and a quality of horror and doom very nearly related to that of Elizabethan tragedy."

723. Their Eyes Were Watching God

Zora Neale Hurston, a major figure of the Harlem Renaissance, received criticism as well as praise for her 1937 novel, which traces the history of the African-American community through the story of Janie Woods. As in her other work, the origins of black culture and the status of black women are prominent themes in *Their Eyes Were Watching God*. A celebration of uniquely African-American mores and institutions, the novel was nevertheless dismissed by some noted blacks as a trivialization of the suffering caused by white oppression. The book sank into obscurity for decades, but Hurston's prodigious talent as a storyteller would not be denied. In the 1970s, black and feminist critics rediscovered *Their Eyes Were Watching God* as an important literary achievement that, despite its faults, portrays the positive side of African-American history.

Zora Neale Hurston.

724. The Heart Is a Lonely Hunter

The first of Carson McCullers's darkly idealistic works, *The Heart Is a Lonely Hunter* appeared in 1940, when its author was twenty-three years old. Its protagonist, the teenaged Mick Kelly, is an aspiring musician and a troubled romantic unwilling to accept the constraints of small-town life in the American South. She longs for a world where her society's outcasts are no longer shunned, and her timeless adolescent angst draws her into increasingly disturbing and even dangerous events. The novel immediately established McCullers as a major talent in the Southern Gothic tradition; her subsequent works would include *The Ballad of the Sad Café* (1944) and *The Member of the Wedding* (1946).

725. The Golden Notebook

Generally recognized as British-South African Doris Lessing's masterpiece, this daringly structured 1962 novel explores the inner life of women in the second half of the twentieth century. A short novel, *Free Women,* provides the book's basic framework and depicts the friendship of Anna and Molly. Segments of the novel alternate with four notebooks kept by Anna, each addressing a different part of herself. Both the novel and the notebooks follow Anna's breakdown in the face of modern social forces, while a fifth notebook—the golden notebook—portrays the reintegration and healing of Anna's psyche. Appearing simultaneously with the birth of the women's liberation movement, *The Golden Notebook* was embraced by feminists as an epic of the war between the sexes. But Lessing eschewed that characterization, insisting she meant merely to document the emotional world of modern women. Either way, the novel remains a powerful feminist work, capturing the essence of women's life in a particular time and place.

726. Wide Sargasso Sea

Haunted by Charlotte Brontë's *Jane Eyre,* Jean Rhys published this vividly surreal reflection on women and madness in 1966. *Wide Sargasso Sea* melds the character of Bertha Rochester with the legendarily demented Creole heiresses of Rhys's native West Indies to create Antoinette Bertha Cosway, who shares Mrs. Rochester's fate. Rhys looks back to her protag-

onist's childhood, coming of age and early marriage to contemplate the origins of her insanity. In so doing she creates a work of breathtaking horror and beauty. The result is a profoundly disturbing commentary on women's oppression and its fruits.

727. Warrior Woman

Part autobiography and part fiction, Maxine Hong Kingston's 1976 book unites two literary forms largely forged by women. The autobiographical sections recall the Chinese-American narrator's California childhood, while the fictional sections conjure Chinese myth and history. Subtitled "Memoirs of a Girlhood Among Ghosts," the work depicts an Asian-American girl's perceptions of the white American "ghosts" among whom she lives and explores the enduring power of ancestral Chinese influences in her consciousness. Throughout, the theme of the female avenger is sounded again and again, shedding light on Chinese attitudes toward women. The book was critically acclaimed not only for its innovative approach to an uncommon subject but for the fierce, lyrical clarity of its prose.

728. Beloved

Winner of the 1988 Pulitzer Prize for Fiction, Toni Morrison's eerie novel concentrates on the shattering impact of centuries of African-American enslavement on a single Ohio household a few years after the Civil War. Haunted by the memory of the baby daughter she killed rather than hand over to white men, the escaped slave Sethe takes in the enigmatic Beloved. Crossing the boundaries between the living and the dead, Beloved's identity slowly reveals itself to the occupants of the house. Past and present overlap in the narrative, illuminating slavery's cruel legacy for African-Americans, especially African-American women. *Beloved* awed an enormous readership, finally bringing Morrison the wide attention she deserved. In 1993 she became the first black woman to receive the Nobel Prize for Literature.

729. *Push*

The debut novel by African-American poet Sapphire, *Push* (1996) is the story of a young girl struggling to overcome the brutal realities of her life in Harlem. Pregnant with her second child by her father, Precious leaves public school to enter a special program where she can finally learn to read. Encouraged by a teacher's kindness—the first she has experienced—she perseveres in her quest for education despite continued abuse by her mother. Precious's path to self-respect and independence mirrors some of the classic themes of literature in an unflinchingly postmodern glass.

THE NOVELISTS

730. *Maria Edgeworth* (1767–1849)

Unlike most women writers of her time, who wrote in spite of male expectations, Maria Edgeworth wrote in order to please her father. The Irishman painstakingly educated his daughter, moving with her from England back to his homeland in 1782. Thirteen years later she published *Letters for Literary Ladies,* an epistolary novel, launching one of the more distinguished careers in Irish literature. Another epistolary novel and a satirical essay on feminine wiles followed, as well as two sitting-room novels, *Belinda* (1801) and *Ormond* (1817). Two other works, however, represent her most significant contributions to Irish literature: *Castle Rackrent* (1800) and *The Absentee* (1812), which use an innovative realism to examine daily life under the landlord system and to criticize abusive Irish landowners.

731. *George Sand*
(1804–1876)

Amandine-Aurore Lucille Dupin, Baronne Dudevant, contributed a large and significant body of work to the Romantic movement under a masculine pseudonym. The feminism that showed up in her work also informed her life, which was unconventional to say the least. She married in 1822, but she grew restless and left her husband for the artist's life in Paris. Surrounded by friends like Balzac, Chopin and Liszt, she sported men's clothing and carried on a series of love affairs. All this was a backdrop for her work; the year she arrived in Paris she published *Rose et Blanche* (1831), a novel written with Jules Sandeau and released under the pseudonym Jules Sand. She then adopted her famous pseudonym and started generating a long string of influential and popular novels that champion women's rights, free love and humanitarian ideals. Among them are *Lélia* (1833), *Les sept cordes de la lyre* (1840) and *Les maîtres sonneurs* (1853); she also wrote two volumes of autobiography, *Histoire de ma vie* (1855) and *Elle et lui* (1859).

732. *Emily Brontë* (1818–1848)

The sister of Charlotte Brontë, author of *Jane Eyre*, Emily Brontë is best known as the author of the equally famous *Wuthering Heights*. With Charlotte and Anne, her other surviving sister (as well as a brother, Branwell), Emily shared a childhood filled with stories and elaborate fantasies, some of which they turned into tiny, hand-lettered books. The sisters' earliest attempt at publication, a collaborative collection of verse pseudonymously called *Poems by Currer, Ellis, and Acton Bell* (1846), failed miserably. Today, however, the merits of Emily's poetry are widely appreciated. But the sisters decided to turn their hands to fiction, producing *Jane Eyre, Wuthering Heights* and *Agnes Grey* (written by Anne) in 1847. The tale of passionate, amoral Heathcliff, who not only broke with but transcended social convention, *Wuthering Heights* appalled some reviewers as a story not fit for decent readers. But later critics came to recognize its literary excellence and its significance as an adroit blend of romance and mysticism. Brontë died of consumption soon after publishing her masterpiece.

733. *Sarah Orne Jewett*
(1849–1909)

A native of Maine, Jewett preserved in fiction the lives of ordinary women facing the challenges of rural life amid the austere beauty of the New England landscape. She started publishing stories in the late 1860s, in magazines such as the *Atlantic Monthly,* and came out with her first collection, *Deephaven,* in 1877. *A White Heron* (1886) and *The King of Folly Island* (1888) followed, earning her the respect of writers such as Harriet Beecher Stowe and John Greenleaf Whittier. But it is *The Country of the Pointed Firs* (1896) that stands as Jewett's masterpiece, a noted contribution in its own right to American letters and a lasting influence on younger writers such as Willa Cather.

734. *Katherine Mansfield*
(1888–1923)

This New Zealand expatriate long ranked as the only writer from her homeland to enjoy international acclaim. Her short-story collections, from *In a German Pension* (1911) to *The Garden Party and Other Stories* (1922), embrace a satiric darkness that reflected the rootlessness, sexual confusion and infirmity of her short life. She died of tuberculosis at the age of thirty-five.

735. *Elizabeth Bowen*
(1899–1973)

The author of more than twenty novels and volumes of short fiction, Elizabeth Bowen won accolades in England as one of Ireland's leading literati. She lived most of her life in England, moving from place to place to live with relatives after her father suffered a nervous breakdown and her mother died of cancer. Not surprisingly, her fiction is filled with frightened children and anxious adults facing unsettled or confusing circumstances. Among her novels are *The Hotel* (1927), *The Heat of the Day* (1949) and *Eva Traut* (1969); her story collections include *Encounters* (1923) and *The Demon Lover* (1945).

736. *Anaïs Nin* (1903–1977)

Born in Paris to a Spanish father and a French-Danish mother, Nin grew up in New York City.

Fascinated with the working of her own psyche, she started keeping extensive diaries in 1914. She returned to Paris and published her first book, *D. H. Lawrence: An Unprofessional Study,* in 1932, then moved on to fiction. Nin's first novel, *House of Incest,* appeared in 1939, the year before a wealthy patron hired her to write erotica for a dollar a page. This patron came to her via the novelist Henry Miller, whom she viewed as her male counterpart in the literary exploration of sexuality. Nin accepted the challenge and produced a body of work that was published under the title *Delta of Venus* upon her death. Published from 1966 through 1980, her massive diaries represent her most familiar work, but she also deserves attention for her numerous worthy novels, including *Children of the Albatross* (1947), *Spy in the House of Love* (1954) and *Seduction of the Minotaur* (1961).

737. Gallic Gals

Four women shine in the constellation of eminent French novelists of the twentieth century: the fantastically prolific psychological realist Colette, author of the Claudine books (1900 on), the Chéri books (1920 on), *Gigi* (1945) and many other works; her literary opposite, Nathalie Sarraute, exponent of the anti-novel and author of *Portrait d'un inconnu* (1947), *Vous les entendez?* (1972) and others; Françoise Sagan, best known for *Bonjour triestesse* (1954); and Marguerite Yourcenar, author of *Mémoires d'Hadrien* (1951) and *Souvenirs pieux* (1973) and the first woman ever elected to the Académie Française.

738. Eudora Welty (1909–)

Renowned as a Southern regionalist, Welty has created a body of work populated by colorful female characters. Her work takes both the mundane and the peculiar as its subject matter, yielding tales memorable for their warmth and optimism. Welty has written short stories, such as those in her first book, *A Curtain of Green, and Other Stories* (1941), and remarkable novels such as *The Robber Bridegroom* (1942) and *The Ponder Heart* (1954). *The Optimist's Daughter* (1972) won the Pulitzer prize; more recently Welty published a short but rich memoir, *One Writer's Beginnings* (1983).

739. Flannery O'Connor (1925–1964)

Convinced that most readers represented a "hostile audience" for her religiously informed fiction, O'Connor justified the intensity of her stories as necessary: "To the hard of hearing you shout, and for the almost blind you draw large and startling figures." Her Southern roots—she was born in Georgia—and ardent Roman Catholicism gave her ample raw material for her novels and short stories. *Wise Blood* (1952), her first book, introduced O'Connor's savage wit to the world and was followed by a collection of stories, *A Good Man Is Hard to Find* (1955). Filled with bizarre imagery, tormented characters and savage action, her fiction illuminated the imperative for and obstacles to spiritual redemption. O'Connor sustained these themes in her second novel, *The Violent Bear It Away* (1960), and in her second story collection, *Everything That Rises Must Converge* (1965), before dying of lupus at the age of thirty-nine.

740. La Famiglia

Two Italian women, both writing about Italian family life, made important contributions to twentieth-century world literature. The family sagas of Elsa Morante, such as *Menzogna e sortilegio* (1948) and *La storia* (1974) became quite popular in Italy. Poet and novelist Natalia Levi Ginzburg created delicate, unadorned images of modern women and children at home in works that included *Le voci della sera* (1961) and the autobiographical essays of *Lessico famigliare* (1963).

741. Isabel Allende (1942–)

The niece of Chilean president Salvador Allende, Isabel Allende started her literary career as a journalist. She boldly covered controversial social and political topics, until she was exiled from Chile when a military junta overthrew her uncle. Settling in Caracas, Venezuela, she published her first novel, *House of the Spirits,* in 1982. Punctuated with surrealist elements, it tells the story of a Latin American family living amid political and economic turmoil. The juxtaposition of private and public concerns also appears in her later works, the novels *Of Love and Shadows* (1984) and *Eva Luna* (1987), as well as a short-story collection, *Stories of Eva Luna* (1992). Allende returned to Chile in 1988, when a democratically elected president took office.

742. Joyce Carol Oates (1938–)

This astonishingly prolific writer has published dozens of short stories, novels, poetry collections and essays on topics as far-ranging as the Victorian age and boxing. Born in Upstate New York, she graduated from Syracuse University in 1960 and earned a master's degree in English at the University of Wisconsin. She published the first of her books in 1963: *By the North Gate,* a volume of short stories. Her first novel, *With Shuddering Fall,* appeared in 1964 and the novel *them* (1969) won the National Book Award. Oates has since produced a steady stream of work even while teaching English at various colleges, including Princeton University. Her oeuvre includes *The Goddess and Other Women* (1974), *Bellefleur* (1980), *Because It Is Bitter, and Because It Is My Heart* (1990) and *Foxfire: Confessions of a Girl Gang* (1993). Often violent or even morbid, her stories probe the dark corners of the human psyche and the underside of contemporary society.

743. Anne Rice (1941–)

A true publishing phenomenon, this bestselling novelist has a huge cult following that reads everything she writes. Early in her career, before achieving superstardom, she wrote erotica such as *Exit to Eden* and the *Sleeping Beauty* trilogy under the pseudonyms Anne Rampling and A. N. Roquelaure. She has written a variety of fiction under her own name, ranging from *Cry to Heaven,* the story of a castrato in Renaissance Italy, to *The Feast of All Saints,* a family saga set in nineteenth-century New Orleans. She's had her greatest luck, however, with her supernatural series. Her "Vampire Chronicles," four titles—including the original *Interview with the Vampire*—center around the vampire Lestat, and have achieved a popularity that defies description. Shifting her focus to black magic, Rice has also produced an enormously successful series about a family of witches, starting with *The Witching Hour.*

744. Dorothy Allison (1949–   )

In 1992, Dorothy Allison's novel *Bastard Out of Carolina* was a finalist for the National Book Award. The story of a poor, white girl growing up in the American South, the book garnered wide attention for its regional flavor and its frank treatment of the topic of incest. Before publishing *Bastard Out of Carolina,* Allison was known chiefly as a poet and writer of short stories that combined themes of lesbianism and violence. Her first book, a collection of poetry entitled *The Women Who Hate Me* (1985), was followed by *Trash* (1988), a volume of short fiction. Most recently, Allison published the novel *Cavedweller* (1998).

Part

EIGHT

Arts and Entertainment

THE CASTING COUCH

745. *Caryatids*

Dating from 500 B.C.E. caryatids were Greek columns carved in the shape of women. The columns were functional, serving as supports for roofs or beams that rested on the heads of the carved women. They were made in memory of the defeat of Caria and subsequent enslavement of its women.

Caryatids.

746. *Lysistrata*

In 411 B.C.E. the twentieth year of the Peloponnesian War, Greek theater audiences first encountered the leader of an unusual women's anti-war protest. Aristophanes' masterpiece, *Lysistrata,* narrates the events that unfold when the women of Athens and Sparta, in an effort to end a long-running war, suspend sexual relations with their husbands. The tactic works, the war ends and spouses reunite. At face value the play seems to celebrate female initiative, but Lysistrata, the leader of the revolt, attributes her cleverness to male mentors. Consumed by sexual frustration, the women ac-

tually suffer more than their husbands, who turn to prostitutes and to each other for gratification. Jokes characterize women as gluttons and drunks, and old women are ridiculed as repulsive nymphomaniacs.

747. Carmen

George Bizet's Carmen is an opera bad girl, defiant from her first entrance until her final-act death. Unafraid to stand up to men—unafraid in general, it seems—she is even unafraid of death. And die she does, rather than allow a man to determine her fate.

748. Nora Helmer

Henrik Ibsen's play *A Doll's House* (1879) portrays the effects on one woman of emotional abuse by her husband. Isolated from the world by her husband, Torvald, Nora Helmer finally finds the will to leave him. The play begins some years after Nora has forged her father's name in order to gain much-needed money while Torvald was ill. One of Torvald's employees now threatens to expose the forgery to Torvald, prompting Nora to tell him herself. When the employee then threatens to blackmail Torvald, he turns on his wife. His incessant, brutal castigation of Nora finally convinces the employee to take pity and drop his plans. Realizing the utter bankruptcy of her marriage, Nora subsequently leaves Torvald.

749. TV Moms

Television has been a powerful purveyor of social norms that keep women "in their place," that is, at home. As a result, women's roles on television were for many years restricted to wives and mothers of male characters. In the 1950s, Jane Wyatt played the perfect helpmeet to Robert Young in the aptly titled *Father Knows Best,* and on *Leave It to Beaver* Barbara Billingsley played the ever-patient, ever-devoted TV mom June Cleaver. *The Adventures of Ozzie and Harriet* brought the real-life Nelson family to the small screen, where they served up another dish of faux-family fare. At least *The Donna Reed Show* was named for its female star, who was permitted mild acts of feminist rebellion—as when she stirred up the neighborhood with her offense at the phrase *"just* a housewife." But even these small rebellions were put down by episode's end, reminding women that feminism is futile. Lucille Ball accomplished a more lasting insurrection, becoming the first TV mom to actually appear onscreen while pregnant. The 1950s and 1960s icons would have more liberated 1970s and 1980s counterparts, mostly superwomen with career and family firmly in hand. Phylicia Rashad's Clair Huxtable on *The Cosby Show* was one of these; Candice Bergen's Murphy Brown became a small-screen single mother by choice. But it was left to Roseanne to shatter and overtly question the mythic TV mom. Over the years her show has made frequent sarcastic references to these forerunner fakes. On one episode of *Roseanne,* she gathered a group of former TV moms in her kitchen and delivered the last word: "On my show, I'm the boss, and father knows squat."

750. Women with Powers

In the television sitcoms *Bewitched* (1964–1972) and *I Dream of Jeannie*

(1965–1969), women have supernatural powers that the merely mortal men in their lives struggle to control. Both shows reinforce a sexist stereotype: For all men's blustering dominion, it is women who actually control events but only through furtive manipulation. Of course, Samantha and Jeannie usually use their powers to provide selfless, invisible support to their men.

751. The Girl from U.N.C.L.E.

The title of this 1966 spin-off of *The Man from U.N.C.L.E.* pretty much says it all. Stefanie Powers starred as April Dancer, "girl agent," for all of one season.

752. Thelma and Jessie Cates

In *'Night Mother*, Marsha Norman's 1983 drama, the hazards of the mother-daughter relationship come to light. Divorced and unstable, Jessie tells her mother she is going to commit suicide. Thelma Cates initially does not take her daughter seriously, but mother and daughter enter a long discussion about their troubled relationship to each other. This conversation does nothing to cheer Jessie up; at the end of the play she kills herself.

753. Women Cops

Cagney & Lacy (1982–1988) proved women cops on TV had come a long way when, in a later episode of the long-running show, the two fictitious NYPD detectives are assigned to escort a television actress who plays a cop on TV. In a classic example of television self-commentary, the "actress" on the episode has more than a few parallels to Pepper Anderson, Angie Dickinson's character on *Police Woman* (1974–1979). In the episode, Sharon Gless's Christine Cagney criticizes the actress for playing a policewoman who frequently goes undercover as a hooker. This is a charge feminist media critic Susan Douglas and others repeatedly lobbed at Dickinson's Pepper Anderson, who always seemed to be going undercover as a porn actress, stripper or prostitute, only to get in over her head and require rescue by her male colleagues, often from rape. That *Cagney & Lacy* went on the air just three years after *Police Woman* seems remarkable.

754. Thelma & Louise and Beyond

In the 1980s and 1990s the movie heroine and villainess evolved from sweet or sexy to tough. Although preceded by other films, such as *La Femme Nikita* (1988), with strong female leads, *Thelma & Louise* (1991) was the first major Hollywood smash featuring women protagonists who used violence to get what they wanted. The image of physically strong, gun-toting, aggressive women appeared in film after film, from Sigourney Weaver in the *Alien* films to Linda Hamilton in *Terminator 2* (1991) to the animated lead in *Tank Girl* (1995) to Demi Moore in *G.I. Jane* (1997).

METHODS AND MEDIA

755. Ancient Performers

As early as 1200 B.C.E., professional women musicians worked in Egypt, Assyria and Babylonia. In 50 C.E. records showed more than three thousand women working as musicians in Athens, though by 300 C.E. the number had dropped so much that men fought one another in the streets to engage the few that remained.

756. Whistling While They Work

Greek statuettes dating from 500 B.C.E. depict women workers dancing to the accompaniment of a woman playing a flute. Over the next thousand years in Africa and Europe, the work song emerged as a uniquely female form.

757. Bharata Natya

Bharata Natya is an intricate classical Indian dance form sometimes compared with Western ballet. Its origins are religious—created by the Hindu god Brahma as a devotional rite for his followers. But Bharata Natya is an exclusively female province. A lone woman performs the dance with brisk, forceful steps that delineate a complex rhythm. Simultaneously, elaborate arm and head movements combine with precise hand and facial gestures to convey nuances of emotion as well as narrative.

758. Kabuki

Kabuki, a form of Japanese theater, originated as dance. Kabuki's invention is credited to a woman: Okuni, who lived from 1573 to 1614. In 1603, Okuni collaborated with a comedian and began to perform a kind of dance theater heavily rooted in mime and often based in religious themes. Okuni was known for appearing in priest's robes and sporting two swords in her sash. Her fondness for playing priests and other male roles established a standard feature of Kabuki where men play female characters and women play male parts.

759. En Pointe

Dancing en pointe emerged during the 1800s as an integral feature of ballet's Romantic period. Ballet in this era sought to conjure a sublime otherworld inhabited by carefree nymphs and fairies. The ballerina became crucial to this fanciful construction and dancing en pointe, in toe shoes, reinforced the desired illusion. A ballerina en pointe appears to float through an ethereal paradise. But creating this illusion is hardly paradise for the ballerina. To dance en pointe requires intense control of both mind and body. It also causes inevitable injuries. Thus, while the Romantic period allowed ballerinas to take center stage, it was only at great physical cost. The modern ballerina pays not only in chronic foot injury, but also in the hundreds of dollars a week it costs to buy the fragile toe shoes that inflict so much damage.

760. Dance Marathons

Alma Cummings made history in 1923 when she and her partner set a world record in America's first dance marathon. They danced nonstop for twenty-seven hours.

761. The Museum of Modern Art

In 1929, three philanthropic women—Lizzie Plummer Bliss, Abby Greene Aldrich Rockefeller and Mary Quinn Sullivan—founded the Museum of Modern Art.

762. Girl Groups

The Chantels, the Shirelles, the Marvellettes, the Chiffons—even the names given to early girl groups conjured the feel-good sound that thrived during an otherwise dead period in rock. The girl-group songs, written by an army of songwriters (Carole King among them), were transmitted to the public most often by slickly beautiful black women in matching outfits. But between the songwriting and the record release came the most crucial piece of the girl-group jigsaw—the producer. Giants like George Goldner and Phil Spector dominated the girl-group sound, which was entirely producer dependent. So were the "girls" in the groups, who had no artistic control. The central focus of the songs? Boys. Still, this exploitative setup manufactured musical gold, both artistically and commercially.

763. Performance Art

During the late 1970s and early 1980s, downtown New York saw the emergence of a number of small, independent performance spaces. These included The Kitchen, Dixon Place, the Limbo Lounge, Performance Space 122 (P.S. 122), La Mama and the Women's One World (WOW) Cafe. Though WOW was the only specifically woman-oriented space, women performance artists found audiences at all of these venues. Through performance art, women explored issues of gender, sexual identity, sexuality, sexual abuse and sexual excess. Pioneers included Peggy Shaw, Lois Weaver and Deb Margolan, all of whom had long, ongoing associations with WOW Cafe, and others such as Karen Finlay, Holly Hughes and Kate Bornstein. Over time, performance art has been both ridiculed and co-opted by mainstream U.S.A. Laurie Anderson, who fell somewhere between a performance artist and an alternative musician, was one of the few who managed to cross over. She attained a degree of celebrity for her trademark combinations of sights, sounds, quirky vocalizations and overall electronic enhancement. But even for artists who don't attract huge audiences, performance-art spaces continue to offer a home for cutting-edge work.

764. Censorship

In the early 1990s, performance artists Holly Hughes and Karen Finlay achieved notoriety as girls in a political war over public funding of the arts. They boldly, and often graphically, dealt with issues of sexuality in their work, challenging and sometimes mocking conventional sexual mores. Both Finlay and Hughes had been selected to receive grants from the National Endowment for the Arts. But charges were made, most loudly by North Carolina Senator Jesse Helms, that their work was obscene or indecent, or in any case, not fit for public consumption. Both women would lose their grants as well as much time and energy to the ensuing and continuing controversy.

765. Guerrilla Girls

The anonymous Guerrilla Girls emerged in 1990, launching a campaign to end gender inequities in the art world. Part political activists, part performance artists, they make strategic strikes to call attention to discrimination against and underrepresentation of women and minorities in museums and galleries. They use a variety of weapons in their covert war, including posters and personal appearances and performances made in gorilla masks.

FINE ARTISTS

766. Guan Daoshang
(1262–1319)

Guan Daoshang, a calligrapher and painter, remains the most celebrated woman artist in Chinese history.

767. Renaissance Painters

A period of enormous growth in the fine arts, the Renaissance produced a number of significant women artists and helped establish art as an acceptable pursuit for women. Barred from formal training in academies, women of this period had little opportunity to learn of the contemporary debates concerning art. Some women artists came from artistic families, as was the case with Lavinia Fontana (1552–1614) and Artemisia Gentileschi (1590–c. 1642). But most came from noble families, where art was just one of a number of subjects that made up a girl's tutelage. The royal courts also commissioned art from women, as when Henry VIII hired Lavina Bening Teerline, a Flemish artist, to paint miniatures. By the end of the Renaissance it had become almost ordinary for women to pursue artistic careers.

768. Properzia de' Rossi
(c. 1490–1530)

De'Rossi is one of the earliest known European women artists. A Bolognese sculptor, she attained great popularity and, as a result, the envy of her male colleagues.

769. Emma Stebbins
(1815–1882)

In 1873, Stebbins unveiled her sculpture *The Angel of the Waters* as part of the Bethesda Water Fountain in New York City's Central Park. It became her best-known work.

770. Grandma Moses
(Anna Mary Robertson, 1860–1961)

Although she did not even begin to paint until she was seventy-seven, Grandma Moses first exhibited her paintings at the Museum of Modern Art two years later.

771. Käthe Kollwitz
(1867–1945)

In 1919, printmaker and painter Käthe Kollwitz was the first woman to become a member of the Prussian Academy of the Arts. Her work depicted the great human suffering that resulted from economic and political upheaval in Europe during the first half of the twentieth century.

The Crushed by Käthe Kollwitz, 1923.

772. Georgia O'Keeffe (1887–1986)

In 1916, the work of Georgia O'Keeffe was exhibited for the first time at Alfred Stieglitz's 291 Gallery in New York. O'Keeffe went on to a distinguished, seventy-year career that earned her accolades as one of the greatest artists of the twentieth century.

773. Dorothea Lange (1895–1965)

Born in Hoboken, New Jersey, Lange is best known for her haunting Depression-era photographs. Taken throughout the 1930s, these images, "White Angel Breadline" and "Migrant Mother" among them, captured the profound suffering of America's Dust Bowl migrants. In 1939, Lange published them in a collection entitled *An American Exodus.* Just as powerful but far less known are the photographs she made in the early 1940s, when she put her considerable talents to work documenting the internment of Japanese-Americans in concentration camps. Lange also did a number of photo-essays for *Life* magazine, including *Mormon Villages* and *The Irish Countryman.*

Ranch woman, photo by Dorothea Lange.

774. *Margaret Bourke-White*
(1904–1971)

As a prominent photojournalist, Bourke-White became the first Westerner to photograph the industrial heart of the Soviet Union. During World War II, while working for *Life* magazine, she became the first female war correspondent to cover the front lines. Over her long career, she used her camera to record social injustice at home and abroad. Her photographs brought the public's attention to poverty in America's South, the incomprehensible atrocities of Nazi concentration camps and apartheid in South Africa. Her pioneering work not only represented a gain for women, but also brought increased respect to the art of photography.

775. *Frida Kahlo* (1907–1954)

Crippled in a traffic accident while young, this Mexican painter created works that reflect the constant physical pain she endured. They also reveal her passion for famed muralist Diego Rivera, her lover of many years. The first major exhibition of her work took place in Mexico in 1953, the year before she died.

776. *Diane Arbus* (1923–1971)

Born Diane Nemerov, Arbus grew up in a prosperous New York City family, the daughter of a Fifth Avenue department store owner. She met Allan Arbus when she was just fourteen and married him at eighteen; the two became successful fashion photographers. Arbus would continue this work until 1959, when she studied with Lisette Model. Model is credited with encouraging Arbus to pursue her artistic vision, which produced the photographs for which she became famous. The first exhibition of this work, part of a project Arbus called *American Rites, Manners and Customs,* took place in 1967 as part of the "New Documents" show at the Museum of Modern Art. Critics immediately acclaimed her dark and disturbing images of America. Four years later, Arbus committed suicide.

777. *Judy Chicago* (1939–)

Founder of the Feminist Art Program at the California Institute of the Arts, the first such program in the United States, Chicago started her best-known work in 1973. *The Dinner Party,* a sculpture consisting of a triangular table set with thirty-nine ceramic plates dedicated to ancient goddesses, took six years to complete.

My Prenatal Life by Frida Kahlo, 1936.

THE APPLIED ARTS

778. Illuminated Books

Although monks have traditionally received most of the credit, nuns laboring in medieval convents produced some of that era's renowned illuminated books. In the pages of *The Spanish Apocalypse,* a book made in 970 and now kept at the Gerona Cathedral, are the earliest known examples of illuminations signed by a woman; up to that time the creators of these works of art had remained anonymous.

779. The Bayeux Tapestry

The great tapestries of the Middle Ages were created by noblewomen who received their education in convents. Such women, and the nuns who taught them the art of needlework, anonymously produced the remarkable Bayeux Tapestry, a rendering of the eleventh-century Battle of Hastings.

780. Navajo Crafts

Nomadic hunter-gatherers for many centuries, the Navajo adopted an agricultural way of life about the same time the Spanish arrived in the American Southwest. Women assumed responsibility for making things, from building homes to baking bread. Their crafts have endured as some of the finest examples of Native American artwork. Coiled basketry and fired pottery feature distinctive geometrical designs, as do the wool rugs for which they are most famous. The Navajo did not have wool until the Spanish introduced sheep; rather than butchering the animals for meat, the people raised them for wool. The women took blanket-weaving to a high art form, never creating two blankets exactly alike.

781. Jane and Mary Parminter

Architects Mary and Jane Parminter designed a unique, sixteen-sided house in their native England. Built in 1795, the famous structure featured an open octagonal center.

782. Gertrude Jekyll (1843–1932)

This English landscape architect originated a style of garden design that determined the direction of modern gardening. Informal and flowing, it featured recurrent motifs of shape and color, as at Hestercomb, England. Jekyll explained her approach in numerous books, including *Wood and Garden* (1899) and *Colour in the Flower Garden* (1908).

783. Elsie de Wolfe (1865–1950)

A turn-of-the-century American interior decorator, De Wolfe swept away the prevailing Victorian aesthetic of dark woods and cluttered knick-knacks, supplanting it with her own light and airy vision. Signatures of her design style were pale colors, lightweight fabrics and the use of mirrors.

784. Julia Morgan (1872–1957)

Born and raised in the San Francisco Bay area, Morgan became enthralled with architecture at an early age. Determined to enter the field, which few women had attempted, she began her studies at the University of California at Berkeley, graduating in 1894 with a B.S. in civil engineering. She then went to Paris, where she was the first woman to study architecture at l'École de Beaux-Arts. Upon receiving her certificate in 1901, she returned to California and earned her architect's license in 1904. Her initial commissions came from various women's organizations; she also hired women whenever possible, particularly young designers. The more than seven hundred buildings she designed during her fifty-year career included William Randolph Hearst's San Simeon estate.

785. *Adelaide Marriot* (1883–1980)

Continuing the ageless tradition of women working in the applied arts, Marriot played a crucial role in organizing craftsworkers in Canada. In 1931 she merged the Handicrafts Association of Canada with the Canadian Handicrafts Guild to ensure equitable treatment of artisan laborers.

DANCERS

786. *Isadora Duncan* (1877–1927)

This innovator's work greatly influenced many modern dancers and choreographers, particularly in Europe. Born in San Francisco, she studied ballet briefly in childhood but had little formal training. In 1899 she went to Europe with her family. There, she created a kind of dance that rejected the traditional modes of ballet and theater, replacing them with improvisations inspired by nature and Greek art. She combined dance with her love of classical music, often dancing barefoot accompanied by the works of master composers. Eccentric to the end, she died by strangulation while driving, when her long scarf became entangled in one of the car's wheels.

787. *La Argentina*
(Antonia Mercé, 1890–1936)

Born in Buenos Aires into a family of dancers, La Argentina was an accomplished ballerina by eleven and the "premiere danseuse" of the Madrid Opera. But while still a teenager she left ballet behind to study traditional Spanish dance. Her mother acted as her teacher and by eighteen La Argentina was touring internationally, displaying her unparalleled command of Spanish dance. She viewed castanets as a crucial component of her performances and devoted much attention to perfecting her technique. She is considered the greatest Spanish dancer of all time.

788. *Josephine Baker* (1906–1975)

Outrageous in every respect, American-born Josephine Baker first found fame in Paris. A frequent performer at the Folies Bergère, Baker took the stage wearing nothing more than a few strings of pearls and a banana skirt. By the 1930s, dancing in New York's Ziegfeld Follies, she wore a tusked bikini that foreshadowed the bustiers created by Jean-Paul Gautier for Madonna's *Blond Ambition* tour. But while Baker loved to shock, she was not without substance. Her Paris appearances broke color barriers, and she was the first black performer to become a star in France. Soon afterward she attained worldwide celebrity, touring internationally. She spent World War II in France, becoming a member of the French Resistance as well as a French citizen. In 1954 she adopted the first of twelve children of various ethnic backgrounds who would make up her "Rainbow Tribe." The Rainbow Tribe was a deliberate and very conscious attempt on Baker's part to prove that all races and nationalities could live together in peace.

789. *Ruby Keeler* (1910–1993)

At thirteen, Ruby Keeler began her professional tap dancing career in New York, appearing in a George M. Cohan production of *The Rise of Rose O'Reilly.* Her continued successes on Broadway, in nightclubs and in the Ziegfeld shows led to Hollywood. At eighteen she arrived in Los Angeles, where she soon became the screen's first tap-dancing movie star. She also became Al Jolson's wife. Important films included *42nd Street, Gold Diggers of 1933* and *Footlight Parade;* she had a long professional association with Busby Berkeley. At sixty she made a successful comeback on Broadway in 1970's *No, No, Nanette.*

790. *Margot Fonteyn*
(Margaret Hookham, 1919–1991)

This English ballerina enjoyed a long career at the pinnacle of ballet, both in Great Britain and throughout Europe. Indeed, she is credited with raising dance to new heights in England. A favorite of ballet fans the world over, Fonteyn combined strong technique with grace and professionalism. She honed her talent first under Vera Volkova and then at the Sadler's Wells Ballet School, whose company (later known as the Royal Ballet) she joined. She worked closely with the choreographer Frederick Ashton dur-

ing the 1940s and 1950s on productions of *Symphonic Variations, Cinderella, Sylvia, Ondine* and many others. In addition to her work with the Royal Ballet, Fonteyn performed as a guest artist with many companies worldwide. Partnered with Rudolf Nureyev, she achieved continued acclaim late in her career.

791. *Tanjore Balasaraswati*
(1920–1984)

At four, Balasaraswati began studying Bharata Natya, an intricate Indian dance form performed only by women. By seven she began touring India and then internationally, attaining renown as her era's most accomplished Bharata Natya performer.

CHOREOGRAPHERS AND COMPANIES

792. *Ida Rubinstein* (1885–1960)

A ballerina in the Ballets Russes for six years, this Russian worked under the direction of Serge Diaghilev. When she broke with the Ballets Russes to form her own company, some saw her move as a direct challenge to Diaghilev's dominance. Her company produced work by Bronislava Nijinska and Léonide Massine, among others.

793. *Mary Wigman* (1886–1973)

In 1919, Mary Wigman began giving dance recitals that challenged the conventions of ballet in her native Germany. Her innovative style of free dance soon became internationally known, and she herself achieved a devoted following. She toured the U.S. individually and with her so-called "girl dance group."

794. *Marie Rambert* (1888–1982)

Originally from Poland, Marie Rambert founded a ballet school in London in 1920. She later formed a ballet company that used her school as a talent pool from which she selected dancers and choreographers. After going through a series of names, the company became known simply as Ballet Rambert in 1935. Not herself a choreographer, Rambert's contribution was as a company director. She knew talent and used her knowledge to produce the works of such choreographers as Frederick Ashton and Antony Tudor. She applied this same keen sense to exceptional dancers: Her company showcased the talents of Celia Franca, Peggy van Praagh and many others.

795. *Martha Graham* (1893–1991)

Martha Graham's impact on modern dance and the arts as a whole was tremendous. Her innovative, distinctive technique influenced a host of dancers and choreographers, Merce Cunningham and Paul Taylor among them. But her technical contributions to dance represent only one part of a complex vision. Cited by dance critics for its fierce intelligence, her dance explored a wide range of subject matter. She paid particular attention to women, creating pieces about the lives of Emily Dickinson and Charlotte and Emily Brontë. In many of Graham's pieces, women appear as a conscience or moral witness.

Martha Graham.

796. *Hanya Holm* (1898–1992)

Born in Germany, Holm first studied dance at the Dalcroze Institute in Frankfurt-am-Main and in 1921 joined Mary Wigman's company. Wigman mentored Holm for the next decade and encouraged her, in 1931, to open the Mary Wigman School in New York. Holm soon came into her own as a choreographer and teacher. Within five years she established her own modern-dance company. In the 1940s, she branched into musical theater, directing and choreographing a number of smash-hit Broadway musicals, including *Kiss Me, Kate, My Fair Lady* and *Camelot.* She continued her work on Broadway into the 1960s, balancing it with teaching at a number of different American colleges and universities.

797. Katherine Dunham
(1912–)

Not your typical dancer, choreographer or dance teacher, this African-American was also an anthropologist and social reformer. She integrated her diverse skills to create dance that incorporated movements rooted in African and Haitian traditions (she'd done ethnographic fieldwork in Haiti). She also used her dance company as an instrument of social reform in an effort to break down racial barriers. Her dance had an impact not only because her company toured the American South, but because it gained immense popularity, allowing her to reach wide and diverse audiences. In addition, Dunham established a number of dance schools in places as diverse as Manhattan, Haiti and East St. Louis.

798. Anna Sokolow (1912–)

With a background that included training at the School of American Ballet and nearly a decade performing in Martha Graham's company, Sokolow founded the first Mexican modern dance troupe in 1939. She emerged in the 1940s as a choreographer with a mission, who proclaimed that dancers need to experiment and who criticized peers she felt were not willing to take risks. Her own work often explored Mexican and Jewish themes; the provocative subject matter for 1961's *Dreams* was Nazi Germany and the concentration camps.

799. Alicia Alonso (1921–)

This ballerina founded her own ballet company in her native Cuba in 1948. Originally Ballet Alicia Alonso, it later became the Ballet Nacional de Cuba. Though she trained in the U.S. at the School of American Ballet, and danced both on Broadway and with the American Ballet Theater, Alonso proclaimed herself a revolutionary when Castro came to power in Cuba in 1959. In addition to running her company, Alonso opened a ballet school in Havana, but these commitments did not prevent her from dancing. She continued to perform both at home and abroad, forming a notable partnership with Igor Youskevitch, a Russian dancer and teacher.

800. A Page of History

In 1925 Ruth Page, who was both a choreographer and a ballerina, founded the Chicago Ballet. The ballet's progressive productions included collaborations with major creative figures such as Marc Chagall.

801. Twyla Tharp (1941–)

During the 1960s and 1970s, Twyla Tharp played a major role in generating popular interest in dance in the U.S. Her background was eclectic: She studied ballet, modern and popular dance, as well as music and even baton twirling. Her choreography reflects her disparate background and has long appealed to wide audiences. She has also choreographed for Broadway shows, as well as films.

802. Meredith Monk (1943–)

Meredith Monk's work incorporates the venue as part of the creative process. So integrated is her dance to the space in which it is performed that she will often refuse to restage a work in a new location. In some of her works she integrates the audience as well, asking them to follow the dancers from one set to another or inviting audience members to take part in the piece. She employs text, film, sound and lighting to augment her work and is especially known for composing music to accompany her pieces.

803. *Pioneering Choreographers*

In 1947, two American women—Virginia Sampler and Valerie E. Bettis—were the first choreographers to create a modern dance piece for a classical ballet company.

804. *Jane Goldberg* (1948–)

Part dancer, part historian, Jane Goldberg founded the Changing Times Tap Dancing Company in the mid-1970s. Her company combines performances by tap's elder statesmen with those of younger tap dancers. Goldberg has kept the tradition of tap alive, not only through performance but also by collecting oral histories from many grand old hoofers. While clearly respectful and cognizant of tap's traditions, her own dance incorporates a decidedly modern slant. She choreographs "topical" tap dances where she "raps" while she taps, covering a range of topics, including sex and feminism.

DRAMA QUEENS

805. *Go West, Young Soprano*

In 1850, British soprano Anna Hunt Thillon (1819–1903) became the first person to produce opera in San Francisco.

806. *Eva Le Gallienne* (1899–1991)

This English-born American actress, director and producer founded the Civic Repertory Theatre in 1926 to bring new plays and theatrical classics to the public at reasonable prices. Her early career in the U.S. was highlighted by performances as Julie in *Liliom* (1921) and as Princess Alexandra in *The Swan* (1923). Once she'd established the Civic Repertory Theatre, she directed and acted in productions throughout the company's seven-year history. She authored *At 33* (1934) and *With a Quiet Heart* (1953).

807. *Ariane Mnouchkine* (1938–)

This French director heads Théâtre du Soleil, a theater group known for its original works. Mnouchkine has piloted such Théâtre du Soleil productions as *1789* (1970), *1793* (1972), *The Golden Age* (1975), *Mephisto* (1979) and *Norodom Sihanouk* (1985).

808. *JoAnne Akalatis* (1937–)

An innovative director known for her experimental work, Akalatis presented plays across the U.S. and in Europe. The director and a founder of New York City's Mabou Mines theater company, she briefly served as artistic director of Joseph Papp's New York Shakespeare Festival in 1991.

809. *Elizabeth LeCompte* (1944–)

Both a director and playwright, LeCompte has served since 1979 as the artistic director for the Wooster Group, an experimental theater company in New York. In 1984 she was named associate director of the American National Theatre at the John F. Kennedy Center for the Performing Arts in Washington, D.C.

ACTRESSES

810. *Sarah Bernhardt*

(Henriette Rosine Bernard, 1844–1923)
This French actress became an international star for her emotional portrayals and extraordinary voice. She began her career with the Odéon Theater in 1866 and continued it with the Comédie-Française in 1872. Playing roles in such plays as *Kean, Le passant, Zaire* and many others, she rose to early renown. She parted with the Comédie-Française in 1880 to form her own company, which toured Europe, England and the U.S. Bernhardt performed in a variety of roles, including Marguerite in *La dame aux camélias,* then became the proprietress of the Théâtre de la Renaissance in 1893. In 1899 she leased a building and opened the Théâtre

Sarah Bernhardt.

Sarah-Bernhardt. Although her leg was amputated in 1915, she continued to perform until her death.

811. *Eleanora Duse* (1858–1924)

Duse was born in Italy and began performing with traveling companies while still a child. At the age of twenty she gained attention while acting in Zola's *Thérèse Raquin in Naples.* Before long she found wide fame acting in the works of the younger Alexandre Dumas, Verga and Ibsen. In 1886, she formed her own company, Dram-

matica Compagnia della Città de Roma. She toured extensively with the company, making her American debut in New York in 1893. A year later Duse began a five-year liaison with the Italian author Gabriele D'Annunzio, who wrote four of his five plays for her. She finds her place in history as one of theater's greatest tragic actors.

812. *Minnie Maddern Fiske*
(Marie Augusta Davey, 1864–1932)

Born in New Orleans, Fiske began performing as a child and grew to become one of America's greatest stage actresses. She also directed and wrote plays and promoted the plays of others, most notably Henrik Ibsen. She debuted in New York in 1882, and in 1890 married Harrison Fiske, the theatrical manager and director of the Manhattan Theatre. She appeared in her husband's play *Hester Crewe,* under his direction, and in many plays her husband produced, notably *Tess of the d'Urbervilles.* Her stage credits include roles in *A Doll's House, Rosmersholm, Ghosts, Pillars of Society* and *Hedda Gabler.* She became Ibsen's principal champion in America, as well as a champion of realism in general. Her last New York appearance was in the 1930s' *It's a Grand Life.*

813. *Fanny Brice*
(Fannie Borach, 1891–1951)

Born in New York, Brice was a popular star of musical comedy and appeared in many Broadway revues, most notably *The Ziegfeld Follies.* A born comedienne and comic singer, Brice also successfully performed torch songs. Appearances in musicals include *Honeymoon Express* (1913), *Nobody Home* (1915), *The Music Box Revue* (1924–1925), *Fioretta* (1929), *Sweet and Low* (1930) and *Crazy Quilt* (1931). She also appeared in films such as 1936's *The Great Ziegfeld* and had a long radio stint in "Baby Snooks" (1936–1951).

814. *Stella Adler* (1901–1992)

The daughter of the great Yiddish actor Jacob Adler, Stella Adler had the theater in her blood. She joined Harold Clurman's Group Theatre in 1931 and gained attention for her roles in that company's productions of *Awake and Sing!* (1935) and *Paradise Lost* (1935). Her acting career ended in 1945 with an appearance in *He Who Gets Slapped,* but she went on to found an acting school, the Stella Adler Conservatory, in 1949. Her lasting contribution as an acting teacher may perhaps have surpassed her career as an actress.

815. *Marlene Dietrich*
(Marie Magdalene Dietrich, 1901–1997)

The German-born Dietrich began her career in theatrical revues, moving to film in 1923. Her major breakthrough came in 1930, when she played Lola-Lola in Josef von Sternberg's *The Blue Angel.* In Hollywood, she worked with Sternberg at Paramount for the next six years, polishing her on-screen persona—the cross-dressing temptress no man, and few women, could resist—in such films as *Morocco* and *The Devil Is a Woman.* Quixotic, exotic, erotic, Dietrich had enough star power to fuel her career through fifty-three films. During World War II she performed extensively for American troops; in the 1950s, as her film days wound down, she began performing a cabaret act.

816. Tallulah Bankhead
(1903–1968)

Born in Huntsville, Alabama, this acerbic actress made her Broadway debut in *Squab Farm* in 1918. Her big breakthrough came five years later in London, with her appearance in *The Dancers,* followed up by roles in *The Green Hat* (1925) and *They Knew What They Wanted* (1926). Back on Broadway in 1939, she starred as Regina in Lillian Hellman's *The Little Foxes.* She won various critics' awards and then went on to make films, including 1944's *Lifeboat* and 1945's *A Royal Scandal.* As famous for her offstage antics as her onstage acting, she called herself "the foe of moderation, the champion of excess." Her scandalous behavior secured her a place among the most famous rabble-rousers of her generation.

817. Hattie McDaniel

Hattie McDaniel made history as the first African-American, male or female, to win an Academy Award. Her Oscar was for Best Supporting Actress in 1939's *Gone With the Wind,* in which she played the stereotypical "mammy."

818. Diana Sands
(1934–1973)

With appearances in *A Raisin in the Sun* (1959), *Blues for Mister Charlie* (1964) and *The Owl and the Pussycat* (1964), Diana Sands became one of the first African-American actresses to play major roles on Broadway.

819. Vanessa Redgrave (1937–)

Born into a British family of actors, Redgrave made her stage debut with her father Michael Redgrave in *A Touch of the Sun* (London, 1958). Her major roles include Rosalind in *As You Like It,* Nina in *The Seagull,* Jean in *The Prime of Miss Jean Brodie,* her 1976 Broadway debut as Ellida in *The Lady from the Sea,* and Lady Torrance in *Orpheus Descending.* Most recently she appeared as Vita Sackville-West in a 1995 production of *Vita and Virginia,* a two-woman show with Eileen Atkins. In addition to her extensive theater work, she has appeared in many films and on television. She is also known for her controversial politics, such as her anti-Zionist support of Palestine.

820. Mary Tyler Moore

Long before *The Mary Tyler Moore Show* and even *The Dick Van Dyke Show* appeared on the air, Mary Tyler Moore had a brief stint in *Richard Diamond, Private Eye.* The show ran from 1957 to 1960, but Moore stayed only thirteen weeks, playing a secretary shown only as a pair of legs. *The Dick Van Dyke Show* came next, running for five years during the 1960s. But the 1970s were the Mary decade. *The Mary Tyler Moore Show* dominated the CBS Saturday night lineup until its self-imposed cancellation in 1977. Meanwhile, Moore and Grant Tinker's MTM Productions flourished, producing easily digestible fare.

821. Diahann Carroll

When she starred in the NBC sitcom *Julia* (1968–1971), Diahann Carroll broke television's color barrier. She was not the first black TV star, but she was the first black actor to have a show built around her. Against the odds, *Julia* became a bona fide hit.

822. Sigourney Weaver
(Susan Weaver, 1949–)

Born the same year as Jessica Lange and Meryl Streep, Sigourney Weaver has built an eclectic film career that may wind up with the most staying power. Her unusual path to success made her the hero of the *Alien* trilogy, in which she gave real dimension to a smart and tough-minded sci-fi character (she also co-produced the third feature). In both *Ghostbusters* and *Ghostbusters II,* she played comedy. *Gorillas in the Mist* won her an Oscar nomination for her fierce and frightening portrayal of zoologist Dian Fossey. Her role as a comically vicious yuppie in *Working Girl* earned her a Best Supporting Actress nomination. Her commanding presence served her well in her role as Queen Isabella in *1492: Conquest of Paradise* (1992), while her knack for comedy again shone in 1993's *Dave.* Her recent films include Roman Polanski's *Death and the Maiden* (1995), in which she delivered an intensely disturbing performance as a torture victim who confronts her torturer, and the thriller *Copycat* (1995), which cast her as an agoraphobic forensic psychiatrist.

823. Roseanne Barr (1952–)

Roseanne became a household name as the mother of all TV moms, Roseanne Connor. Her path to television fame was defiant and hard fought. A single mother of three by age twenty-six, she lived in Colorado working as a window dresser, maid, and waitress while slowly building a comedy act. As a cocktail waitress, she slung wisecracks as well as drinks to the customers, who lapped it up. She then tried stand-up at a club for new comedians and honed her stage presence as the MC at a strip club; meanwhile, she worked at a women's bookstore and became immersed in academic feminism. Banned at one point from performing at the stand-up club, she organized a "Take Back the Mike" night and enlisted other feminist comics. The club invited her back, material intact. From the beginning, Roseanne's comedy has been about telling the sometimes ugly truth from the standpoint of her own brand of no-holds-barred feminism. She appeared on national television, on *The Tonight Show,* for the first time in 1985 and did an HBO special in 1987. In 1988, her series, *Roseanne,* began its run on ABC. She battled with writers and producers to maintain her distinctive, if caustic, voice in the show, and secured creative control after a series of early standoffs. Its ninth episode hit number one in the ratings, and the show has remained in the top ten ever since. Today, Roseanne vies with Oprah Winfrey for the mantle of most powerful woman in the entertainment industry. Although their styles contrast sharply, they share a history of child sexual abuse and a passion to speak the truth about that history.

824. Jodie Foster
(Alicia Christian Foster, 1962–)

There are many unforgettable things about Jodie Foster, but the first of these was certainly her 1976 appearance as Iris in Martin Scorsese's *Taxi Driver.* She played the role at thirteen but was already a seasoned pro, having appeared in commercials, on TV and in six other films. She acted in fifteen more films before giving her first Academy Award–winning performance, in 1988's *The Accused.* In the interim she graduated from Yale University, where she became the object of John Hinckley's obsession. Hinckley said his 1981 assassination attempt on President Ronald Reagan was a bid for Foster's attention. The episode made Foster somewhat media-shy, but she transcended her identity as child star and historical curiosity not only in *The Accused* but in 1991's *The Silence of the Lambs.* For her role in that film she won her second Oscar; she was still only twenty-nine. The same year she made her directorial debut with *Little Man Tate,* a film she also starred in. Another Foster vehicle, *Nell* (1995), was the first film from Egg, her production company.

PLAYWRIGHTS AND SCREENWRITERS

Forc'd Marriage, The Rover, False Count and *The Roundheads.* She also did translations and wrote poetry and novels. Her best known non-dramatic work was *Oroonoko,* an autobiographical novel based on her life in Surinam.

Aphra Behn.

825. *Aphra Behn* (1640–1689)

Considered the first Englishwoman to make a profession of writing, "the Incomparable Astrea," as she was known, grew up in Surinam, West Indies. This colorful figure served as a spy in Antwerp, though her efforts went unrewarded and she was subsequently imprisoned for debt. Throughout the 1670s and 1680s, Behn wrote raw and lively dramatic comedies, including

826. *Mae West* (1893–1980)

Mae West was a bombshell in every sense. Her name conjures instant images and her quips have become national treasures, but many fans overlook her creative essence: She was a writer from her start in vaudeville and through much of her film career. Her smash hit plays *Sex, The Drag* and 1928's *Diamond Lil* broke social taboos, much as West broke Hollywood taboos in 1933. Approached by the ailing Paramount studio to do a film version of *Diamond Lil,* she demanded final cut and total creative control. She chose Lowell Sherman to direct, and cast then-unknown Cary Grant as her co-star. The resulting film, *She Done Him Wrong,* was an unqualified success. Subsequent screenplay credits include *Belle of the Nineties* (1934), *Goin' to Town* (1935), *Go West, Young Man* (1936), *Klondike Annie* (1936), *Every Day's a Holiday* (1939) and *My Little Chickadee* (1940). The only thing that got in her way was the establishment of the Production Code in 1934, the year West's income was the second highest in the nation. *Klondike Annie* generated so much controversy that the censors took aim and sent West's career into a marked decline. Ironically, it was newspaper magnate William Randolph Hearst—the one American to earn more than her in 1934—who sicced the censors on West.

827. Lillian Hellman
(1905–1984)

Born in New Orleans, Hellman became a prolific playwright as well as an outspoken advocate of leftist causes. Her first play was 1934's *The Children's Hour.* Its exploration of and preoccupation with the dark, even evil side of human nature set the tone for works to come. These would include *The Little Foxes* (1939), *Watch on the Rhine* (1941), *Another Part of the Forest* (1946) and *Toys in the Attic* (1960). Embroiled in the anti-Communist witch-hunts of the McCarthy era, Hellman sent a letter to the House Committee on Un-American Activities in 1952, saying that she was willing to answer questions about herself but would not inform on friends. From this letter came her famous phrase, "I cannot and will not cut my conscience to fit this year's fashions." She had a thirty-year relationship with the mystery writer Dashiell Hammett.

828. Alice Childress
(1920–)

When her 1952 play *Gold through the Trees* was produced, this playwright became one of the first African-American women to have her work performed on a New York stage. Her later plays include *Trouble in Mind* (1955), *The Wedding Band* (1966) and *Wine in the Wilderness* (1969).

829. Ruth Prawer Jhabvala

A kind of silent partner to the Merchant-Ivory producer/director team, Jhabvala has adapted novels such as *The Remains of the Day, Maurice, Howards End* and *The Bostonians* for the screen. Merchant-Ivory's first joint effort was an adaptation of Jhabvala's own novel, *The Householder.*

830. Beth Henley
(1952–)

A playwright in the Southern Gothic tradition, Henley crafts darkly comic plays. In 1981, her *Crimes of the Heart* won the Pulitzer prize. Later works include *The Wake of Jamey Foster* (1982), *Am I Blue?* (1982) and *The Miss Firecracker Contest* (1984).

COMPOSERS AND SONGWRITERS

831. *Fanny Mendelssohn*
(1805–1847)

Though nearly all her music remains unpublished, German composer Fanny Mendelssohn (the sister of Felix Mendelssohn) wrote some five hundred works.

832. *Ethel Smyth* (1858–1944)

In 1898, English composer Ethel Smyth created *Fantasio,* an opera for which she also wrote the libretto. The pioneering artist went on to compose an anthem for the suffrage movement entitled *March of Women* (1916). She also continued her classical work, earning respect for such contributions as the opera *The Boatswain's Mate* (1917). In 1920, Smyth was named Dame Commander of the British Empire.

833. *Ma Rainey*
(Gertrude Melissa Nix Pridgett, 1886–1939)

The "mother of the blues" didn't just sing blues songs, she wrote and recorded them. Her music, representative of very early blues, treats subjects such as love, hardship and the suffering of women.

834. *Carole King* (1942–)

With husband Gerry Goffin, Carole King wrote hit after hit for New York's famed Brill Building music mill during the 1960s. So highly regarded were the duo that when the Beatles came to New York for the first time, they made sure to meet their idols and hit them up for songwriting tips. King's songs from this era include "Will You Still Love Me Tomorrow," "Take Good Care of My Baby," "Run to Him," "The Loco-Motion," "One Fine Day," "Oh No Not My Baby," "Don't Bring Me Down," "Pleasant Valley Sunday" and "A Natural Woman," most written for other artists. In 1968 King and Goffin divorced and King went on to a successful career as a singer/songwriter. Although she released several albums, she never topped the success of her first LP, 1971's *Tapestry,* which became the most popular album of the 1970s.

835. *Joni Mitchell*
(Roberta Joan Anderson, 1943–)

Canadian-born Joni Mitchell performed in Calgary folk clubs before moving to New York City in 1966 and signing with Reprise. Her first two albums received little attention, but *Clouds* (1969) yielded the hit songs "Both Sides Now," "Circle Game" and "Songs to Aging Children Come." Even before the album was released, Judy Collins did a cover of "Both Sides Now" that put it into the top ten. *Ladies of the Canyon* came next, with the songs "Woodstock" and "Big Yellow Taxi." "Taxi" made the charts as a single, while "Woodstock" became the after-the-fact, yet haunting and enduring, anthem of the epic festival Mitchell hadn't attended. *Blue* (1971) made it to number fifteen on the charts, and *For the Roses* (1972) made it to number eleven. This pattern continued with 1974's *Court & Spark,* which went to number two and featured "Help Me," Mitchell's only top-ten single. *Miles of Aisles,* a live album released the same year, also hit number two, marking Mitchell's peak. An experimental departure, 1975's *Hissing of Summer Lawns,* landed a respectable number four slot, but *Hejira* and *Don Juan's Reckless Daughter* were defiantly noncommercial. Regardless, commercial success has never seemed to be Mitchell's goal. Her progression as an artist and her continued production of quality music, even once her heyday had passed, attests to something deeper at work than a mercenary desire to make the charts.

VOCALISTS AND MUSICIANS

836. *Bessie Smith* (1894–1937)

The Empress of the Blues got her start with Ma Rainey, the Mother of the Blues, in 1912 and toured with her in 1915. Smith then appeared in her own revue in Atlanta and began recording in the early 1920s, although the exact date is unclear. What is clear is that she recorded for Columbia Records from 1923 to 1931. In fact, her recording sales are credited with keeping Columbia out of bankruptcy. But when the Depression hit, Columbia simply dropped Smith, effectively ending her career. The company tried to give her another chance in 1933, but it didn't work. She died from loss of blood after a car accident, prompting rumors that she was refused hospital treatment because she was black. Those proved untrue.

837. *Marian Anderson* (1899–1993)

This African-American contralto broke color barriers in the rarefied world of opera. In 1939, after the all-white Daughters of the American Revolution (DAR) refused to let her sing at Constitution Hall, she sang a historic concert at the Lincoln Memorial, before an audience of more than 75,000. The DAR's racist treatment of Anderson prompted Eleanor Roosevelt to resign from the group, drawing international attention to the event. In 1955, Anderson achieved another breakthrough when she sang Ulrica in *A Masked Ball* at New York's Metropolitan Opera, becoming the first African-American singer to appear there.

838. *Billie Holiday*
(Eleanora Fagan, 1915–1959)

Arriving on the scene hard on the heels of Bessie Smith, Holiday recorded her first record—with Columbia—the same year Smith recorded her last. Like Smith, Holiday, too, would die young (Smith died at forty-three, Holiday at forty-four). While Holiday listened to Smith as a child, her style would be uniquely her own. She is considered by many to be both the first and the greatest jazz singer. Of her debut at Harlem's Apollo Theater in 1935, MC Ralph Cooper reportedly said, "It ain't the blues—I don't know what it is, but you got to hear her."

839. *Edith Piaf*
(Edith Giovanna Gassion, 1915–1963)

This French vocalist began her career as a Paris street singer before being discovered in 1930 by Louis Leplee, a cabaret owner who changed her name to Piaf, French slang for "sparrow." Piaf achieved international renown as a chanteuse, interpreting melancholy torch songs. *"Les trois cloches"* and *"L'hymne a l'amour"* were among these, though she is perhaps best known for her rendition of *"La vie en rose."*

840. Maria Callas
(1923–1977)

Shortly after she made her debut with the National Opera in Athens, Greece, New York–born Callas broke out at the age of eighteen with her performance as Tosca. Five years later she debuted in Italy, the world capital of opera, in the title role of *La Gioconda.* She went on to perform for over a decade at La Scala (1950–1962), returning to New York in 1956 to make a stunning debut with the Metropolitan Opera, singing the title role in *Norma.*

841. Ella Fitzgerald
(1918–1997)

A master of the jazz singing form known as scat (in which a vocalist uses nonsense syllables for rhythmic and melodic effect), Ella Fitzgerald attained popularity and influence as great as any other jazz musician's. She started her career after winning a 1934 talent contest at the Apollo Theater in Harlem. Over the course of a more-than-sixty-year career, she recorded with the likes of Count Basie and Duke Ellington, but she did the bulk of her work as a soloist. Her renditions of "A-Tisket A-Tasket," "Laura," "How Long Has This Been Going On?" and many others remain some of the best-loved recordings from the golden age of jazz.

842. Sarah Vaughan (1924–1990)

Called the Divine One, Vaughan was one of this century's greatest singers. As a child she played piano and sang in her church choir. She won kudos at an Apollo Theater amateur night in Harlem before joining the Earl Hines Band in 1944. Leaving Hines a year later, she formed a group with Billy Eckstine, also a Hines expatriot. Soon she was recording under her own name, and the rest is history. Her spectacular career spanned more than four decades.

843. The Andrews Sisters

This 1940s vocal trio, comprising Laverne, Maxine and Patti Andrews, sold 60 million records.

844. Patsy Cline
(Virginia Petterson Henley, 1932–1963)

Ten years after her death, Cline was inducted into the Country Music Hall of Fame. In her tragically short career, she was the first woman to cross over from country to pop, challenging the great Kitty Wells's position as the first lady of country music. But unlike most women in country, Cline was no honky-tonk angel. She could booze and brawl with the best of them—and she often did. She died in a plane crash in 1963.

845. First Chair

In 1952, Doirot Anthony Dwyer became the principal flautist of the Boston Symphony Orchestra, the first woman ever to hold first chair in a major orchestra.

846. Diana Ross & the Supremes

Along with Mary Wilson and Florence Ballard, two friends from her Detroit housing project, Diana Ross got her start in a girl group they formed in the 1950s. They named themselves the Primettes after meeting a boy group called the Primes, later known as the Temptations. Ballard, their original leader, renamed the group the Supremes shortly before they signed with Berry Gordy's Motown in 1961. Once there, they became the ultimate crossover sensation, with hit after hit in the 1960s. As Ross eclipsed Ballard as a performer, tension escalated within the group; Ballard left in 1967 and was replaced by Cindy Birdsong, recruited from Patti LaBelle's Bird Belles. Now known as Diana Ross & the Supremes, the group continued hit making for another few years. Ross left the group in 1970, but the Supremes kept going for nearly a decade afterward. The hits, however, followed Ross: She had thirty-three between 1970 and 1985.

847. Joan Baez
(1941–)

As famous for her politics as for her voice, folk singer Joan Baez has recorded classic and original songs since the late 1950s. After making the hits "Mary Hamilton" (1960) and "There But for Fortune" (1965), she gained ascendancy among the popular musicians, such as Bob Dylan, who used their work to protest the Vietnam War. Baez was a featured performer at Woodstock and went on to record successful albums such as *Diamonds and Rust*. In recent years her political energy has focused on human rights in Latin America.

848. Aretha Franklin (1942–)

With her first monster hit, 1967's "I Never Loved a Man," Aretha Franklin skyrocketed to the top of the charts and stayed there, with "Respect," her signature song, released shortly thereafter. Though she achieved superstardom at only twenty-five, her arrival was bumpy and indirect. At eighteen, with years of gospel circuit touring already behind her, she signed with Columbia Records. There, as the latest "find" of producer John Hammond—who had made such stars as Bessie Smith and Billie Holiday—Franklin's career foundered. By the time her contract expired in 1966, she'd honed her vocal skills, but more important, she'd determined she could no longer allow others to dictate to her. When she signed with Jerry Wexler, then vice president of Atlantic, she gained control in the studio, choosing songwriters, arranging songs and singing them the way she wanted to. Her phenomenal success came only once she was in charge.

849. Helen Reddy
(1942–)

Though not strictly a one-hit wonder, Reddy will be best remembered for 1972's "I Am Woman." Writer of much of her own material, including "I Am Woman," she had a string of fourteen top-forty hits between 1971 and 1977. Among these were "Delta Dawn," "Angie Baby" and "I Don't Know How to Love Him." Eight of her albums reached the top twenty.

850. Janis Joplin (1943–1970)

Joplin's death by heroin overdose in October 1970 came less than a month after the death of

Jimi Hendrix; Jim Morrison would join them within two years. Together, they would form a triumvirate within the dead-rock-star pantheon. Joplin's place in death—sandwiched between the baddest boys of 1960s rock—appropriately mirrors her place in life. Rock critic Ellen Willis places Joplin "second only to Bob Dylan in importance as a creator/recorder/embodiment of her generation's history and mythology" and calls her "the only woman to achieve that kind of stature in what was basically a male club, the only Sixties culture hero to make visible and public women's quest for individual liberation, which was very different from men's."

851. Women Drummers

Perhaps the only thing Maureen Tucker and Karen Carpenter have in common is that they played the drums. The music they made—with the Velvet Underground and the Carpenters, respectively—couldn't have been more different. In the late 1960s, the Velvet Underground played minimalist art rock and achieved a cult following. "Mo" Tucker stayed behind her kit, so anonymous and androgynous that at first it was unclear if she was male or female. Conversely, Karen Carpenter and her brother Richard dominated 1970s pop. During their reign, the Carpenters perfected their squeaky-clean personas and highly produced sound. Karen played drums for a while, on stage if not in the studio. But it was her voice that made the difference, as she became the duo's lead singer. While Karen Carpenter was likely to be found on a network TV show in a long white gown, Maureen Tucker dressed mostly in black and traveled with Andy Warhol's Exploding Plastic Inevitable.

852. Operatic Leader

In 1976, Sarah Caldwell became the first woman conductor at New York's Metropolitan Opera.

853. Marianne Faithfull (1946–)

Entering rock via her boyfriend Mick Jagger, Faithfull struggled for years to transcend that identity. Sighted at a Rolling Stones party by the group's manager, she became a famous English girl singer at just eighteen. Her recording of the Jagger/Richards song "As Tears Go By" hit number nine on the charts, followed by more hits and her much publicized affair with Jagger. In 1969 she wrote the lyrics for "Sister Morphine" and cut a single of the song, but her record company pulled it within two days of its release in an attempt to preserve her lighter pop persona. By then, however, Faithfull had a drug problem; shortly after the death of Stones member Brian Jones, she attempted suicide. She later said that at the time she saw suicide as the only way out of her relationship with Jagger. "Sister Morphine" appeared on the Stones' *Sticky Fingers* (1971), but Jagger and Richards got the credit for it. Faithfull's first comeback came in 1979, with *Broken English,* an album that forced critics to take her seriously. *Dangerous Acquaintances* (1981) and *A Child's Adventure* (1983) were less successful, but in 1987 *Strange Weather* was a tremendous critical success, presenting her more as a chanteuse than a rock singer. On *Blazing Away* (1990), a live album, Faithfull reclaimed the entire body of her work from under the Stones' mantle and showed new work. The 1990s also found her singing Kurt Weill's *Seven Deadly Sins* and writing her autobiography, *Faithfull* (1994).

854. *Patti Smith* (1946–)

Starting out as a writer of lyrics for Blue Oyster Cult (she was Allen Lanier's girlfriend), Patti Smith got proper credit for her work right off the bat. Also unlike Marianne Faithfull, she eclipsed her boyfriend almost immediately. She began making records in the mid-1970s while in her late twenties, rather than in the mid-1960s while in her late teens, as Faithfull did. Dark-haired, gaunt and androgynous in the extreme, she never suffered under the sex-kitten image of her counterpart. Instead of sexy, she was, more accurately, sexual, borrowing her guise from men like Elvis, Keith Richards and Jim Morrison. Unapologetically raunchy and outrageous, she was also the undisputed leader of The Patti Smith Group. Their 1974 debut album, *Horses*, was a critical success that instantly put Smith on the map, if not the charts. The ensuing years were more difficult. Critics panned her second album, *Radio Ethiopia* (1976), complaining that Smith had given in to the worst influences of her band. In 1977 she fell off a stage and broke her neck, and doctors said she would never perform again. But she was back a year later with an "out of traction/back in action" mini-tour, and then released her most popular album, *Easter.* The album's "Because the Night" went to number thirteen on the American charts and made number five in the U.K. After cutting the far less successful *Wave* in 1979, Smith married MC5 guitarist Fred "Sonic" Smith, set up house in Detroit and had children. Smith released *Dream of Life,* a comeback collaboration with her husband, in 1988, but she did not tour. After her husband's sudden death in 1995, Smith resurfaced and resumed recording. In 1996 she released *Gone Again* and in 1998 *Peace and Noise*.

855. *Star Wives and Widows*

It's not easy to be married to a rock star, particularly if you're a rock star yourself; it's harder still if your husband dies violently. Blamed for breaking up the Beatles, among many other supposed sins, Yoko Ono was the wife, then widow, of John Lennon. She has had to fight hard to be taken seriously as an artist in her own right, and it's questionable whether she'll ever win, or if she ever had a chance of winning. Courtney Love has fared somewhat better, so far. Though initially seen as a gold digger clinging to the coattails of husband and Nirvana front man Kurt Cobain, Love has emerged since Cobain's 1994 suicide as a superstar of sorts. Her second album with her band, Hole, *Live Through This,* was a critical and commercial success. It remains to be seen whether rock fans will stay behind Love or turn on her, as recent rumblings about her star trip may signal the beginning of a serious backlash. But it's worth noting that Love's star quality is what put Hole on the map to begin with, and she has established a core following that is unlikely to desert her.

856. *Madonna*

(Madonna Louise Ciccone, 1958–)

Born in Rochester, Michigan, Madonna studied dance at the University of Michigan. After working briefly in Paris as a backup singer for a French disco star, she moved to Manhattan, where she was a drummer for the Breakfast Club and lead singer for Emmy, two new-wave groups. A demo tape cut with Emmy earned

Madonna a contract with Sire records, which released her first album in 1983. Since that smash-hit debut she's remained at the top, despite controversy and criticism. A consummate entrepreneur and entertainer, Madonna just keeps coming back, in different guises and with different musical styles.

857. Nadja Salerno-Sonnenberg
(1961–)

At age ten, violinist Nadja Salerno-Sonnenberg debuted with the Philadelphia Orchestra. At twenty she won the Naumberg Violin Competition, becoming the youngest performer ever to do so. Her future was secure, if not without controversy. In the conservative world of classical music, Salerno-Sonnenberg shocked aficionados by appearing onstage in pants and establishing a radical stage persona. She has drawn criticism for the intense movements and facial expressions she makes while performing; offstage, she is equally confounding. Her fondness for playing pool, smoking cigarettes and drinking whiskey continues to underscore her uniqueness among classical musicians, but the music world has come to respect her genius.

BEHIND THE CAMERA

858. Natalie Kalmus
(1892–1965)

In 1915, Natalie Kalmus and her husband, Herbert T. Kalmus, invented the Technicolor process. Far more than her husband, Kalmus understood from the outset that Technicolor would become an industry standard. She meticulously perfected color separations, creating the tones upon which Technicolor's distinctive natural look depended. In 1939, she supervised color processing on two standouts of her career—and of film history: *Gone With the Wind* and *The Wizard of Oz*.

859. Margaret Booth
(1989–)

Margaret Booth was the supervising editor at the MGM movie studio from 1937 to 1968. In need of cash, she signed on as a cutter for D. W. Griffith right out of high school. She then moved to Louis B. Mayer's studio, which became MGM in 1924. Her eye was so keen that she came to the attention of MGM production supervisor Irving Thalberg, who told her she should consider directing, but she declined. When Thalberg died in 1936, Mayer named Booth supervising editor. With the transition to sound film, she developed a sound editing process by trial and error; her innovations became guideposts for others. In her long career with MGM and later working for Ray Stark, she put her stamp on countless films.

860. Brianne Murphy

Brianne Murphy continues to make history as the only woman director of photography in IATSE, the Hollywood Feature Film Union.

MOVIE DIRECTORS AND PRODUCERS

861. Early Directing Women

While much is rightly made of the difficulties women have breaking into the male bastion of film directing, a woman—Alice Guy Blache (1875–1968)—is credited as the first director in history to make a narrative film, *The Cabbage Fairy* (1896). French-born Blache took an immediate interest in the technological advancements of her time, which included Lumiere cameras, and soon employed them in the first of her many hundreds of short and feature films. In the early twentieth century, women had more license in film than they have enjoyed since, but the contributions they made have been slighted, or discredited entirely. No matter how actually subversive, their work is generally dismissed as encompassing "domestic" themes. Women of Blache's era, Mary Pickford among them, were forced to walk a tightrope, careful not to alienate the public by revealing too much power behind the camera. These and later women directors—such as Dorothy Arzner, Lois Weber and Elaine May—all played the tradeoff game in order to pursue their craft. Strategies included disavowing the suffragist cause, carefully retaining a "ladylike" public persona, complaining about working with other women behind the camera, or bashing their on-screen female characters. Ida Lupino (1918–) stated publicly and emphatically that she'd rather be a good wife and mother than do the "career thing."

862. Mary Pickford

(Gladys Marie Smith, 1894–1979)

The Canadian-born Pickford began her stage career at five, and by sixteen she was already a major draw at the box office, in leading roles in the silent films of D. W. Griffith. In contrast to the little orphan ingenue she often played on screen, Pickford was a powerhouse behind the camera. The savviest of businesswomen, she was deeply involved in film production and distribution. A founder of United Artists (with Douglas Fairbanks—her second husband—and Charlie Chaplin), Pickford ran the studio from all angles, serving as star, studio owner, director and executive producer. Her mother is credited for putting Pickford on the star track early, demanding for her daughter ten thousand dollars a week when the going rate was twenty-five and pegging her daughter's salary to Charlie Chaplin's. Pickford was the first actor, male or female, to become a millionaire.

863. Leni Riefenstahl (1902–)

A looming figure relegated to the shadows of film history, Riefenstahl is the creator of such films as *The Blue Light, Victory of Faith, Day of Freedom, Olympia I* and *II, Tiefland, Schwarze Fracht* and, most infamously, *Triumph of the Will.* Her place in film and in history remains ambiguous because of her affiliation with the Nazis. Hitler recognized Riefenstahl's talent and recruited her to make the films he proposed. Before World War II broke out, *The Blue Light, Olympia* and *Triumph of the Will* won European film prizes. According to Riefenstahl, "at that period, Hitler had acquired a certain credit in the world, and he fascinated a certain number of people, among them Winston Churchill," and *Triumph of the Will* "showed what everyone was witness to or had heard about. Everyone was impressed by it. I am the one who fixed that impression, who captured it on film." A reminder of the prewar world's admiration for Hitler and his programs, the film has since earned Riefenstahl condemnation as a sympathizer. In response, she has always denied knowledge of Nazi atrocities, both before and during the war. Of those who denounce her, she asks how "I, I alone, I should be able to foresee that one day things would change?" Her films, in her words, are a reminder that "One saw things before the war out of different eyes than after."

864. *Kinuyo Tanaka*
(1909–1977)

Like many other women directors, Tanaka, Japan's first, began as an actress. By the early 1930s she was a star; twenty years later she began her short directorial career. She made her first film, *Love Letter,* in 1953 and followed it with *The Moon Has Risen,* her only other film, in 1955. Despite her star status and the support of Yasujiro Ozu (her director in ten features), she could not survive as a director within Japan's studio system. Kenji Mizoguchi, then head of the Japanese directors' organization, proclaimed the conventional wisdom that women should not make films. That Mizoguchi had directed Tanaka in fourteen films and that the two had been lovers since 1947 only underscored the irony and futility of Tanaka's position. Her relationship with Mizoguchi didn't last much longer than Tanaka's directorial career; she returned to acting.

865. *Julia Phillips*

The co-producer of *Taxi Driver, Close Encounters of the Third Kind* and other films, Phillips was the first woman in history to win an Academy Award for Best Picture, for 1973's *The Sting.*

866. *Barbra Streisand* (1942–)

With 1983's *Yentl,* Barbra Streisand became the first woman ever to produce, co-author, direct, sing and star in a feature film. In 1991, she was nominated for an Academy Award for Best Director for *The Prince of Tides.*

867. *Penny Marshall* (1942–)

Penny Marshall made her first directorial efforts on the small screen. While starring in the hit television series *Laverne and Shirley,* she directed a few episodes of the show, which was produced by her brother Garry Marshall. In 1986, three years after the demise of *Laverne and Shirley,* she made her big-screen directorial debut with *Jumping Jack Flash,* a vehicle for comic actress Whoopie Goldberg. Marshall's breakthrough film, 1988's *Big,* was just that, right where it counts: the box office. The film's success secured her future: She went on to direct *Awakenings* (1990), *A League of Their Own* (1992) and *Renaissance Man* (1994).

868. *Euzhan Palcy* (1957–)

Euzhan Palcy was not only the first black woman to direct a Hollywood feature film (1989's *A Dry White Season*), she also worked on *La Messagère* (1976), the first film ever produced in her native Martinique. Palcy was just nineteen when she went to Paris and found a mentor in François Truffaut. Truffaut supported her next film project—one she'd dreamed of from the age of fourteen—1983's *Sugar Cane Alley.* Spurred to pursue a film career out of anger with the typical depictions of blacks in the movies, she was criticized for *A Dry White Season*'s focus on a white character's struggle with apartheid. About this choice Palcy is matter-of-fact, saying she "knew Hollywood would not do a film about black people unless the main character was a white man."

869. To Name Just a Few

Recently, women have produced dozens of Hollywood's most successful films, including:

Circle of Friends (Arlene Sellers)
Clockers (Rosalie Swedlin)
Fatal Attraction (Sherry Lansing)
Forrest Gump (Wendy Finerman)
Free Willy 2 (Lauren Shuler-Donner)
The Joy Luck Club (Janet Yang)
Kids (Christine Vachon)
Mrs. Doubtfire (Marcia Garces Williams)
Seven (Lynn Harris)
The Shawshank Redemption (Liz Glotzer)
Sleepless in Seattle (Lynda Obst)
Something to Talk About (Paula Weinstein and Anthea Sylbert)
Waiting to Exhale (Deborah Schindler)

TELEVISION PRODUCERS

870. Lucille Ball (1911–1989)

With appearances in more than thirty films, Lucille Ball was no newcomer when she and husband, Desi Arnaz, took over American television with their *I Love Lucy* sitcom in 1951. The show's success and Ball's popularity were phenomenal. Arnaz is credited with initial business savvy, retaining ownership of the huge body of work they would create. This move was crucial to the establishment of the Desilu empire, which gobbled up RKO studios within a few years and turned it into a TV production house.

Lucille Ball.

Despite Arnaz's crucial early input, it was Ball who would rule for the next two and a half decades. *I Love Lucy* ran until 1957; Ball and Arnaz then presented a monthly comedy hour until their divorce. In 1960 Ball emerged from the divorce as president of Desilu, having bought out Arnaz. She returned to TV in 1962 with *The Lucy Show*, which ran through 1968. That year she sold Desilu for $17 million and launched another sitcom, *Here's Lucy*, which ran until 1974. The long run of her three sitcom vehicles, each of which aired on Monday evenings at 9:00 P.M., assured CBS dominion over Monday night for many years.

871. Jane Cahill Pfeiffer

From 1978 to 1980, Jane Cahill Pfeiffer was chairman of NBC and a board member of NBC's parent company, RCA. With these positions she broke through the glass ceiling, reaching the highest level yet attained by a woman in broadcasting.

872. Oprah Winfrey (1954–)

Oprah Winfrey started out as a television newscaster in Nashville, Tennessee, and hosted a talk show in Baltimore before moving to Chicago in 1984. After two years there, her morning talk show, *AM Chicago,* was revamped, renamed *The Oprah Winfrey Show* and nationally syndicated by King World. It met with immediate success as an afternoon program and Winfrey soon became a household name. She maintained ownership of the show and now owns her own production company—Harpo (Oprah spelled backward) Productions. Winfrey has the highest earnings of any woman in the entertainment industry—currently believed to exceed $40 million a year. In addition to hosting her talk show, she also acts and produces. She had a supporting role in *The Color Purple* and a leading role in *The Women of Brewster Place,* the latter of which she also produced.

873. TV Movie Queen

At one time the executive producer for ABC's Movie of the Week, Lillian Gallo went independent to produce such TV movies as *Hustling, What Are Best Friends For* and *Stranger Who Looks Like Me.*

874. Lucie Salhany

Beginning as a secretary at a local TV station, Salhany ascended to the position of chairman of Twentieth Television in 1991, the culmination of a twenty-year career. Her position gives her control over all of Fox's production and distribution for network, syndication and cable.

Part

NINE

Sports and Adventure

RULES OF THE GAME

875. Taking the Cure

Conventional medical wisdom at the turn of the twentieth century posited that the human body contained a finite amount of energy. Thus, whatever part of the body was used drew energy from other parts. This theory was used to deny women education because if women "used their heads" they drained energy from their reproductive organs, perhaps even causing damage to them. Doctors, however, were also concerned with the physical frailty of middle- and particularly upper-class white women. In order to ensure the propagation of the white upper classes, they prescribed exercise as a solution. Advocates of women's intellectual and physical education used the exercise "cure" to their advantage, arguing that exercise circulated and balanced energy in the body. If women exercised they could safely pursue academic pursuits.

876. Title IX

Title IX of the Education Amendments of 1972 prohibits sex discrimination in federally funded educational programs. The law includes athletics, although its opponents in Congress tried to exempt sports from the anti-discrimination provisions. By 1978, just six years after Title IX was passed, women's participation in intercollegiate sports increased by almost 600 percent. A 1984 Supreme Court decision gutted Title IX, but its essentials were reinstated by Congress as part of the Civil Rights Restoration Act of 1988.

While Title IX was great for women athletes, it had an ironic effect for women coaches and athletic directors. The Association for Intercollegiate Athletics for Women was subsumed by the National Collegiate Athletic Association in 1983, and colleges combined separate men's and women's programs into one department. In the wake of the consolidation, women coaches and administrative staff were usually the ones fired. And as more money poured into women's college sports, male coaches became increasingly interested in the field and claimed many of the jobs.

877. Athletics and Femininity

Throughout this century, physically active women have walked a tightrope between being "manly" athletes and feminine women. Balancing these two images has required a complex acrobatic act on a string that couldn't be strung any tighter. Some women athletes have simply refused to walk the walk. Of those who have refused to toe the line, none stands out so much as tennis great Martina Navratilova, who seemed incapable of being anyone other than who she really was. Her trials reached their zenith when at the height of her career she was painted not only as unfemale but inhuman: She won so many victories and so dominated the sport in the 1980s that it seemed drugs or technology had to share the credit. Navratilova's openness about her sexuality only fueled the flames, but her endurance and integrity eventually won her the respect and even affection of those who once attacked her.

For all the overt abuse encountered in the muddy trenches beneath the high wire, the battle of those balanced above may be no easier. The latest example is power volleyball player and fashion model Gabrielle Reese, who has attracted wide media attention precisely because she embodies the current ideals of physically fit feminine beauty. For the first time it seems possible that a new generation of gutsy girl athletes may not have to choose between their identities as women and as competitors.

ALL-AROUND ATHLETES

878. *Atalanta*

One of the great heroes of classical mythology, Atalanta ranks alongside Perseus, Theseus and Hercules. Her legend starts when her father, bitterly disappointed that she was not a boy, abandoned her as an infant to die of exposure on a mountainside. A female bear found the baby and raised it as her own, feeding and sheltering it. When a group of hunters found the wild girl, they took her to live with them and taught her how to hunt. Atalanta followed up her first heroic feat, the downing of two centaurs, with the famed hunt of the Caledonian boar. The boar terrorized Caledon until that country's king called upon the hunters of Greece to kill it. A band of brave hunters, including Atalanta, tracked and surrounded the vicious creature. It killed three men before Atalanta wounded the boar with an arrow, allowing the king's son to kill it with his knife. The honors of the hunt went to Atalanta, to the dismay of most of the men. Some accounts claim that Atalanta sailed with Jason and the Argonauts, although others dispute this. She is known to have defeated Peleus, the father of Achilles, in a wrestling match, among other adventures. Her athletic prowess and great beauty won her many suitors, but she put them off by declaring she would only marry someone who could beat her in a footrace—something she knew no man could do. Many young men raced her and lost, until one suitor by the name of Melanion showed up with three apples of pure gold. As they raced, Atalanta began to outdistance him, but he tossed one of the golden apples in front of her and she slowed to pick it up. He pulled alongside her and threw the second apple, forcing her to fall behind as she grabbed for it. Still, Atalanta caught up with Melanion as the finish line approached. He rolled the last apple into the grass beside the race course, distracting her as he reached the goal. Atalanta had no choice but to marry Melanion and give up her life of sport and freedom. She bore a son, Parthenopaeus, before she and her husband were turned into lions when they offended either Zeus or Aphrodite.

879. *Eleanora R. Sears*
(1881–1968)

In 1910 the press proclaimed Sears "the best all-around athlete in American society." The daughter of a shipping and real estate tycoon, Sears had the time and money to pursue a wide variety of sports. Because of her daredevil streak, many of her sporting accomplishments came as the result of bets or dares. She was one of the first women to race a car or fly a plane. She was the first person to swim from Bailey's Beach to First Beach in Newport, Rhode Island. She skippered yachts, raced speedboats, skated and played both baseball and football. She trained and rode show horses and played polo on an all-male team, unheard of for a woman of that time. She also played squash and tennis competitively. As she grew older she began long-distance walking. She walked from Newport to Boston, a distance of seventy-three miles, in seventeen hours.

880. Babe Zaharias
(Mildred E. Didrikson, 1914–1956)

Nicknamed Babe by the boys she played softball with as a teenager—she hit a lot of home runs—Zaharias earned world renown as the greatest athlete of her time. One sportswriter said of her, "She was probably the most talented athlete, male or female, ever developed in our country. . . . I never encountered any man who could play as many different games as well as the Babe." At the 1932 Olympics she set world records in the javelin and the eighty-meter hurdles. After she was barred from amateur competition for appearing in a car advertisement, she started and toured with her own basketball team. She also toured with the House of David baseball team, as well as playing billiards matches. As an amateur, she won the 1935 Texas Women's Golf Championships. She went on to dominate the women's tour, winning forty tournaments in four years. She was a founder of the LPGA and one of its early stars, earning nearly a million dollars. She also won tennis, diving and bowling competitions. Even after she was diagnosed with cancer, she came back to win the U.S. Women's Open golf tournament in 1954.

THE UNEXPECTED

881. Bull Leaping

Minoan artifacts from the fifteenth century B.C.E. depict women participating in bull leaping or bull dancing, a sport where one person is tossed between the horns of a bull and caught by another. Women are shown both being tossed and acting as catchers. Around 500 B.C.E., women in Crete also participated in bull leaping.

882. Women Wrestlers

In ancient Sparta (500 B.C.E.), girls regularly trained as athletes alongside boys. Part of the training involved naked wrestling with young men.

883. Girl Gladiators

The so-called gladiatrices of second-century Rome fought professionally, for both private and public entertainment. Their battles pitted them against each other in groups; individual women also battled dwarfs.

884. Annie Oakley
(Annie Moses, 1860–1926)

Annie Oakley grew up shooting game for her family's dinner table in Greenville, Ohio. Her talent as a marksman was apparent to one and all, and in 1875 neighbors raised funds to send her to Cincinnati, where she defeated Frank Butler in a shooting match. Butler, who had a traveling show, signed her up and gave her the name Annie Oakley (they later married). In 1884 "Little Sure Shot" joined Buffalo Bill Cody's Wild West Show and became its star attraction. An exceptional trap shooter well into her old age, Oakley could easily shoot one hundred clay pigeons in a row. But her trick shooting was the attention getter. She'd hit a dime in the air, shoot the ashes off a cigarette in someone's mouth, plug a playing card from thirty paces, and most astonishing, while lying on her back she'd fire at six glass balls thrown into the air at the same time, shattering all six with a double-barreled shotgun before they hit the ground.

885. *The Extra Mile*

Sent by the Christian Missionary Society to found a mission in Persia late in the 1800s, Mary Bird was the organization's first female envoy. Traveling alone, she rode five hundred miles on a camel to reach her destination.

886. *Parachute Jumping*

In 1913, Georgia Broadwick became the first woman to make a parachute jump.

887. *Touché*

Helene Mayer, a German Jew, won a gold medal in fencing at the 1928 Olympics. After competing in the 1932 Olympics in Los Angeles, she was ousted from the Offenbach Fencing Club during a Nazi purge of Jewish athletes. The

Amateur Athletic Union voted to boycott the Berlin Olympics of 1936 unless Jewish athletes were allowed to compete for Germany at the games. In response to the threat of boycott, Germany invited Mayer to compete with the German fencing team. She agreed to, and won the silver medal.

OVER THE NET

888. *Tennis, Anyone?*

In 1874, while vacationing in Bermuda, Mary Ewing Outerbridge learned to play lawn tennis. When she returned home to America, she taught the game to her society friends, thus introducing tennis to the United States.

889. *First Star*

In 1938, Chilean tennis star Anita Lizana became the first South American player to be ranked among the world's top ten players.

890. *Althea Gibson* (1927–)

Althea Gibson grew up in New York City's Harlem playing basketball, stickball and paddle tennis. In 1939 she won a Police Athletic League/Parks Department paddle tennis tournament, attracting the attention of musician Buddy Walker. Through Walker, Gibson met a member of the Cosmopolitan Club, Harlem's prominent African-American tennis club. Seeking ways to bring more black players into tennis, the club recognized Gibson's talent and offered her membership. Under the club's ban-

Althea Gibson.

in Wilmington, North Carolina; Gibson lived with his family from 1946 to 1949 and practiced tennis on his private court. In 1947 she began her ten-year dominance of the ATA women's singles championships, but she assumed competing against the famous white players was an out-of-reach fantasy. Her supporters, however, saw Gibson as African-American players' ticket to the all-white United States Ladies Tennis Association (USLTA). With their help, she was invited to play in two USLTA national indoor tournaments in 1949. She made it to the quarterfinals of both tournaments but was still barred from the more prestigious outdoor tournaments, held at exclusive all-white country clubs. In 1950, she won one indoor tournament and placed second in another, prompting veteran tennis great Alice Marble to lobby on her behalf before the USLTA. Marble got Gibson in the door to the U.S. National Championship at Forest Hills that year. The color barrier was broken, but it would be a while before Gibson began winning grand slam titles. By 1956, she'd won both the French and the Italian Opens; the next year she became the first black player to win Wimbledon and the U.S. Nationals. She won Wimbledon and the U.S. Nationals again in 1958 and began playing exhibition matches at halftime during Harlem Globetrotters' games, broadening the African-American audience for tennis.

ner she won a series of girl's singles titles in tournaments sponsored by the all-black American Tennis Association (in the 1940s, blacks were barred from competing against whites). These early wins gained her another benefactor, a wealthy African-American doctor

891. Ping-Pong Patriot

In the mid-twentieth century, Ruth Hughes Aarons had a spotless four-year career in table tennis, winning every single match she played.

She is the only American, male or female, to attain a world table tennis championship.

892. Billie Jean King
(Billie Jean Moffitt, 1943–)

First picking up a tennis racquet at the age of eleven, King reached number nineteen in the women's national rankings within five years. That's when she started working with tennis great Alice Marble, who like King had learned to play on public courts and was largely self-taught. Because she lacked confidence in her back-court strokes, Marble had been the first woman player to develop a serve-and-volley game. Under her tutelage, King, too, became known as a serve-and-volleyer, and her ranking went to number four in under a year. In 1961, she won the women's doubles crown at Wimbledon, the first of her record twenty Wimbledon titles; three consecutive Wimbledon singles titles came in 1966, 1967 and 1968, followed by three more in 1972, 1973 and 1975. King also won the U.S. Open four times, the Australian Open in 1968 and the French Open in 1972. A great champion on the court, King also championed women's tennis and women's sports off the court. She co-founded the Virginia Slims Circuit and the Women's Tennis Association, and was a founder of the Women's Sports Foundation. The leading advocate of prize-money parity for women, she also invented Team Tennis to bring the sport to a wider, less elite audience. Perhaps best known was her trouncing of Bobby Riggs in 1973's "Battle of the Sexes" match, which put her on the cover of *Sports Illustrated* as Sportswoman of the Year. King not only came a long way on her own, she brought a lot of women with her.

893. Flo Hyman
(1954–1986)

A star volleyball player for the University of Houston from 1974–1976, Hyman left school to play for the U.S. national team. At six feet, five inches tall, she led the 1984 U.S. women's volleyball team to a silver medal in the Olympics, their best finish ever. She was the first American woman to play for the All-World Cup team, and was named best hitter at the World Cup Games in 1981. While playing professional volleyball in Japan in 1986, she died suddenly of congenital heart disease; she was only thirty-two. Hyman is a member of the International Women's Sports Hall of Fame.

894. Martina Navratilova
(1956–)

Considered by many to be the greatest tennis player of all time, Navratilova began playing tennis at six and won the Czech women's singles title at sixteen. She played in the United States for the first time the following year, 1973. Accusing her of becoming "Americanized," Communist Czech officials nearly refused to let her play in the 1975 U.S. Open. Navratilova decided to take no chances with her career and defected to the U.S. immediately following the 1975 Open. Two years later she won six tournaments, and in 1978 and 1979 she won her first Wimbledon singles titles. In the early 1980s she began her domination of international tennis, taking the number-one world ranking from Chris Evert, her longtime friend and rival.

Navratilova won Wimbledon again in 1982, inaugurating a reign that would last for six consecutive years. She won the U.S. Open four times, the French twice and the Australian three times. In 1990, when her heyday was waning, she won her ninth Wimbledon singles title. She

Martina Navratilova. *(Photo by Carol Newsom)*

retired in 1994 with a record 161 singles titles and record prize-money earnings of nearly $20 million.

ON THE LINKS

895. *Patty Berg* (1918–)

Worried that their incurably athletic daughter was too old to continue quarterbacking for a boy's neighborhood football team, Berg's parents encouraged her to take up golf when she was fourteen. By sixteen, she was Minnesota's amateur champion. Over the next seven years Berg won twenty-nine titles, becoming the best-known woman golfer in the U.S. She went pro in 1940, at just twenty-two years old, working for the Wilson Sporting Goods Company to promote a line of Patty Berg golf clubs. Playing exhibitions and running clinics, she also competed in the few women's pro tournaments of the era. In 1941 she was in a car accident, but she returned to golf in 1943, winning the Western Open and All-American tournaments. She then joined the marines and served until the end of World War II. In 1946 she returned to golf again, winning the Women's U.S. Open. Two years later she helped found the Ladies Professional Golf Association (LPGA). A fixture on the LPGA tour for the next eleven years, Berg won thirty-nine tournaments and was a leading money winner. Throughout her career she worked diligently on behalf of golf, particularly women's golf, and was known for helping to advance the careers of young professionals. The LPGA now gives an annual Patty Berg Award to honor outstanding contributions to women's golf.

896. The Birth of the LPGA

In 1950, Patty Berg, Babe Zaharias and a group of professional women golfers founded the Ladies Professional Golf Association. Twenty-eight years later, the LPGA tour boasted thirty-six tournaments and prize money totaling $3.4 million. Today, women's professional golf is one of the fastest-growing spectator sports in the U.S.

897. Pat Bradley
(1951–)

Pat Bradley made history as the only golfer to win all four of the major LPGA tournaments. She joined the tour in 1974 and won her first tournament two years later, but her career did not take off until 1980, when she won her first major tour title, the Peter Jackson Classic. The next year she took the U.S. Women's Open. In 1986 she won three major championships—the Dinah Shore, the Du Maurier Classic and the LPGA championship. Setting a record that year for single-season prize-money earnings—$492,021—she also became the first woman to pass the $2 million mark in total career earnings. She would surpass the $3 million mark just four years later, in 1990, and raked in another million in prize money the following year.

898. The Queen of Golf

The most famous woman athlete in Japan, Hisako Higuchi Matsui is known in her native country as "the queen." Winning the European Open and Japanese National golf tournaments in 1976, she won the LPGA title the following year. By 1981, two hundred Japanese women played golf competitively, most of them on the U.S. pro tour.

899. Nancy Lopez (1957–)

Taught by her father, Lopez played golf from the age of eight and started competing at twelve. She left college to join the LPGA tour and in 1978 won nine events—including the championship—earning recognition as Rookie of the Year, Player of the Year and the Associated Press Female Athlete of the Year. A steady string of successful seasons followed, notably 1985, which brought her second Player of the Year and AP Athlete of the Year awards and another LPGA championship. Lopez won a third championship in 1989; by 1993 her career earnings neared $4 million. She has been inducted into the LPGA Hall of Fame and the World Golf Hall of Fame.

ON ICE AND SNOW

900. Nineteenth-Century Nordic

In 1893, Sweden held the first cross-country skiing competition for women.

901. Sonja Henie (1912–1969)

Sonja Henie was not only a great figure skating champion but also a shrewd businesswoman. She began her phenomenal and lucrative career while still a child, winning the Norwegian championship at ten. At eleven she competed in her first Olympic Games and at thirteen she won the first of ten consecutive world championships. At her second Olympics, in 1928, she won the first of three consecutive gold medals, the only skater ever to accomplish this. After the 1936 Olympics, she turned professional and displayed her talents in her own Hollywood Ice Revue and in ten movies for Twentieth Century Fox. At her death in 1969, her net worth exceeded $47 million.

Sonja Henie.

902. *Suzy Chaffee* (1947–)

A skier from the age of three, Chaffee was captain of the 1968 U.S. Women's Olympic ski team. She pioneered in freestyle skiing, which became a professional sport in 1971. At that time the sport had no women's division, so when Chaffee joined the pro circuit, she competed against men. She won the world championship three years in a row (1971–1973), a feat that encouraged more women to join the sport. In 1973 a women's division was created, some say because Chaffee's dominance of the sport embarrassed her male competitors. Chaffee became a board member of the U.S. Olympic Committee in 1976. In that capacity she continued to advocate for freestyle skiing, specifically that it be included as an Olympic sport. In 1988 freestyle was added to the Olympics as a demonstration sport, and in 1992 it became an official Olympic sport.

903. *Peggy Fleming* (1948–)

Peggy Fleming began skating competitively at eleven, and five years later she won the first of a five-year string of U.S. championships (1964–1968). She began a three-year reign as world champion in 1966, and in 1968 won the gold medal at the Olympics. That year, the Associated Press named her Female Athlete of the Year. Fleming then turned pro, appearing with the Ice Follies and Holiday on Ice, and in her own television specials.

904. *Long Jump*

In 1975 Norwegian skier Anita Wold made history with the longest recorded jump in the history of women's skiing. She made the 321-foot, 5-inch jump at Oukura Sapporo in Japan.

905. A Final Frontier

In 1985 Libby Riddles became the first woman to win Alaska's Iditarod sled-dog race. The race is an arduous test of skill and endurance, arguably the most grueling sporting event on earth.

906. Susan Butcher
(1954–)

The Iditarod sled-dog race takes competitors over 1,162 miles of Alaskan wilderness, often while temperatures sink to fifty below zero. Susan Butcher has won the Iditarod four times—in 1986, 1987, 1988 and 1990—a record number of wins. She also set the course record with her 1990 win, turning in a time of eleven days, one hour and fifty-three minutes. Known for her modesty, Butcher credits her dog teams for her wins.

907. Bonnie Blair
(1964–)

In 1988, speed skater Bonnie Blair set a world record when she won the 500-meter sprint at the Olympics. At the 1992 Winter Olympics, she won the 1,000-meter event and again won the 500-meter sprint. Her second gold in the 500-meter event marked the first time a skater won it in two consecutive Olympics.

908. Debi Thomas
(1967–)

The first African-American figure skating champion, Thomas won both the world championship and the U.S. national singles championship in 1986. That year, the Women's Sports Foundation named her Amateur Sportswoman of the Year.

Injuries plagued her the following year, but she nonetheless took the silver in both the world and national championships. She won the U.S. national singles championship again in 1988 and took the bronze medal at the Olympics. A premed student at the University of Colorado, Thomas spoke openly about the pressures of balancing education with competitive skating. She retired from figure skating after the Olympics to study medicine at Stanford University.

909. Kristi Yamaguchi
(1971–)

In 1992, Japanese-American figure skater Kristi Yamaguchi won the U.S. national championship, the world championship, and the Olympic gold medal. A real crowd-pleaser, she executed her free-skating programs with apparent effortlessness despite their difficulty. She was known for incorporating as many as seven triple jumps into a single routine. After the 1992 Olympics, Yamaguchi turned pro.

910. A Different Kind of Skater

Manon Rheaume, a Canadian, made history in 1993 as the first woman to play in the National Hockey League. In a pre-season game, she started for the Tampa Bay Lightnings as a goalie. During the 1994–95 season she played for the Las Vegas Thunder, a minor league team in the International Hockey League.

TRACK AND FIELD

911. *Track Record*

In 1922 the Amateur Athletic Union (AAU) founded the National Track and Field Championships for Women.

912. *Wilma Rudolph*
(1940–1994)

The victim of polio as a child, Rudolph only began to walk at eight, with the aid of a leg brace. But by sixteen she was a high school basketball and track star and a member of the 1956 Olympic track team. After helping the U.S. 4 x 100–meter relay team win the gold medal, she competed for the track team at Tennessee State College. In 1959 she won the first of four straight AAU outdoor 100-meter championships and in 1960 she set two world records, in the 100-meter and the 200-meter. At the Olympics that year she won three gold medals. She re-

tired from competition in 1962 and started the Wilma Rudolph Foundation, which sponsors athletic events for youngsters and helps underprivileged children.

913. *Wyomia Tyus* (1945–)

In 1964, this African-American won the Olympic gold medal in the 100-meter sprint, tying Wilma Rudolph's world record of 11.2 seconds during the preliminary heats. Returning to the Olympics in 1968, Tyus set a new world record in the 100-meter, running it in eleven seconds flat and winning the gold medal. This made her the only sprinter to win the same event at two different Olympics. She also won a gold medal as part of the 4 x 100–meter relay team. At the medal ceremony, she was joined on the platform by African-American teammates John Carlos and Tommie Smith, who had won their own medals. As the national anthem played, all three bowed their heads and gave the black power salute to protest racial injustice in the United States.

Wilma Rudolph (far left).

914. Jackie Joyner-Kersee
(1962–)

An outstanding high school and college competitor in basketball and track, Joyner-Kersee won the NCAA pentathalons in 1982 and 1983. She won an Olympic silver medal in the 1984 pentathalon and set college long-jump and pentathalon records in 1985. In 1986 she broke the women's world pentathalon record and then topped herself by breaking it again. The next year she broke the world record in the long jump and was named the Associated Press Female Athlete of the Year. Joyner-Kersee took Olympic gold medals in the long jump and heptathalon in 1988, and in 1992 won the heptathalon gold again, along with a bronze in the long jump.

915. Gaining Speed

In 1992, researchers announced that the speed of female runners is increasing at a much faster rate than that of male runners. They predicted that women could reach parity with men in marathon running by 1998.

GYMNASTICS

916. Clara M. Schroth (1920–)

A member of the 1948 and 1952 U.S. Olympic teams, this gymnast won thirty-nine national championships from 1941 to 1952. She is considered the best gymnast of her era, an era very different from today. Throughout her gymnastic career, Schroth worked a day job as a secretary and trained at night. She also competed in track and field and won the standing broad jump at the AAU indoor championships in 1945.

917. Acrobatic Archetype

In 1972, Russian gymnast Olga Korbut performed the first backward somersault on the uneven parallel bars.

918. The Perfect Ten

Nadia Comaneci made history again and again at the 1976 Olympic Games. This Romanian gymnast earned a succession of perfect scores that left audiences and competitors stunned. Never before had any gymnast—or any athlete in any Olympic sport—scored the elusive and seemingly unobtainable ten. But Comaneci, just fourteen at the time, erased the world's assumptions about women's gymnastics.

919. Power Play

Mary Lou Retton challenged the status quo in women's gymnastics, bringing power and muscle to the sport. The results were astonishing. Although no American woman had ever won an individual gymnastics medal at the Olympics, she medaled four times at the 1984 games in Los Angeles: She took the gold in the all-around competition, the silver in the vault, and bronzes in the uneven bars and floor exercise. Some critics slighted her accomplishments because of the absence of the mighty Soviet team, but no one could deny that she had changed the face of American and world gymnastics. Her sturdy muscularity presaged the demise of the anorectic look, and the rise of the more fit and solid-looking gymnast.

IN THE SWIM

920. *Noble Navigator*

In 1876, Lady Anna Brassey and her crew set sail in her yacht *Sunbeam* and voyaged around the world.

921. *Gertrude Ederle* (1906–)

In 1926, Gertrude Ederle became the sixth person and first woman to swim the English Channel. She swam from France to England in fourteen hours and thirty-one minutes, breaking the established record by more than two hours. A New York City native, Ederle returned home to a ticker-tape parade attended by more than 2 million people. She then hit the vaudeville circuit, traveling with a collapsible swimming pool. But her life was hardly fun and games. She became deaf as a result of the channel swim and had a nervous breakdown in 1928. She also spent four years in a body cast because of a back injury. Nothing if not resilient, by 1933 she had a new career working as a swimming teacher for deaf children.

922. *Patricia McCormick* (1930–)

Daredevil diver Patricia McCormick consistently performed the most difficult and dangerous dives at a time when women were banned from using them in international competition. Her dangerous diving was not without consequences. In 1951, while training eight hours a day and doing all the housework, shopping and cooking for her family, she went to a doctor and complained of exhaustion. The doctor not only diagnosed fatigue but found welts on her back, a loosened jaw, lacerations on her arms and legs, scars on her scalp and back and healed rib and finger fractures. None of these injuries deterred McCormick, whose career was just about to take off. In 1952 the ban on risky dives was lifted and she won two gold medals (springboard and platform) at the Olympics. She won golds in both events again in 1956, becoming the first diver—male or female—to do so in two Olympics.

923. *Donna de Varona* (1947–)

Long before she became a founder of the Women's Sports Foundation, or became the first woman to do television commentary for the Olympics (1968), or became the first woman sportscaster for network television (1965), Donna de Varona was an Olympic swimmer. She was a member of the U.S. Olympic team at thirteen, and while she did not take a medal that year (1960), she came back four years later to win the gold in the 400-meter and swim on the gold medal–winning 4 x 100–meter relay team. The Associated Press named her 1964's Female Athlete of the Year.

Gertrude Ederle.

924. Waterskiing

In 1970, at just seventeen, Sally Younger set the women's world speed record for waterskiing, reaching 105.114 mph.

925. Supreme Stamina

In 1978 Diana Nyad set a world distance record in swimming when she became the first person to swim from the Bahamas to Florida. The eighty-nine-mile trek took twenty-seven hours and thirty-eight minutes.

926. Trailblazing Mariner

In 1978, British sailor Naomi James sailed around the world solo, becoming the first woman to do so.

A MAN'S WORLD?

927. The All-American Girls Professional Baseball League

In 1943 Phillip K. Wrigley, the owner of the Chicago Cubs, founded the All-American Girls Baseball League. He hoped to keep Americans interested in professional baseball during World War II, when many players and male fans went overseas to serve in the military. Ten teams made up the league, which showcased the talents of Sophie Kurys and others. The league lasted for a decade, then petered out as American women were expected to confine themselves to home and marriage.

928. Janet Guthrie (1938–)

Before she became a race car driver, Janet Guthrie was one of the first women to be se-lected as a NASA astronaut candidate. She got her pilot's license at seventeen and majored in physics at the University of Michigan. But she turned her attention to auto racing in 1964, and by 1976 she passed the rookie test for the Indy 500. She didn't qualify for that year's race, so she raced in NASCAR and ranked third in NASCAR's 1977 Rookie of the Year standings. That year, Guthrie first drove in the Indy 500, becoming the first woman ever to do so. Forced out by engine trouble, she didn't finish the race. She came back in 1978, finishing ninth in only her second Indy 500. Entering eleven IndyCar races, she earned $84,608 in prize money. Her best pro finish—fifth place—came in her last major race, 1979's Milwaukee 200.

929. Kathy Kusner

(1940–)

In 1968, after a yearlong battle, Kathy Kusner became the first woman to obtain a jockey li-cense. When her initial application, made in Maryland in November 1967, was refused, she told the press, "Horse riding is more a game of technique and skill than strength. It's the same as playing chess with men, so I don't intend to give up the fight." Not until a judge ruled that she had been discriminated against did her li-cense come through. Kusner won her first race in September 1969 at Pocono Downs. Her career would be fairly short, though, as she had diffi-culty meeting weight requirements.

930. Joan Joyce (1940–)

In her twenty seasons with the Raybestos Brakettes, softball star Joan Joyce pitched 105 no-hitters and thirty-three perfect games, winning 509 of 542 games. She threw pitches at over 116 mph, and in exhibition matches struck out two male baseball legends—Ted Williams in 1962 and Hank Aaron in 1978. After leaving softball in 1973, she joined the LPGA tour. She is considered a rival to Babe Didrikson Zaharias for the title of greatest woman athlete of all time.

931. *Shirley Muldowney*

(Shirley Roques, 1940–   )

This drag racer has battled sexism every step of her way to championship. At seventeen she married amateur drag racer Jack Muldowney and soon began racing herself for grocery money; her marriage lasted as long as she remained content with amateur escapades. But in 1972, she turned pro and became a top driver in "funny car" drag racing under the management of Conrad Kalitta. When her manager tried to promote her as "Cha Cha," she switched from funny cars to top fuel dragsters and made her manager her crew chief. In 1977 she won three consecutive national competitions and became the first woman to win the Winston World Championship—all in her hot-pink car. She won the Winston championship again in 1980, becoming the first driver, male or female, ever to win two world championships. In 1982 she won the U.S. Nationals, but in 1984 a serious accident sidelined her. She returned to competition in 1986.

932. *Shoulder Pads*

In 1974 the National Women's Football League was founded to support professional competition by women in American football.

933. *Shot Down—Almost*

Margaret Murdock made history in 1967 when she won a gold medal in the small-bore rifle division at the Pan American Games. Shooting a score of 391, she set a world record and became the first woman ever to exceed a men's record in any sport. She won another gold at the 1975 Pan American Games and tied with Lanny Bassham at the 1976 Olympics. The judges ruled in Bassham's favor, deciding he had edged out Murdock. He took the gold and she the silver, but to protest the decision, Bassham shared the victory platform with Murdock during the national anthem. Murdock is a member of the International Women's Sports Hall of Fame.

934. *Putting on the Brakes*

In 1976 Kitty O'Neil set the women's land speed record, hitting 612 mph, compared with the men's record of 627.287 mph. Since warned not to compete against men, she is barred from attempting to beat even her own record.

935. *First Draft*

Lucy Harris made history as the first woman to be drafted by an NBA team. In 1977, the New Orleans Jazz picked Harris, who'd had an outstanding women's collegiate career, in the seventh round of the NBA draft. Harris never played for the Jazz, though she did play in the Women's Professional Basketball League for the

Houston Angels. Harris also made history in 1975 as the first African-American homecoming queen at Delta State University.

936. *Nancy Lieberman* (1958–)

At just seventeen, this basketball star played on the silver medal–winning 1976 U.S. Olympic team. She then began her career in college basketball, playing for Old Dominion. During her stint at Dominion, the team won two consecutive national championships, in 1979 and 1980—the same years Lieberman twice won both the Wade Trophy and the Broderick Cup as Best Collegiate Woman Athlete. In 1979 she was also named Outstanding College Woman Athlete, winning the Honda Broderick Cup. She made the Olympic team again in 1980, but never played because of the U.S. boycott of the games in Moscow. Moving on to the pros, she signed with the Dallas Diamonds as a first-round draft choice and was named Rookie of the Year. But the Women's Professional Basketball League soon collapsed and the sidelined Lieberman spent the early 1980s as part of the so-called "team Navratilova." Along with Rene Richards and Mike Epstep, she helped coach tennis great Martina Navratilova into top form. When the Women's American Basketball Association League was formed, Lieberman signed a three-year contract, again with Dallas, but again the league folded. So she became the first woman player in men's professional basketball, signing with the U.S. Basketball League in 1986. In 1987 she joined the Washington Generals, the team that tours with the Harlem Globetrotters, achieving another female first.

937. *Mounted Medalist*

In 1984 Leslie Burr rode with the first U.S. equestrian team to win a gold medal at the Olympics. The year before, she had set a record in the sport, in which women and men compete on equal footing. She won three consecutive Grand Prix events and was named the 1983 Mercedes Rider of the Year.

938. *League Leader*

In 1990 Kelly Craig became the first girl to pitch in a starting lineup at the Little League World Series. A member of the Canadian Team of British Columbia, she was only the third girl in history to play in the series. Little League began admitting girls as players in 1974.

939. *Gridiron Girls*

During the 1994–95 school year, 328 girls numbered among the 955,000 high school football players in the United States. Two girls in particular stood out as place kickers on their teams: Heather Sue Mercer kicked proficiently for Yorktown (New York) High in 1993. In 1995 Sara Mergenthaler gained attention as an exceptional place kicker for Marlboro High in New Jersey. Mergenthaler is also a basketball and soccer star at Marlboro.

940. *Alone on the Team*

Kathy Klope, a place kicker for the University of Louisville, is the only woman on a NCAA I-A football team.

Up in the Air

941. First in Flight

Harriet Quimby was the first woman to obtain a pilot's license. She received it from the Aero Club of America in 1911.

942. Lofty Records

In 1923 French stunt pilot Adrienne Bolland performed a record ninety-eight loop-de-loops in fifty-eight minutes. That same year, flier Bertha Horchem set a women's altitude record of 16,300 feet.

943. Amelia Earhart

(1897–1937?)

Much is known about Amelia Earhart's pioneering efforts as a woman pilot, but it is less known that she was a persistent and compelling advocate of commercial air travel. Her interest in commercial aviation dated back to 1927, when she became a sales representative for a commercial airport as well as a stockholder. She co-founded Boston and Maine Airways, one of the first commercial airlines. All this predated her marriage to publisher George Palmer Putnam, who would play a role in her later aviation ventures. But flight remained a passion of hers, not his.

944. The Ninety-Nines

Amelia Earhart planted the seeds of the Ninety-Nines, an association of women fliers, in 1927 when she wrote to Ruth Nichols, another pilot. "What do you think of the advisability of forming an organization composed of women who fly?" she asked. The women corresponded about the prospect until 1929, when the organization took shape in the wake of a women's air derby. Earhart was the first president of the Ninety-Nines, named for the number of its charter members. Fellow pioneers included Clara Trenchmann, who worked for the Curtis Flying Service; Jacqueline Cochran, who supervised hundreds of women pilots in the Women's Air Service during World War II; and Olive Anne Beech, who owned Beech Aircraft.

945. Adventure Aloft

In 1934 Jeanette Piccard, an American, became the first woman to pilot a hydrogen balloon into the stratosphere. She took her 175-foot zeppelin to an altitude of 57,559 feet.

Amelia Earhart.

946. Self-Propelled

Lois McCallin, an American, set an endurance record in the *Eagle,* a ninety-two-pound pedal-powered plane.

UPHILL BATTLE

947. Getting a Foot Up

In 1837 Lady Jane Franklin climbed Mount Wellington in New Zealand, becoming the first woman to make the four thousand-foot ascent.

948. Annie Smith Peck

(1850–1935)

This indefatigable suffragist and mountaineer climbed the Matterhorn in 1895. Two years later she became the first woman to climb Mexico's Mount Orizaba, and in 1902 she helped found the Alpine Club for mountaineers. When she scaled Peru's Mount Coropuna in 1911, she unfurled a banner at the summit. It read: "Votes for Women."

949. Fanny Bullock Workman

(1859–1925)

Scientists and mountaineers, Workman and her husband mounted seven expeditions through the northwest Himalayas, mapping and photographing the Karakorum mountain range. They also recorded altitudes, temperatures and glacial movements. Workman set a number of altitude records for women climbers, and she and her husband made the first descent of the Himalayas' Kalberg glacier. Like her fellow mountaineer Annie Scott Peck, Workman was a woman's suffrage advocate and took a "Votes for Women" banner into the Himalayas on one of her treks. In 1925 she endowed Smith, Radcliffe, Wellesley and Bryn Mawr colleges.

950. The Pinnacle of Success

Part of a 1975 expedition of fifteen Japanese women who set out to conquer Mount Everest, Junko Thaei was the only one to reach the top. Her feat made her the first woman in history to climb the 29,028-foot peak.

Annie Smith Peck setting out from New York with three colleagues.

Part

TEN

Wild Women

THE WILD WEST

951. Range Rules

The women who drove cattle or operated ranches in the old American West developed a set of guidelines concerning how and when to use guns. Different from the cowboys' gun creed in many respects, the rules reflected the particular dangers that confronted women on the range:

1. Strange men will do to shoot.
2. Shoot first, ask questions later.
3. If you shoot a man in the back, he rarely returns fire.
4. Scare a man to death even if you do not intend to kill him.
5. If a man needs killing, do it.

952. Belle Starr

(Myra Belle Shirley, 1848–1889)

The "Bandit Queen" dressed alternately in male drag and velvet gowns, stealing countless horses and captivating and discarding many lovers. She headed a gang in Oklahoma—then called Indian Territory—and with Sam Starr, a Cherokee whose name she took, was convicted as a horse thief and did some jail time. On other occasions she teamed up with the notorious James-Younger gang, the baddest bad guys of the old West, and harbored the fugitive Jesse James. She kept on rustling and stealing the finest livestock in the West until her murder by a bushwhacker in 1889.

953. Calamity Jane

(Martha Jane Canarray, 1852?–1903)

A cohort of Wild Bill Hickok, Calamity Jane endures as a legendary Wild West figure. She often passed as a man and claimed to have worked a variety of jobs, including mule skinner, cattle driver, Indian scout for Custer, prospector, innkeeper, teamster, rancher and Pony Express rider. It is hard to separate fact from myth where she is concerned, but she certainly made a reputation as a boozer and brawler, famous in saloons throughout the American West. When she died she was buried beside Hickok in Deadwood, South Dakota's Boot Hill Cemetery.

Calamity Jane.

954. The Last of a Dying Breed

In 1899, famed Wild West bandit Pearl Hart pulled the last stagecoach robbery in U.S. history.

BANDITS

955. *Nieh Yin-niang* (d. c. 700)

This Chinese warrior learned how to handle a sword from a nun. She went on to become a kind of Robin Hood, avenging criminals and defending the poor and downtrodden.

956. *Mary Frith* (1584?–1659)

This cross-dressing criminal was the first professional woman thief on record in England. Mary Frith dressed as a man to pull off highway robberies that earned her such monikers as Moll Cutpurse and the Queen of Misrule.

957. *Madame Hon-Cho-Lo* (c. 1600)

After her pirate husband's death, this Chinese bandit took over his business as a river pirate. Her exploits and ferocity earned her the title Terror of the Yangtze.

958. *Co-Pirates*

In the early years of the eighteenth century, Mary Reade and Anne Bonney ambushed and ransacked trading ships that plied the waters of the West Indies. Mary Reade began her seafaring career dressed as a man and serving with the British navy (she had also served in the British army by posing as a man). But crime was her true calling, and she joined up with a group of pirates on their way to the West Indies. Among them was Anne Bonney, an Irish pirate who had disguised herself as a man to join the dastardly band. Reade and Bonney joined forces and set off on their own to plunder and terrorize the West Indies. They were finally captured in 1720 and sentenced to be hanged, but both successfully avoided execution by claiming to be pregnant. When released, they fled.

959. *The Diamond Necklace Affair*

In 1785, Comtesse Jeanne de la Motte pulled off one of history's most famous cons. She entreated her lover, the disgraced Cardinal Louis-René-Édouard de Rohan, to regain the support of Marie Antoinette by procuring a diamond necklace for the French queen, and he went to a Parisian jeweler. Thinking the couple was acting on the queen's authority, the jeweler gave them a necklace made of five hundred diamonds. The comtesse hired a prostitute to pose as the queen, thereby stealing the stolen goods. The jewels promptly disappeared; one theory holds that De la Motte's husband took it to a fence in London. When the jeweler was not paid, the cardinal and the comtesse were convicted of fraud. Rohan was sent into exile and De la Motte was whipped, branded and sentenced to life in prison. She escaped, though, and retired to England to write her memoirs. The episode intensified popular disgust with the aristocracy, contributing to the outbreak of the French Revolution.

960. *Sophie Levy Lyons* (1848–1924)

Lyons achieved worldwide notoriety for her swindles and bank robberies. She later gave up this lucrative line of work to make history as America's first society columnist.

961. Train Heist

In 1901, American bandit May Churchill was the brains behind the legendary robbery of the *Parisian-American Express.* Churchill's aliases included May Lambert and Chicago May; some called her the Queen of the Badgers.

962. Bonnie Parker (1910–1934)

Partnered with fellow Texan Clyde Barrow, Bonnie Parker capped a career of crime with a two-year robbery and murder spree during the Great Depression. Originally a waitress, she wrote poetry and shocked people by smoking cigars before she met Barrow in 1930. Starting in December 1932, she and her partner stole cars, held up gas stations and restaurants and robbed banks across the Southwest. Along the way the duo killed twelve people, mostly lawmen. Frank Hamer, an ex-Texas Ranger, finally caught up with them near Arcadia, Louisiana, in May 1934. Attempting to drive through the ambush with their guns blazing, both were shot dead by police.

KILLERS

963. The Papin Sisters

These French sisters worked together in the same nineteenth-century household as servant girls. Perhaps fed up or bored with housework, they killed their employer's wife and daughter while he watched, paralyzed by fear and dismay.

964. Lizzie Andrew Borden
(1860–1927)

Lizzie Borden, America's most famous ax murderer, was acquitted of the 1892 murders of her father and stepmother. A week after the butchered bodies were discovered—both had been beaten to death—police arrested Borden and a sensational trial ensued. Although she was found not guilty, Borden remained an outcast in her hometown for the rest of her life. The question of whether she did the deed—not to mention the deed itself—continues to fascinate generation after generation. The incident has since been memorialized in books, movies, the famous children's rhyme, an opera and Agnes de Mille's 1948 ballet, *Fall River Legend.*

965. Typhoid Mary
(Mary Mallon, 1870–1938)

A carrier of typhoid—but immune to it herself—Mary Mallon worked as a cook in New York City knowing she would pass on the disease. Even when her condition became known, she used aliases to get new jobs as a food handler. As a result, New York City suffered an outbreak of typhoid in 1903. When authorities finally tracked her down, she refused to stop spreading the disease. She was thus institutionalized on North Brother Island in New York City from 1914 until her death in 1938.

966. Alice Mitchell (1873–?)

Born to a wealthy Memphis family, Alice Mitchell had a teenage romantic liaison with Freda Ward, two years her junior. According to

Mitchell, their devotion to one another was so complete that they agreed to kill each other if they were forced to separate. Mitchell made good on her part of the pledge in 1892. Then nineteen years old, she had been prohibited from seeing Ward or even speaking her name. To add insult to injury, Ward had returned an engagement ring Mitchell had given her. Alice Mitchell then cut Freda Ward's throat.

967. *Joan Little* (1954–   )

Arrested and jailed for shoplifting in 1974, Joan Little killed a prison guard when he sexually abused her. The incident made headlines throughout the U.S.

968. *Aileen Wuornos*

Touted and tabloided as the first female serial killer, Aileen Wuornos may never emerge from the sensationalism surrounding her case. A prostitute, she says she had a steady and safe clientele until Desert Storm shipped out her soldier regulars. She then resorted to hitchhiking along the interstate in Florida to find customers. Aware of the dangers, Wuornos packed a gun for protection. She says her string of killings—which began in 1989 and continued for a year before she was caught in 1991—was set off when a client became sadistic and she had to kill him in self-defense. After that, she says, if a customer became threatening, she would shoot. During her trial, her self-defense argument was largely ignored. The jury never heard that the first man she killed had served time as a sex offender and had a pattern of violent behavior consistent with her claims. Meanwhile, attorneys and officials involved in

the case were trying to sell the first female serial killer to Hollywood. Although she confessed to killing seven men, Wuornos insisted she was not a serial killer—she had simply killed a number of men. Unlike stone-cold Ted Bundy, automaton Jeffrey Dahmer or psychotic Son of Sam, Wuornos killed in the heat of the moment and displayed the wide range of feelings generally associated with that behavior. The jury is still out on whether or not Wuornos is a serial killer, or if her case represents a paradigm that distinguishes male and female serial killers.

EVIL QUEENS

969. *Two Athaliahs and a Jezebel*

The name of Jezebel, a ninth-century B.C.E. Phoenician princess, survives today as an emblem of wanton immorality, and little wonder. Wife of Ahab, the king of Israel, she viciously harassed the Hebrew prophets and forced the worship of Baal on devout Jews. Her daughter Athaliah married the king of Judah and, after her husband and son died, she murdered all her grandchildren in order to claim the throne. As disrespectful of Judaism as her mother, she was executed on order of the high priest after she defiled the temple. Four centuries later, another Athaliah became queen of Judah on the death of her son. She persecuted the prophet Elijah and dictated that her subjects worship Baal. To protect her crown against the claims of her grandsons, she had them killed. But one survived to mount a rebellion against her, and she was executed in 437 B.C.E.

970. Fredegunde and Brunhilda

Feuding Frankish queens, Fredegunde of Neustria (now a region in France) and Brunhilda of Austrasia (now part of France, Belgium and Germany) engaged in a power struggle replete with intrigues and assassinations. Fredegunde died in 597, to be remembered as one of the most bloodthirsty queens in European history. Brunhilda's sister was among Fredegunde's victims. For her part, Brunhilda briefly ruled all of Neustria and Austrasia, but was soon forced to flee to Burgundy. She continued rousing rabble until she was captured by Chlotar II. He executed the eighty-year-old Brunhilda by having her dragged behind a wild horse.

971. Elfrida (d. 970?)

The widow of Saxon King Edgar, Elfrida arranged for the murder of her stepson, King Edward the Martyr. She then had her own son, Ethelred, placed on the throne in Wessex.

972. Mary Tudor (1516–1558)

The daughter of Henry VIII and Catherine of Aragon, Queen Mary I ruled England and Ireland from 1553 to 1558. In 1555 she reestablished Roman Catholicism and proclaimed Protestantism a form of heresy. To encourage her subjects to be good Catholics, she persecuted Protestants. Three hundred were executed during her reign, earning her the nickname Bloody Mary.

973. Marie Antoinette (1755–1793)

The much-despised wife of King Louis XVI of France was reviled for her profligate ways in a time when her subjects suffered widely from poverty. Known as Mme. Déficit and Mme. Veto, the queen provoked the public with her extraordinary greed and her contempt for ordinary citizens. Marie Antoinette, as a caricature of all that was wrong with monarchy as a form of government, became one of the great villains of the French Revolution. She was guillotined as a traitor.

974. Ashraf Pahlavi (1919–)

Twin sister of Mohammed Reza Pahlavi, the Shah of Iran, Ashraf Pahlavi has been called the

Mary Tudor.

shah's evil genius, the power behind the throne and the Black Panther of Iran. Along with her mother, referred to as the Dowager Empress, she is credited with exerting tremendous if not total control over her brother's brutal rule of Iran. Shortly before her father's death, he told her to tell her "brother not to be afraid," and said, "I know you can be strong . . . I want you always to be strong for your brother." Since her childhood, her father had openly declared he'd rather Ashraf had been his son and her weaker brother his daughter.

SICK MINDS

975. *Inés de Castro* (c. 1320–1355)

Not necessarily a wild woman herself, Inés de Castro nonetheless figured in one of the more bizarre episodes in history. The mistress and later wife of Pedro, heir to King Alfonso IV of Portugal, de Castro was executed by Alfonso in 1355. Two years later when he became king, Pedro had de Castro's body exhumed and placed on a throne so she could receive the honor and adulation his father had denied her.

976. *Countess Nadasdy*
(Elizabeth Báthory, 1560–1614)

Known as the Bloody Countess, this Hungarian believed that bathing in human blood would ensure eternal youth. Toward that end she killed 610 servant girls for her blood baths.

977. *Ilse Koch*
(1907–1967)

This German served a life sentence in prison for the atrocities she committed and promoted in Nazi concentration camps. Among other pursuits, Koch collected lampshades made from human skin.

978. *Eva Braun*
(1912–1945)

The mistress of Adolf Hitler achieved eternal infamy as the mistress of evil incarnate. The companion, and some say advisor, of the Nazi dictator throughout World War II, Braun married him as the Russians marched on Germany. The next day, with defeat imminent, she committed suicide by cyanide capsule with Hitler and his inner circle in the chancellery bunker in Berlin.

979. *Eyewitness News*

Chris Chubak was the anchorwoman of Sarasota, Florida's WXLT-TV morning show, *Seacoast Digest*. On July 15, 1974, she opened the show with the announcement, "In keeping with Channel Forty's policy of bringing you the latest in blood and guts in living color, you're going to see another first—an attempt at suicide." Chubak then pulled out a gun, put it to her head and killed herself on camera.

ASSASSINS AND SPIES

980. *Lucusta*

Living in Rome in the first century A.D., Lucusta made her living as a professional assassin. Clients included Agrippina, who hired her to poison Claudius, and Nero, who hired her to poison Britannicus. Her career ended when she was executed by Emperor Galba.

981. *Elizabeth L. Van Lew*
(1818–1900)

This Virginian operated as a secret agent for the federal government during the Civil War. In 1863 she infiltrated Libby Prison to collect military intelligence for the Union army.

982. *Mary Surratt*
(Mary Eugenia Jenkins, c. 1820–1865)

Mary Surratt ran the boardinghouse in Washington, D.C., where John Wilkes Booth and others plotted the assassination of President Abraham Lincoln. Her son had become a friend of Booth while serving as a dispatch rider for the Confederacy. Following the assassination, Surratt was charged and convicted as a conspirator. She was hanged in 1865, though there is some question whether the government proved its case against her. Her son, meanwhile, is known to have been active in the conspiracy, but was not arrested until 1866. Unable to get an indictment, the government released him in 1868. The question of whether Mary Surratt was executed for the crimes of her son and others, or whether she actively participated in Lincoln's assassination, will likely never be answered.

Mary Surratt.

983. *Belle Boyd* (1844–1900)

A Confederate spy during the Civil War, Belle Boyd worked as a courier for both General

Belle Boyd.

Beauregard and General Jackson. In 1862 she delivered information to Jackson that allowed him to retake a Union-held city. She was captured in 1865 by the Union army and imprisoned.

984. *Anonymous Assassin*

In 1881, after numerous other terrorists had failed in their attempts, a nameless woman revolutionary assassinated Czar Alexander II of Russia. A member of the Narodnaya Volya (People's Will), she threw a bomb into his carriage as he rode by.

985. *Mata Hari*

(Margaretha Geertruida MacLeod, 1876–1917)
Originally from Holland, this infamous seductress was educated in a convent. In 1895, at the age of eighteen, she married Campbell MacLeod, a Dutch military officer, and lived with him in Java and Sumatra until 1902. The marriage proved unhappy and she divorced MacLeod, changing her name to Mata Hari and moving to Paris. There, she created an identity for herself as a Javanese dancer and earned a living performing risqué dances for an exclusive clientele. In 1907 Germany recruited her as a spy and trained her in espionage. Her popularity with the gentlemen came in handy during World War I, when her intimate relationships with Allied officers allowed her to gather sensitive information for the Germans. Arrested by the French and charged with espionage, she was executed by firing squad in October 1917.

WARRIORS

986. *Penthesilea*

(d. 1187 B.C.E.)

Greek legend tells of this Amazon queen, noted for her courage and skill during the Trojan War. She was killed at the siege of Troy by Achilles, who grieved over killing one so courageous and beautiful. According to Pliny, she invented the battle-ax.

987. *Amazons*

Greek historian Herodotus wrote of Amazon warriors who came from Asia and twice besieged Athens. The Amazon kingdom was said to

Mata Hari.

be in western Tibet and so strong that even Alexander the Great could not conquer it. According to the legends, these women warriors would kill a man as a prenuptial ritual and kept only their female children. Amazons supposedly cut off their right breasts to perfect their skill with bows and arrows.

An Amazon.

988. *Boadicea* (d. 62)

Queen of a Celtic tribe called the Iceni, Boadicea (or Boudicca) led an army of 200,000 in an uprising against Roman domination of Britain in the first century. Her rebellion began after the death of her husband, who left part of his fortune to Nero, emperor of Rome. Unimpressed, the Romans assaulted Boadicea, raped her daughters and enslaved her nobles as

they moved in to annex her kingdom. Her army raged through the countryside burning Roman army camps and towns such as Colchester and London, reportedly killing seventy thousand Roman settlers. She crushed the Ninth Legion on the battlefield before provincial governor Suetonius Paulinus arrived and routed her. She died before she could be taken to Rome and displayed in a triumphal parade; some accounts state that she poisoned herself.

989. *Queen Nzinga Mbande Ngola* (1582–1663)

This ruthless African warrior fought Portuguese slavers whose trade threatened to destroy her people, the Matamba of Ndongo. She first negotiated a treaty with the Portuguese, but later she formed an alliance with the Dutch and repudiated the agreement. When the Portuguese defeated her in battle, she retreated to the rain forest and fought a guerrilla war for eighteen years. Famed for her brutality, she reputedly cannibalized those she captured in battle, and promoted infanticide among her female warriors so they would not be burdened by domestic concerns. Into the nineteenth century, European observers recorded accounts of such all-woman African armies, which were said to fight better than men.

990. *Lakshmi Bai* (c. 1835–1858)

When British colonizers attempted to annex her kingdom after the death of her husband, the Rhani (queen) of Jhansi took up her sword. She raised an army of fourteen thousand to fight in the Sepoy mutiny, donned a uniform herself and rode into battle alongside her soldiers. Her fiercely pitched fighting won her a grisly reputation. Before a British hussar killed her in hand-to-hand combat, she helped take the city of Gwalior. The British considered her "the most dangerous of rebel leaders."

991. *No Trespassing*

In 1897 Augusta Main was arrested for assault with intent to kill. Owner of a farm in Berlin, New York, she had a strict policy against allowing men on her property. If she needed labor, she simply hired "strapping young women," as she put it. One day she assaulted a male neighbor, resulting in her brush with the law. Explaining her actions, she said she "never sees men or dogs but what I aches to kill them."

CROSS-DRESSERS

992. *Hatshepsut*
(d. 1482 B.C.E.)

Although her father, Thutmose I, declared her his successor, Hatshepsut first ruled as her half-brother's queen and then as his illegitimate son's regent. In 1503 B.C.E. she decided to claim her rightful place and pronounced herself Egypt's supreme monarch, thereby becoming the first female pharaoh. She also proclaimed herself a god and a man. Dressed in pharaoh's regalia and addressed as His Majesty, she ruled for twenty years.

993. *James Miranda Barry*
(1799–1865)

Barry passed as a man for at least fifty years; only her death revealed her true gender. A medical doctor, she worked as the inspector general of the British Army Medical Department.

Dr. James Barry.

994. *Charley Parkhurst* (1812–1879)

Parkhurst passed as a man and worked as a stagecoach driver during the California gold rush. In fulfillment of her duties, she killed at least one would-be robber.

995. *Murray Hall* (d. 1901)

Murray Hall kept her sex a secret until she developed breast cancer at the age of seventy. She was part of the Tammany Hall political machine and excelled at whiskey drinking, cigar smoking, card playing and womanizing. Her first wife left her because Hall had such a wandering eye.

996. *Billy Tipton* (d. 1989)

A jazz-piano and -saxophone player, Tipton passed as a man to enter the all-male enclave of 1930s swing bands. Taking a male identity, Tipton worked as a musician her whole life and even formed her own trio. She married a woman and adopted her sons. Tipton's gender was discovered only when she died in 1989. Even her wife claimed not to have known her husband's true sex.

DAREDEVILS

997. *Lady Godiva* (d. 1080)

Lady Godiva appealed to her husband Leofric, Earl of Mercia, to reduce taxes in Coventry because she believed they placed an unfair burden on the people. Her husband agreed to do so only if his wife would ride naked through the public marketplace at noon. Lady Godiva accepted the dare, touring the streets of Coventry clothed only in her long hair. No welsher, her husband reduced taxes. Lady Godiva was also responsible for building and endowing monasteries in Coventry and Stowe.

998. *Lillian Gish* (1893–1993)

Starting out with director D. W. Griffith in 1912, this actress had a long career in the movies, culminating in 1987's *The Whales of August*. Appearing in such silent classics as *The Birth of a Nation* (1915) and *Orphans of the Storm* (1921), she proudly did all her own stunts. This was not uncommon in the early days of film, but Gish seemed truly to delight in the challenge. She gleefully put her head in guillotines, lay facedown on ice floes or did whatever the picture called for. Her boldness as an actress belied the often distressed and helpless characters she portrayed.

Lady Godiva.

999. Occupational Hazards

Betty Danko exemplified the rugged stunt-woman of Hollywood's golden age. In 1939 she stood in as the wicked witch in *The Wizard of Oz* and, while shooting one of the witch's famous smoke-puff exits, she was badly burned when a tech assistant used too much gunpowder. Stunting for Patsy Kelly in another movie, Danko wound up clawed and bitten in a scene with a lion.

1000. Rough Going

Jean Criswell, a Hollywood stuntwoman in the 1940s, agreed to do a scene in which she would grab a bull by the tail and let it drag her across a field. The going rate for stuntwomen at that time was $35 a day, so Criswell figured $150 was good money for the job. Another woman was to ride the bull and keep it under control, and Criswell assumed that would be the case. But in take after take, the rider kept falling off and the bull kept running, dragging Criswell behind until it tired of the game. The episode went down in stunt-player history as an example of someone who really earned her pay.

1001. Wendy O. Williams

In the late 1970s and early 1980s, Wendy O. Williams and her band the Plasmatics took what they called "pornography rock" to as yet unmatched extremes. Williams, often clad only in whipped cream, a body stocking or black pants and strategically placed electrical tape, smashed television sets on stage and was handy with a chainsaw. On at least one occasion she used her saw to cut through a plugged-in guitar. Not satisfied with merely making a few sparks fly, Williams moved on to full-scale demolition and began finishing shows by blowing up cars. The Plasmatics were fun while they lasted, but they didn't last long.

For Further Reading

Alic, Margaret. *Hypatia's Heritage: A History of Women in Science from Antiquity through the Nineteenth Century.* Boston: Beacon Press, 1986.

Anderson, Bonnie S., and Judith P. Zinsser. *A History of Their Own: Women in Europe from Prehistory to the Present.* New York: Harper & Row, 1988.

Covey, Alan. *A Century of Women.* Atlanta: TBS Books, 1994.

D'Emilio, John, and Estelle B. Freedman. *Intimate Matters: A History of Sexuality in America.* New York: Harper & Row, 1988.

Ehrenberg, Margaret. *Women in Prehistory.* Norman: University of Oklahoma Press, 1989.

Green, Rayna. *Women in American Indian Society.* New York: Chelsea House, 1992.

Greenspan, Karen. *The Timetables of Women's History.* New York: Simon & Schuster, 1994.

James, Edward T., et al. *Notable American Women 1607–1950.* Cambridge, Mass.: Belknap Press of Harvard University Press, 1971.

Jordan, Rosan A., and Susan J. Kalcik. *Women's Folklore, Women's Culture.* Philadelphia: University of Pennsylvania Press, 1985.

Kessler-Harris, Alice. *Out to Work: A History of Wage-Earning Women in the United States.* Oxford, England: Oxford University Press, 1982.

King, Margaret L. *Women of the Renaissance.* Chicago: University of Chicago Press, 1991.

Morgan, Robin. *Sisterhood Is Global: The International Women's Movement Anthology.* New York: Doubleday, 1984.

Olsen, Kirstin. *Chronology of Women's History.* Westport, Conn.: Greenwood Press, 1994.

O'Neill, Lois Decker. *The Women's Book of World Records and Achievements.* New York: Anchor Press, 1979.

Pomeroy, Sarah B. *Goddesses, Whores, Wives, and Slaves: Women in Classical Antiquity.* New York: Schocken Books, 1995.

Read, Phyllis J., and Bernard L. Witlieb. *The Book of Women's Firsts.* New York: Random House, 1992.

Sicherman, Barbara, and Carol Hurd Green. *Notable American Women: The Modern Period.* Cambridge, Mass.: Belknap Press of Harvard University Press, 1980.

Stanley, Autumn. *Mothers and Daughters of Invention: Notes for a Revised History of Technology.* New Brunswick, N.J.: Rutgers University Press, 1993.

Stephenson, June. *Women's Roots: Status and Achievements in Western Civilization.* Napa, Calif.: Diemer, Smith Publishing Co., 1986.

Sterling, Dorothy. *We Are Your Sisters: Black Women in the Nineteenth Century.* New York: W. W. Norton, 1984.

Trager, James. *The Women's Chronology: A Year-By-Year Record, from Prehistory to the Present.* New York: Henry Holt, 1994.

Uglow, Jennifer S. *The Continuum Dictionary of Women's Biography.* New York: Continuum, 1989.

Walker, Barbara G. *The Women's Encyclopedia of Myths and Secrets.* San Francisco: Harper & Row, 1983.

Weiser, Marjorie P. K., and Jean S. Arbeiter. *Womanlist.* New York: Atheneum, 1991.

Photo Credits

Index